Seeker's Guide to Learning Wicca: Training to First Degree in the Southern Hemisphere

Seeker's Guide to Learning Wicca: Training to First Degree in the Southern Hemisphere

Amethyst Treleven

Oak and Mistletoe

Oak and Mistletoe
PO Box 7393, Hutt Street, South Australia 5000, Australia

First Published 2008

National Library of Australia Cataloguing-in-Publication entry

Author: Treleven, Amethyst.

Title: Seekers guide to learning wicca: training to first degree in the
southern hemisphere/ Amethyst Treleven.

ISBN: 9780980581812 (pbk.)

Notes: Includes index.
        Bibliography.

Subjects: Wicca--Handbooks, manuals, etc.
          Witchcraft--Handbooks, manuals, etc.

Dewey Number: 299.94

For further information;
http://www.oakandmistletoe.com.au

For my Oak and Mistletoe Family
Always my inspiration

Table of Contents Page

Acknowledgements

They say that Rome wasn't built in a day and the same philosophy would be true of this book. Having taught Wicca for many years, this book is the end result of many hours of writing, many more hours of editing, hours and countless emails asking my own students for advice, writing some more, and then some more again.

Without my wonderful students, who teach me as much as I teach them, this book would not have been possible. To each one of you, please know that you are my inspiration, my motivation and my joy. Thank you to each and every one of you for teaching me how to teach.

Smiles and blessings,
Amethyst

Introduction

Am I the only one who's sick and tired of reading Wicca and Witchcraft 101 books and finding they're virtually all by northern hemisphere writers who simply don't understand the issues we face about festival dates, circle directions and quarter placements in the southern hemisphere? If you've found the same thing and are fed up too, please raise your arm so I can see you. Yeay! I see you all now. It seems there's quite a few of us!

It was for that reason that I finally wrote this book. As a Wiccan practitioner and teacher, having been taught a lot of the old ways and then having moved into a more eclectic and flexible practice, I just got fed up with 'translating' everything from British and American writers to use down here at the bottom of the world. Don't get me wrong here please. I'm not saying our colleagues at the top of the world have it wrong, not at all. A considerable body of the work produced as teaching material is absolutely superb and I'm in awe of the talents and skills of those writers. But, down here, we also practice Wicca and Witchcraft in surprisingly growing numbers and while most of the books written are fantastic works that teach us so much, they don't address the issues and problems we face trying to implant a foreign religion into its opposite ecology.

Here at the bottom of the world, our summer is chugging along when England and the USA are shivering through winter. They celebrate Samhain on October 31st, partly to mark the harvest, but down here we're planting and not harvesting. So should we stick to the 'script' and do what they do and pretend we're harvesting or do we swap Samhain over with Beltaine? They work deosil (clockwise) in the circle because that's the natural path of the sun across the sky up there but underneath the world down here the sun travels widdershins (anti-clockwise). So do we work in the same direction even though it doesn't reflect the natural cycles down here or swap directions? Up there, the south quarter heads off toward the heat of the equator so the Fire element corresponds with the southern quarter. But down here, the equator is to the north of us so do we swap the southern and northern quarters in our circle casting rites? Not many northern hemisphere writers thoroughly appreciate those problems for us down here and so it's no wonder that learners get so confused reading about things that just don't relate for us at the bottom of the world.

The Seekers Guide to Learning Wicca was written first and foremost as a teaching book and program especially for learners in the southern hemisphere. For years Wiccan teachers in the southern hemisphere have been teaching their students the practicalities of being a Wiccan and Witch at the bottom of the world but there was nothing available that allowed students who couldn't join a face to face coven to learn the Craft for their southern ecology. Instead, they just had to buy British and American texts and then desperately try and work out how to manipulate that into something that worked for them down under. Now, those solitary practitioners don't have to do that. They can use this book to develop a practice relevant to their needs without the confusion and distortion.

For those practitioners with internet access, there's also an online accompaniment to this book available at www.oakandmistletoe.com.au which supplements this work and provides opportunities to link with fellow students and teachers in a supportive, caring and ethical community. I'd encourage you to explore that option as well.

Finally a quick word on traditions. This book reflects the Inclusive tradition of Wicca and is the First Degree training program text for students at Oak and Mistletoe, which is the founding coven of the Community Church of Inclusive Wicca Incorporated. Using this program enables students to reach their First Degree status within the tradition and offers them the opportunity to move on to higher studies and to foster real relationships with likeminded people who hold the same values and principles. Inclusive Wicca stands up for the rights of people who want to learn Wicca and Witchcraft without the need to adhere to the strict regime of oath bound coven teaching and while the program proudly provides students with the underpinning and traditionally available teachings, it also encourages students to look beyond the old dogma and develop a spiritual practice which meets their own personal needs and fosters their unique relationship with the Divine. In other words, the Inclusive tradition teaches you everything you need to know but asks you to turn it into your own religion so that you're not just doing what someone else says you have to do. Inclusive Wicca therefore provides freedom of choice and this is something we're very proud of.

So in conclusion, I genuinely welcome you to our wonderful tradition and community and sincerely wish you well in your learning journey with us. Know always that I'm freely available via email (please go to the web page at www.oakandmistletoe.com.au to contact to me) to answer any questions and to offer personal support and help.

Smiles and blessings,

Amethyst

How to Use This Book

Welcome to the Toward First Degree training program delivered by Oak and Mistletoe, the founding coven of the Community Church of Inclusive Wicca Incorporated. The Inclusive Wiccan tradition is one that emphasises each practitioner's right to adapt their practice to suit their own needs whilst still remaining within the principled confines of the Wiccan religion. What this means is that through this program you'll learn all the skills and knowledge required to live effectively as a Wiccan but you'll also be encouraged to experiment and adapt it so that it becomes *your* practice within the Inclusive tradition. So how does it all work?

There are three ways to learn about this tradition and to become a First Degree within it. The first, and preferred option of course, is face to face training with an Inclusive coven. But for many people that simply isn't possible, either because they don't want to join a coven or because there isn't one locally available to them. So their next two options are to use this book alone or to use this book in conjunction with the online Toward First Degree training program at www.oakandmistletoe.com.au. I'd very much encourage you to consider using the website as well as this book because together they can provide you with a wealth of opportunities to connect and talk with fellow students, to have a tutor assigned especially to you and to access the wealth of resources available for students and for initiated practitioners too.

Please take your time when working through this program. The book gives you all eight lessons so you could speed through it but it won't benefit you to do so. The book has been designed to be done as one lesson at a time and at the pace of one lesson per month. You need this time to be able to practice the visualisations and to use them to develop your connections with the elements and to stretch your own ability to reach outward and to delve more deeply inwards. Mastering a new skill, especially one as esoteric and intuitive as Wicca and Witchcraft doesn't happen overnight and indeed, most practitioners will tell you that they still don't consider themselves masters even after decades of practice.

So each month, focus on one lesson at a time and follow the order of lessons as they appear in this book. Each lesson has been designed to build on the previous month's work so that by the time you reach the end, you will have completed a very thorough, in depth learning program that gives you a holistic set of skills and knowledge to work from.

Each lesson is crammed with not just basic and relevant information within the text, but they're also peppered with a host of activities that you have to attend to. Learning is a two way street whereby you receive information but you also have to work to consolidate that for yourself. As you work through the book, you'll come across three different icons.

The Activity icon signals that you have to do some of your own work rather than just reading. These activities are quite varied and are generally about 'doing' something rather than just reading about it. You'll often be asked to record the result of what you've done in a Learning Journal as well. I'll explain that for you shortly.

The Read icon usually asks you to read a specific text either within this book or located elsewhere and it's used to supplement this program. In learning the Inclusive tradition, we ask you read a number of different approaches so that you can see where the Inclusive tradition fits with all the other traditions and also so that you've got a broader set of readings to base your own personalised practice on.

The last icon, Research, suggests you go and locate other materials and information from as many sources as you can find. Often resource suggestions will be provided for you but the more information you can find to supplement your learning, the more benefit you'll get in the long term.

I'd really encourage you to engage with all these icons because they turn an 'off the shelf' program that a book can only ever be into a much more personalised training program that meets your particular needs. On top of that, the old adage is really true here in that the more you put into this training course, the more you'll get out of it. If you're doing this program online and using this book as a companion to that, then your tutor will want to see the results of your icon activity as well.

Learning Journal
As part of your journey forward, you'll need to find or buy a Learning Journal. Essentially this is simply a book of blank pages like a school exercise book that you can write down the results of your activities and any other information that's important. You can find one available for sale in the Oak and Mistletoe bookshop at www.oakandmistletoe.com.au or you can simply buy a low cost

exercise book from the supermarket. This book will eventually morph into your Book of Shadows but in the meantime it's your tool to capture your important learnings and it's a diary of your journey. For now however, a simple exercise book will suffice.

Alternatively, you can use your computer and record your work in a Word doc or similar. This would also allow you to share that more easily with your tutor if you're learning through the online Toward First Degree program.

Dream, Meditation and Nature Diary.

Just about every student Wiccan and Witch is required to keep note of any significant dream or meditation as they can be windows into insights and knowledge you didn't realise you had. In addition, Wicca is about connecting with the natural world around us so it's absolutely vital to watch nature, take notes and begin to see the depth of your connection, relationship and impact on the natural world. Like the Learning Journal, there is a Dream, Meditation and Nature Diary available in the bookshop at www.oakandmistletoe.com.au but this can also be a simple exercise book if you prefer.

You'll find more information and instructions on these two requirements in the first lesson but for now let me welcome you again to Inclusive Wicca and your Toward First Degree training program. Please feel free to contact me via email (you can do so from the contact page at www.oakandmistletoe.com.au) at any time if you have any queries, concerns or simply need some helpful advice.

Smiles and blessings,
Amethyst

The First Lesson
Wicca versus Witchcraft

elcome to your own, tailor made Outer Court Wiccan journey! You're at the beginning of a very special time in your life when you'll learn lots more about yourself, about the Wiccan world around you and from which you can then determine your commitment to this powerful, dynamic and fast growing religion.

By the time you've finished your first lesson you should be able to;

- Discuss the difference, and the relationship, between Wicca and Witchcraft,
- Talk through the basics of Wicca as a religion,
- Describe the ethics of Wicca including the Rede and the Law of Return,
- Explore the purpose of visualisation and do your first visualising exercise,
- Write in your Dream, Meditation and Nature Diary,
- Explain what a Book of Shadows is.

So let's get started! Make sure you've read the "How to Use This Book' Section so you can get the absolute best out of your Wiccan teaching program before you carry on with these pages.

Wicca versus Witchcraft

So one of the first things we really need to get straight are the definitions of Wicca and Witchcraft. This is important because without it, you won't be able to define yourself as either a Wiccan or a Witch and while at the moment this might seem unimportant, eventually you're going to want to know who and what you are and what your practice is. Depending on the opinions of who you talk to, there are two primary descriptors for the terms Wicca and Witchcraft.

The Initiatory Approach
This opinion is often held by those people who've been initiated into oath bound traditions such as Gardnerian and Alexandrian. Many traditions determine that you cannot identify as a Wiccan unless

you've undertaken the mystery ritual that is initiation into that tradition and coven. Within this approach, Wicca is a religion, the secret knowledge of which is only available after initiation into a teaching coven and only through face to face teaching by an initiated Wiccan of that tradition.

If you follow this line of thought, Witches are those people who have not been initiated and therefore aren't privy to the inner most secrets and practices of Wicca. It also means that you cannot self initiate and much as I hate to admit it, there is a degree of merit with this argument.

Initiation is, by its very nature, a ritual that takes you through three phases. First you're stripped of your previous identity through a variety of means (which isn't quite as scary as it sounds!) Then, through a process that's deliberately not revealed to you, you're introduced to the Gods and Goddesses who will give you secret insights which are meaningful only to you, and finally you come out the other end with a new identity as a renewed spiritual being. Now because initiation is traditionally a ritual that you can't go into knowing what will happen, how can you initiate yourself if you don't know the ritual? Initiation in this traditional sense is a beautiful, mystery experience which allows you to transcend from one stage of life to another and when conducted by a trusted Priest/ess who understands your needs, it can be a life changing, affirming experience.

The counter argument to this approach asks the question 'who initiated the first person?' If you must be initiated by an initiated person, how did the first person become initiated? Furthermore, opponents to this approach argue that it's elitist and excludes people from the religion when they aren't able to be trained or initiated in a face to face coven situation. They argue that religion is a philosophy and you can't exclude people because they're unable to train in a particular manner.

The Religion versus Practice Approach
The more flexible and contemporary approach supposes that Wicca is the religion and Witchcraft is how you practice that religion. In this approach, your title isn't related to whether you've been initiated by someone else or not but is a choice you make. Let's explore this for a moment.

If Wicca is accepted as a religion, just like Christianity or Buddhism is a religion, then you can call yourself Wiccan if you believe the underpinning fundamentals that form that religion. But you can also call yourself a Witch because in this approach, Witchcraft is how you '*do*' Wicca. It's the circle casting, the magickal workings and all the rituals and rites that express your Wiccan religious commitment. Thus your title, Wiccan or Witch or even

Pagan or all three, is up to you and isn't bound by whether you've been initiated or not. We'll talk about Paganism in a moment but first let's also look at another benefit of this approach, that of the potential for self initiation.

If you follow this religion versus practice approach, then you're also free to self initiate. Let me explain. If you can call yourself Wiccan because you believe in the fundamentals of the religion, then you also have the divine right to bless yourself before the Gods and Goddesses and dedicate your life to them. This form of initiation is more akin to a dedication rather than a mystery based initiation but it's valid and effective none the less.

So what does the Inclusive tradition believe? Because we're an embracing tradition, indeed our name is Inclusive Wicca, hence the name, we believe very much that you have your own right of choice. Fundamentally we follow the religion versus practice approach and so you've total control over your title, and how you want to dedicate yourself to your religious and spiritual life. So while we strongly encourage Priest/ess lead initiation into both our tradition and your coven so that you get to experience the wonder and beauty of a mystery initiation, we also fully support self dedication where circumstances suggest that's the best way to go for you.

Ultimately, you alone have the responsibility to manage your own religious life and the way in which you commit yourself to the Divine. That means you also have the responsibility to choose what you call yourself, how you learn about Wicca and how you practice. This tradition will give you the framework in which to fit that knowledge, skills and the responsibility but in the end, you're a grown up and you have the right and the ability to make your own choices about your relationship with the Wiccan religion.

Where Does Paganism Fit in all This?
Yet another term to get your head around! Having worked out what the terms Wicca and Witchcraft refer to, let's have a look at what Paganism means.

Wicca, we've determined, is the name of a religion, while Witchcraft is how we 'do' the religion. Paganism is the umbrella term for religions, philosophies and practices that base their approach in Earth based, ancient or reconstructionist mythology. So Paganism includes religions like Wicca, Druidism and even Asatru.

Most Pagan religions are polytheistic and have a reverence for nature and our planet. They also usually see balance between male and female deities and this contrasts with Christianity, Islam and Judaism which focus heavily on a patriarchal deity. Pagan religions often see the world as being made up of four elements, Earth, Air, Fire and Water and finally, most Pagans prefer to see reincarnation as a component of their religious beliefs.

Activity
So let's put that all together. For me, I'm a Wiccan because I've chosen to live my life according to the rules and ethics of the Wiccan religion. I'm also a Witch because I cast circles and do lots of the 'how to' of Wicca in my commitment to the religion, and all that makes me a Pagan as well so I'm a member of all three groups. What are you going to call yourself? How do you see your place in this complex framework of opinions and approaches? Take a few minutes now to think through what the terms Wicca, Witchcraft and Paganism mean to you and decide what you'll call yourself. Maybe even write this in your Learning Journal.

As a final point to this section, it's worth having a quick discussion around what New-Age means. Are Wiccans New-Agers? Most Wiccans will probably frown at you if you asked them this question! A New-Age practice is an esoteric activity such as tarot, divination or crystal work. Just because you're a Wiccan/Witch/Pagan doesn't mean you automatically read tarot cards, runes or have kitchen witch ornaments hanging off your ceiling! It doesn't mean you have to use herbs, interpret dreams or listen to Tibetan singing bowl meditation CDs all day. Sure you can do all that, but that's not what makes you Wiccan. We'll talk about the fundamental beliefs of Wicca shortly but New-Age crystal healings, ear candles, reiki, chakra points and so on are very often in tune with the natural energies used within Wicca, but they are not inextricably tied to it.

Research
Ok, now that you've read all that, it's time to go and do some research of your own. Using the resources in the back of this book, the internet, your local library and bookshop, online email groups and any Wiccan/Witch/Pagan friends, go and find out what other people think the terms Wicca and Witchcraft mean. Be prepared for some very passionate and utterly devoted opinions as this is a volatile topic in the global Wiccan community! Remember, ultimately you have the right to your own decisions on what these terms mean and you don't have to adhere to anyone else's viewpoint no matter how strongly they argue their point.

So What do Wiccans Believe?
Now that we've got the terms Wicca and Witchcraft sorted out, let's look now at what Wiccans actually believe.

Like many other religions, there are of course variations across different traditions but most of those differences often show up more in the way the religion is practiced rather than in what different Wiccans believe. So even though different Wiccans and different groups might do things slightly differently, essentially the underpinning framework of belief remains the same from one tradition to another.

There's probably six things that underpin Wicca and help define it as a stand-alone religion. Most Wiccans tend to believe in;

* A polytheistic approach to the Divine,
* A Divine gender balance and so they honour both male and female deities,
* Reincarnation as a legitimate, sensible and spiritually valid means of growing and learning about humanity,
* A spiritual and physical connection between the energies and souls of all beings in nature, including the planet itself and the cyclic seasons,
* Magic as a powerful mechanism to bring about desired outcomes,
* The Wiccan Rede as the primary framework to describe religious and general life behaviours.

Looking at polytheism first, we immediately see the most obvious difference between Wicca and the more established Abrahamic religions such as Christianity. As Wiccans we honour a broad variety of Gods and Goddesses, often from different pantheons depending on the tradition. Christians believe only in a single God and so their religion can be classified as monotheistic. One thing is really important to note at this point and that's that the Christian God is *not* one of the Wiccan Gods. He is a representation of Christian divinity and not of Wiccan.

As already mentioned, depending on the tradition, a Wiccan might honour deities from a single or from multiple pantheons. Some Wiccans, particularly those who are reconstructing what they understand from the available evidence of pre-Christian religions, might engage only with a single pantheon like the Celtic or Norse group. The more eclectic Wiccans are more likely to honour the Gods and Goddesses from all manner of pantheons including Greek, Roman and maybe even the indigenous Gods of their own country. Personally, I tend to honour whatever deity is the best representation for my needs at the time but having said that, I do have a soft spot for the Celtic pantheon, given I can trace my family back to the Cornish Celts right back to the 6th century. That's just my preference though and as you develop your relationship with the Gods and Goddesses, eventually you'll probably also develop a fondness for a pantheon or even for a small group or pair of Gods and Goddesses. The essential point here is that you work with the deities that speak to you. Please don't adopt a pantheon or a deity just because your friend does or because you think that's who you're supposed to be honouring. This is *your* spiritual relationship so you need to explore and decide what deities work with you.

The second point, that of gender balance between deities, also highlights for us another difference between the Abrahamic religions and Wicca. While Wiccans see the Gods and Goddesses as being fairly equally represented, Christians tend to focus much more heavily on the patriarchal sense of deity with their God as the Father, Son and Holy Ghost. Wiccans prefer to honour both male and female Gods/Goddesses and they do so with much more balance and even flexibility.

As you become familiar with ritual, you'll probably notice that many Wiccans refer to the 'Lord and Lady' and there are two points to consider with this popular terminology. The first is that this term highlights how Wiccans prefer gender balance in all ritual and that the term doesn't necessarily refer to a single God or Goddess but rather is a generic term that refers to all Gods and Goddesses. Ritual works best when it's rhythmic and poetic. We remember things better in rhyme or when there's a predictable beat to the words. When you hear a song on the radio, no matter how old it is you can usually remember the words and this is because the brain is programmed to better remember tempo, rhythm and beat. Try saying the 'Lords and Ladies' in ritual and you'll quickly see that it just doesn't work as well and doesn't roll off the tongue like 'Lord and Lady'. So when using this term, remember that you are in fact referring to all divine Lords and Ladies, all Wiccan Gods and Goddesses, and not just one of each.

The second point is that just because the term 'Lord and Lady' has the Lord first, doesn't mean he's more important. We use 'Lord and Lady' in this order simply because it is easier to say than 'Lady and Lord' and is easier to remember and fit into the beat of ritual language. If you prefer to say 'Lady and Lord' instead then go for it, but again you must remember that whatever order you place the titles in, neither is more important than the other. Remember, balance of gender is most important!

The third point that underpins Wicca is that of reincarnation. There are so many different viewpoints on the form that this takes with some Wiccans feeling people can be the reincarnation of plants and animals, while others feel we just reincarnate as people. Yet others feel we reincarnate after considering what our next lessons in life will be while others feel we return immediately.

Regardless of exactly how reincarnation might actually operate, the fact remains that most Wiccans tend to adopt the principle that

6

we return in recurrent lives as an underpinning fundamental of the religion.

Activity
Take a few moments now to go and look at how other people, Wiccan and otherwise, view reincarnation. Do a search on the internet and read through some trusted resources so you can get a feel for the broad concepts of reincarnation and how different people view it. Your task is to think through the different forms of reincarnation and decide what you feel to be appropriate for you. Write this in your Learning Journal.

One of the most powerful principles of Wicca is that of connectivity between humans, plants, animals, the very substance of our planet and the natural cycles of life, death and the seasons. Essentially, Wiccans understand that we're all connected, that we all share the same energy, are made of the same energy and in fact trade and swap energies as a natural part of life and existence. The extension to this is that all beings, all plants, all animals, the planet itself and the cyclic seasons of nature are themselves life giving and divine.

The Gods and Goddesses don't live somewhere separate from ourselves. They don't live up in the sky or somewhere remote. They're in fact part of who we are, part of the plants, the animals, the planet and the seasons. To be more precise, they *are* the plants, the animals, the planets, the seasons and also you. It's their energy that makes us who we are and makes our planet as lusciously wonderful as it is. The outcome of this understanding is that you have a responsibility to honour, not just the Gods and Goddesses, but people, animals, plants, the planet and the seasons because they *are* the Gods and Goddesses. *You* are a God or Goddess! Look around you and see the Gods and Goddesses in the environment around you. That's part of being Wiccan!

Given we are therefore divine, magick (with a 'k' so we differentiate it from stage magic) is the most powerful way a Wiccan can generate their own divine future. Wiccans believe that because they're God or Goddess, that means they don't need to seek permission from a remote deity in the sky to grant them what they need. Instead, they have the divine responsibility to manifest it for themselves through the medium of magick.

Many people will argue that magick is the equivalent to prayer in that when someone prays, they're articulating a need and asking for an outcome for that need. Others will argue that prayer is different because it's a request to a remote God while magick is an action designed to bring about a result without the need for a request. Whatever way you look at magick, the fact remains that there are some ethical constraints around the use of magick which we'll cover in the next and final foundational principle of Wicca, that of the Wiccan Rede. This is a fairly intense, extremely important and fundamental principle of Wicca and one that deserves its own heading.

The Wiccan Rede

The Rede (pronounced 'reed') has dubious origins and depending on your source it was first published either by Lady Gwen Thompson or Doreen Valiente. It's commonly known and published as "An it harm none, do what ye will" but history shows that it comes from a much longer poem published in 1974.

Doreen Valiente, in a speech in 1964, was quoted as reciting "Eight words the Wiccan Rede fulfill, An it harm none, do what ye will" and that appears to be the first time the words come to light. Later, in 1974, in the Earth Religion News, a full, 26 line poem titled "The Wiccan Rede" was published with the same two last lines. In the same year a slightly different version was published by Lady Gwen Thompson and it was titled "Rede of the Wiccae". Lady Thompson attributed the poem to her grandmother Adriana Porter and she claimed that the earlier version was a distorted and fabricated version of her grandmother's original.

Whatever the origin, the fact remains that the last line of this poem,

An it harm none, do what ye will

has become fundamental in describing how Wiccans should conduct their religious and life practice. The term 'Rede' is a Middle English term from sometime between the 11th and 15th centuries that means 'counsel' or 'advice'. So the Rede, both as a full 26 line poem and as this more popular single line, is a document that provides us with some advice around how we should behave.

The term 'An' isn't a shortened version of the word 'and' but is rather an old version of the word 'if'. So the Rede is really saying 'If what you do harms nothing or no one, then you can do what you need to do'. That's all very well but it's really hard to live on this planet without harming anything or anyone so it's virtually impossible to live up to the Rede if we take it literally. Let me explain that for you.

Just by breathing, you're killing important bacteria. As you breathe in, bacteria hit the back of your throat and die. By eating vegetables, you're killing the plant and of course even more killing happens when you eat meat. By walking over your lawn, you're potentially standing on ants and other insects and killing them. So you can see that if we take the Rede literally, we simply will never live up to it. So what do we do to be ethical Wiccans then? Good question.

The answer is to look at our lives and really think through what we do, how we interact with the world, with our friends, family, business associates and others, how we talk with others, how we consider the sanctity of life, how we take things for granted, how we act without thinking, how we generally operate as human beings and really consider what the impact of our actions, thoughts and words are on others and on the environment. If we're sensible and don't act as literal fundamentalists in terms of what the Rede says, then we can live our lives ethically and appropriately and still 'have a life'!

Activity
Take some time now to think through and consider how your actions impact on others, on our planet and on yourself.
In your Learning Journal write down all the potentially negative or harmful ways your actions, words and behaviours could impact on other people, on the environment, on the Gods and Goddesses and of course on yourself. What does smoking do to your lungs? What does yelling at your kids do for their self esteem? How does eating all that junk food affect your body? How does your loved one feel after your selfishness? How long will that litter you dropped contaminate the planet?
After you've written your list, take heart, you're only human! Instead, think about a couple of ways you could work towards reducing that harm. Write down two ways you will minimise harm to others, to the planet or yourself.
Once you've done that, think about how you will stop and think before you act or speak now that as a Wiccan, you've got a responsibility to live according to the Wiccan Rede.

Read
The Wiccan Rede is a very important document that underpins ethical and behavioural expectations for Wiccans. So it's really important that you're familiar with what the Rede says and how it underpins everything Wiccans do. Take a few moments now to quietly read through and contemplate all the words of the Rede.

The Wiccan Rede
(Full Version)

Bide within the Law you must, in perfect Love and perfect Trust.
Live you must and let to live, fairly take and fairly give.

For tread the Circle thrice about to keep unwelcome spirits out.
To bind the spell well every time, let the spell be said in rhyme.

Light of eye and soft of touch, speak you little, listen much.
Honor the Old Ones in deed and name,
let love and light be our guides again.

Deosil go by the waxing moon, chanting out the joyful tune.
Widdershins go when the moon doth wane,
and the werewolf howls by the dread wolfsbane.

When the Lady's moon is new, kiss the hand to Her times two.
When the moon rides at Her peak then your heart's desire seek.

Heed the North winds mighty gale, lock the door and trim the sail.
When the Wind blows from the East, expect the new and set the feast.

When the wind comes from the South, love will kiss you on the mouth.
When the wind whispers from the West, all hearts will find peace and rest.

Nine woods in the Cauldron go, burn them fast and burn them slow.
Birch in the fire goes to represent what the Lady knows.

Oak in the forest towers with might, in the fire it brings the God's
insight. Rowan is a tree of power causing life and magick to flower.

Willows at the waterside stand ready to help us to the Summerland.
Hawthorn is burned to purify and to draw faerie to your eye.

Hazel-the tree of wisdom and learning adds its strength to the bright fire
burning.
White are the flowers of Apple tree that brings us fruits of fertility.

Grapes grow upon the vine giving us both joy and wine.
Fir does mark the evergreen to represent immortality seen.

Elder is the Lady's tree burn it not or cursed you'll be.
Four times the Major Sabbats mark in the light and in the dark.

As the old year starts to wane the new begins, it's now Samhain.
When the time for Imbolc shows watch for flowers through the snows.

When the wheel begins to turn soon the Beltane fires will burn.
As the wheel turns to Lamas night power is brought to magick rite.

Four times the Minor Sabbats fall use the Sun to mark them all.
When the wheel has turned to Yule light the log the Horned One rules.

In the spring, when night equals day time for Ostara to come our way.
When the Sun has reached its height time for Oak and Holly to fight.

Harvesting comes to one and all when the Autumn Equinox does fall.
Heed the flower, bush, and tree by the Lady blessed you'll be.

Where the rippling waters go cast a stone, the truth you'll know.
When you have and hold a need, harken not to others greed.

With a fool no season spend or be counted as his friend.
Merry Meet and Merry Part bright the cheeks and warm the heart.

Mind the Three-fold Laws you should three times bad and three times good.
When misfortune is enow wear the star upon your brow.

Be true in love this you must do unless your love is false to you.

These Eight words the Rede fulfil:
"An Ye Harm None, Do What Ye Will"

The Law of Return

Some more ethics to consider now! With the Wiccan Rede telling us to think before we act so that we behave much more ethically, morally and in a way that allows us to live without guilt, the Law of Return follows on from that. This principle says that no matter what you do, no matter what you say, it all comes back to you somehow. This is a little like Karma except Karma talks about the repercussions of actions coming back to you across different lifetimes.

The Law of Return tends to consider repercussions in a shorter time span and says that what you do in this life will come back in this life. So, theory has it that if you live life according to the Rede by minimising harm to yourself and others, then you'll minimise any harm coming back to you from your actions right here and right now.

Let's just make sure we fully understand exactly what will come back to us though. The Law of Return doesn't mean that exactly what you do will come back the same way. So just because you give $20 to charity doesn't mean you'll receive a mysterious envelope in the letterbox next week with $20 in it! Neither does it mean that just because you stood on an ant last week that some mutant, giant insect is going to come and stand on you! That's a flippant example I realise but what I'm trying to say is that the Law of Return is general. Being really generic, it argues that if you try your best and live your life with kindness, respect, generosity, empathy and concern, then you'll live a happy life where others respect you and where you benefit from happiness and wellbeing. Maybe people will be generous to you because you showed them empathy and respect.

Likewise if you live your life selfishly, without any thought for others, disrespecting people and the environment, fail to pay your bills, behave unkindly and unjustly, then life is going to come back and bite you!

One popular version of The Law of Return in Wicca is the Threefold Law which suggests that whatever you do will result in a return three times that which you gave out. One of the problems with this version is how do quantify a return of three on many actions or words? For example, how do you quantify being kind? If you speak kindly to a friend who needs some help, how do you measure that and recognise when three times your kindness comes right back at you? The Threefold Law is a quaint concept but it's probably a little difficult to measure and that's why the Law of Return, which generalises the concept of repercussions for your actions into something a little more workable, is much more sensible.

So now in terms of Wiccan fundamentals and ethics we have two major concepts.

- The Wiccan Rede which prescribes that we live the best way we can and minimise harm as much as possible and,
- The Law of Return that says whatever way we do live our life will come back as repercussions we then have to live with.

Those two concepts are powerful principles that we can use to test our behaviours against Wiccan expectations. The Rede is thus our prescription for life and the Law of Return is what happens to us when we do that. Together with the other points we went through that define what Wiccans believe in, you now should have a much better idea about what living your life as a Wiccan actually means philosophically, ethically, morally and religiously.

Activity
The Wiccan Rede and The Law of Return are the two most important ethical constraints that a Wiccan life imposes on you.
In your Learning Journal, write down a few sentences that explain the Rede and then a few more sentences that explain The Law of Return.

What is Visualisation and Why is it Important?

One of the most important skills to learn, practice and then use as you 'do' Wicca is visualisation. The success and feel of your circle casting and magick is largely dependent on how well you can 'see' what you're trying to create. So developing your skills of imagination and turning them into 'seeing' outcomes is hugely important in Wicca. To begin with it might be quite difficult and if you do find that, don't be too discouraged. Plenty of people find it hard to get to grips with 'seeing' something that they've been told since they were children doesn't actually exist.

The circle for instance is a sacred space that you build using the four elements and spirit so the walls of the circle are firmly planted in a different plane to the physical which as flesh and bone humans we usually inhabit. Casting your circle is done by 'seeing' the circle walls being built, and as a result actually feeling them around you. To anyone else who's not practiced at this art, there may appear to be nothing actually there but you know those walls exist because you 'saw' them into being.

The same is true of magick. In many forms of practical magick, the success of the outcome is determined by how concrete and real you can make it from 'seeing' it in your mind's eye. You create the outcome from your thoughts and internal vision and so you turn a concept into reality. Perhaps your magic might be candle or herb magick, the ingredients are unimportant. What really matters is the outcome you design and 'see' into reality.

But being able to 'see' things takes practice and over the next few months as you go through this Outer Court Wiccan learning journey, you'll gradually hone this skill and become adept at creating real outcomes from simply visualising them in your head and heart. To begin with though, we're going to focus on some simple ways to experience visualisation so you can see that in fact you already do it. Visualisation isn't just about seeing a picture in your mind's eye. It's also about feeling that picture, smelling the smells in it, feeling the heat or cold within it, tasting the food in it and hearing the sounds from it. Visualisation, once you've got it down pat takes you to a whole new plane of being so that you don't just see the picture in front of you but you *experience* it and make it real around you.

Make sure you're well prepared for your visualisations. Take the phone off the hook, lock the cat in the other room, shut the door and make sure you won't be disturbed. Experiment and see if visualising is easier for you with some calming meditation music in the background or maybe by the light of a safely positioned candle. Always start any visualisation by making yourself comfortable and calming yourself. For this first one, read it through and then get prepared and do it.

Your First Visualisation

Activity

Close your eyes, breathe deeply and slowly. Think about a meal you've had recently that you really enjoyed. Maybe it was a dinner out with friends, a romantic meal with your partner, maybe a picnic with the family or a meal at a friend's wedding.

Remember the meal and think about what you ate. What was the food? Remember what it tased like. Was it smooth or crunchy? Was it warm or cool? Was it peppery or sweet? How did it smell? Did you take your time over it or did you indulge in it fully? Taste it in your mouth again now. What does that feel like against your tongue, against the roof of your mouth? Can you smell the meal? How did you feel as you were eating that meal? Happy? Excited? Content? How do you feel now as you remember it?

What was the environment like where you ate? Was it a restaurant? A park? A friends house? What colour were the plates? What sort of cutlery did you use? Were there flowers of the table? Was the area filled with light or was it dusky and romantic?

What sounds were around you? Was it loud and bustling or quiet and peaceful? Was there music in the background or was there lots of laughter and chatter?

Take a few more moments to remember the meal and as many details as you can. Taste the food, smell the smells, see the table and the people you were with, hear the sounds around you and feel the feelings you had.

When you're ready, slowly bring your attention back to the room you're in and gradually open your eyes. When you're ready (take your time) slowly look around you and come back to the here and now. Congratulations on doing your first visualisation!

Your Dream, Meditation and Nature Diary

Well! You've achieved an awful lot already for a start but there's still some more to do and then you'll be set and ready to practice over the next month all that we've been talking about.

Witches become very skilled at listening to their own mind, body and heart. They learn very quickly and thoroughly about the messages they receive through meditations and dreams and it doesn't take long for them to recognise how their own behaviour is influenced or shaped by nature around them.

Most Wiccan teachers will expect their students to write their dreams and meditations down so that the students can begin to see those patterns and start to evaluate what each event means. This program is no different. In addition, you'll also need to write down what you see around you in nature so that you can begin to identify any patterns you see in your behaviour related to those seasonal differences and cycles. This process of recording in your diary is what helps you recognise, analyse and use the information you see within yourself.

Your Dreams and Meditations

Activity
Whenever you have what you think is a significant dream or meditation, write down what happened immediately in your diary. If you have trouble remembering your dreams, before you go to sleep say out loud "I will remember my significant dreams in the morning".
Get into the habit of writing dreams and any meditations down. This habit takes a while to form but it will be invaluable in your learning journey ahead.

Recording Nature

The reason for recording your observations is so that you can begin to see patterns in the seasonal cycles of nature. Wicca is very closely aligned with, and has a strong relationship with, the ecology around us. In order to connect with nature, you need to have a thorough understanding of her behaviours at any given time of year.

Activity
In your diary record what you notice in nature this month. This can be done just as dot points, as a story or even in pictures. You can write once a month but it'll be easier if you write at least once a week. Use the ideas below but remember also that these are examples only and you're encouraged to find your own nature based topics to explore as the year progresses.

Examples
Explain how the weather has been over the last month.
Has it been raining, dry, windy, gusty, calm, stormy, cold, humid, hot, changeable, cloudy or clear?
How has the weather made you feel this month? Was this feeling different from last month and could that be related to the weather? Have you felt restless, joyous, lethargic, hot and bothered, rejuvenated, sad or maybe even happy?
Is this your favourite or least favourite time of year? Why?
What colour have the sunsets been? What does this tell you about the weather?

Are the days getting longer or shorter? Are the nights getting cooler or warmer?

How are the birds behaving this month? Are they noisy, quiet, hidden, playful, waking early?

How are the insects and ants reacting this month? Are they mobile and out in force or nowhere to be seen?

What have you noticed about the local plant life? Are the plants and trees looking healthy, sad, dry, green, vibrant, growing, dormant, wilting, budding, in flower?

How is the grass growing in your lawn? Do you need to cut it more or less often? Is it starved of water, green and luscious, full of weeds, healthy, suffering?

How have your pets behaved lately? Do they change behaviour with the seasons?

Your Book of Shadows

The Witch's Book of Shadows is one of his or her most valued tools and becomes a prized and sacred book. While different Witches use it for different purposes, generally they will write the following things in their Book of Shadows;

* Rituals for Sabbats,
* The Ritual for the Esbat,
* Any magickal workings and the results,
* Rules for that individual or coven that govern how they work.

So this means your Book of Shadows is different to your diary. Your diary holds your dreams, meditations and nature observations while your Book of Shadows is much more sacred and long term.

Each Witch usually has her own Book of Shadows and a coven will often have a communal book as well in which the coven's rituals and rules are kept.

Many Witches have beautiful, often handmade books that are so precious that they almost become works of art. However, a simple school exercise book will do just as well. I usually encourage new seekers to just use inexpensive exercise books to begin with until they get a feel for how they want their final Book of Shadows formatted and what they want to include in it.

For now you don't need a Book of Shadows and in fact you won't need one until we get to lesson 3. However, because it's such a valuable tool to capture your workings and Wiccan experiences, it's worth you doing a little research on them in preparation for when you do have one.

Your Homework This Month

This month, your first as a Wiccan seeker in an Outer Court teaching program, is one of getting used to your diary and practicing the visualisations. Don't place too much pressure on yourself this month, take things slowly and ease yourself into the work. This isn't a race and in fact the more carefully you work at it, the more you'll benefit.

So for the next month ahead;

* Keep practicing the visualisation. Make sure you prepare first and calm yourself. Visualise different meals, and different events around happy meals you might have shared with others. Write the results in your Learning Journal.
* Write regularly in your diary and include any significant dreams you had, any meditations that offered you insights and look at what's happening around you in nature and write that down too.

That's not too heavy a workload is it! Congratulations on getting this far, you're on the road to becoming a Wiccan and Witch and while you'll learn a whole range of new things over the next few months, you've taken a huge step by embarking on your first month's work.

The Second Lesson
Wicca Then and Now

So you survived the first month, well done! Now that you have some underpinning foundations around what Wicca and Witchcraft means, this month we're going to focus on the history of Wicca and how it's morphed into its current genre of coven and degree structures.

By the time you've finished this second lesson you should be able to;

🐚 Describe Wicca's history and discern between the truth and fallacies,
🐚 Explain what the Inclusive tradition is and what makes it different from the others,
🐚 Talk through the popular Outer Court and Inner Court Wiccan degree structures,
🐚 Appreciate how Oak and Mistletoe works,
🐚 Extend your visualisation experience.

Wicca's Problematic History

So our first task is to look at how and where Wicca was started and we need to get the first fallacy out of the way. Contrary to the romantic notion of some people, Wicca is *not* an ancient religion revived from the pre-Christian era. Let's make sure we all fully understand that right now. For too long there's been the proposal that Wicca is an old religion that was rediscovered by Gerald Gardner in the 1940s and that he brought it back to life and released it to the world. Simply not true. So what is true then?

Gerald Brosseau Gardner (1884-1964) was an English civil servant who served both in his home country and overseas, mainly in Malaysia. He was fascinated by magickal systems like the Golden Dawn system, the Rosicrucians and so on and as a means of indulging his own need for a legitimate religious practice, he developed what eventually became called Wicca.

Gardner was the product of the Victorian era which was rife with secret societies and various esoteric experiments. Freemasonry was in its hay day and Thelemic mysticism had been publicised and promoted by Aleister Crowley so the early part of the 20th century was a time of underground popularity of all things mysterious and exotic. To make things even more open for Gardner to foster and promote his new religion, the English Witchcraft Laws were repealed in June of 1951 which allowed more open discussions of esoteric practices.

Gardner claimed that he came across a practicing group of Witches operating in the New Forest in the south of England and he proclaimed that he was initiated into the coven in 1939. Gardner revealed that the coven was lead by a woman called Dorothy Clutterbuck and whilst research has since shown that Dorothy existed, there's no proof that she was actually a High Priestess of any religious group. There's since been a considerable body of research conducted that suggests the woman Gardner claims was the coven's High Priestess may in fact have been Edith Woodford-Grimes or Rosamund Sabine. The truth is that we'll probably never know who this woman actually was and in fact there's still much speculation that there wasn't any coven at all and that Gardner made the whole thing up anyway!

Gerald Gardner

In 1949, ten years after Gardner claimed he was initiated into the New Forest coven, "High Magic's Aid" was published. In it Gardner put forward a supposedly fictional story but prefaced the story with the claim that the rituals described in it were authentic. This was a bold move because the laws in England at the time still prevented Witchcraft so Gardner had to claim the work was fiction.

In 1954, Gardner published "Witchcraft Today" and because by then the Witchcraft Laws had been repealed, he was legally able to refer to the materials he wrote as being legitimate and current experiences. The story gets very muddied though by now because Doreen Valiente and various other writers had come to the fore and described themselves as Wiccans and Witches, related in many ways to, but independent of Gardner. By the 1960s Alex Sanders had entered the ongoing debate and started creating his own brand of Wicca alongside Gardner's. There were considerable public arguments and disputes about the authenticity of people's priestly title, their claims to initiation, their supposed hereditary status and indeed still even the origin and authorship of the whole religion itself. Individual practitioners often had a desire for personal power over rituals, wanted publicity for their own means, disagreed with their coven politics and so on and the religion Gardner claims to have stumbled across gradually fragmented into different groups known as traditions because of their then claim to historical foundations.

Research
The history of Wicca has been researched by a number of well qualified people who have published some very valid accounts of the religion's troubled and clouded development.
Take a few days to source information on Wicca's origins. A very sensible web site is;
http://www.geraldgardner.com/
and the transcript of a wonderful speech by Julia Phillips can be located on that site here;
http://www.geraldgardner.com/History_of_Wicca_Revised.pdf

So by the 1970s we begin to see a growing number of traditions branching out from Gardner's original concepts. Gardnerian Wicca still remains the agreed founding tradition but Alexandrian Wicca (founded by Alex Sanders) quickly grew in popularity around the world. Both these traditions are oath bound in that any initiated practitioners are bound to secrecy on several aspects of ritual and deity. This legitimately means that you can only be trained and initiated into their tradition by an initiated Gardnerian or Alexandrian Wiccan. Many Gardnerians and Alexandrians argue that any training and claim to the title 'Wiccan' is invalid unless that person has undertaken the training and oath bound initiation of that coven. We discussed this in the previous lesson of course but what this means in terms of the history of Wicca is that the fundamentalists would claim that Gardnerian Wicca is the true source and any other non oath bound practitioners are neo-Wiccans instead of being 'true' Wiccans.

Read
You've already spent some time looking at the development of Gardnerian Wicca. To round out your history lesson a little more, please try and locate a copy of "The Triumph of the Moon: A History of Modern Pagan Witchcraft" by Professor Ronald Hutton. It's a long book but well worth a read. It will provide you with a no-nonsense history of Wicca including many of the other traditions that followed on from Gardner's contribution.

So where does all that history leave us now? Humans, being as individual as they are were bound to fragment a single religious concept into different forms to suit their broad range of needs. Just look at Christianity as an example of the vast array of opinions and approaches to what is supposedly a single Abrahamic religion! There are Catholics, Pentecostals, Baptists, Lutherans, Anglicans and the list goes on and on. The same is true of Wicca and with the advent of modern communication systems like the internet, our ability to mushroom and spread in different directions has been exponential over the last thirty years. As well as Gardnerian and Alexandrian, the list of Wicca traditions is massive and growing daily it seems. Some of the more popular and widely known traditions include;

- Correllian
- The Church and School of Wicca
- British Traditional
- Covenant of the Goddess
- Dianic
- Eclectic
- Georgian
- Sacred Wheel
- Seax Wicca
- Discordianism
- Stregheria

Research
Do a search on the internet for different traditions of Wicca. You'll find many sites that provide you with listings of popular traditions and brief summaries of their approach. Spend an hour or so reading through the appraisals you can find on different traditions.

The Inclusive Tradition

So with a greater understanding of how we got to where we are today in terms of Wicca, let's now spend some time looking at our own tradition, the one you're studying now.

While the coven known as Oak and Mistletoe was founded in 2005, the Inclusive tradition which came from that coven was born in 2008 from years of study and practice. As its founder, I was originally trained and initiated into an Alexandrian based eclectic coven but later moved to a much more flexible mode of Wiccan practice where I studied through to eventually gain the High Priestess title.

As part of my vocational research experiences, I studied how Wiccans and Witches learn their Craft and in so doing was awarded a PhD from Curtin University of Technology in Western Australia. This was significant and I was truly blessed because unlike many Wiccans (who are bound to practice only with their own coven), I was allowed to attend the rituals of covens from several different traditions as well as work with my own coven; so that I could gather effective and legitimate data for the research. So I got to work with many different approaches to Wicca and to develop a broad understanding of the wide variety of traditions within the religion.

Having seen how many covens operate and having watched the inflexibility of some traditions, I decided there had to be a better way to teach students that wasn't elitist, discriminatory or based in strict dogma. As a result, I formed Oak and Mistletoe initially as a teaching coven so that people who wanted to learn a flexible, personalised approach to Wicca could do so in a safe and caring, shared environment. Oak and Mistletoe quickly developed into more than just a face to face teaching coven and while it's still growing, it's become known as a community that supports students and practitioners around the world. But what does the tradition that grew out of that hold as its foundation principles?

- We tell the truth,
- Everyone has the right to develop their own relationship with the Divine,
- Wicca is a religion, philosophy, practice and a way of life. It is *not* a dogma,
- All tradition members deserve to be honoured, respected and cared for,
- The real religion of Wicca is more important than the fluffy bunny stuff around it,
- The Wiccan Rede and Law of Return are our prescriptions for appropriate behaviour and consequences,
- Wicca can be eclectic and flexible and still be Wicca.

So let's take some time to explore these points in detail so you're much more informed about what the Inclusive tradition was developed to offer.

We Tell the Truth
Right at the beginning of this lesson we talked about how Wicca is *not* an ancient religion reborn and re-established as some of the more romantic followers of the faith might have you believe. The simple truth is that research and historical records clearly show that Wicca is a modern religion that is based on what is known of old rituals, but it is not of itself an old religion. That's the truth.

Like that example, this tradition strives to always teach its students the truth. The tradition believes that everyone has the right to know the truth about Wicca, about the rituals and about its practice. The only exception to that is the full disclosure of mystery rituals to students and practitioners prior to their participation in them. Rather than spoil the wonder that is a mystery tradition by explaining what happens and how, the tradition prefers to remain silent on them so that the full experience remains special, awe inspiring and personal. Other than that, teachers and students alike are encouraged always to minimise the romantic and untrue stories of Wicca and Witchcraft and instead focus on reality and honesty.

We also follow this methodology in our principles of operation within any covens of the tradition as well. Rules and expectations are transparent and open for anyone to see and contribute to. Covens must have an open charter and set of by-laws that clearly spell out for everyone's benefit what the expectations are, how people should behave with each other and how the coven is structured. Any coven dues or expenses are always open to member scrutiny so that everyone can be free to trust and accept the honesty, integrity and character of any office bearers or coven members. Trust and respect come from honesty and the truth and so the Inclusive tradition upholds that everyone has a right to know the truth and a responsibility to give the truth.

Everyone has the Right to Develop their own Relationship with the Divine

The Inclusive tradition also says that while Wicca is a recognised religion with an underpinning set of base beliefs and foundational practices, the absolute way in which those beliefs and practices are committed to is flexible. This means that we don't prescribe that you *must* do things a particular way, neither must you adhere to the rituals we set out for you. Of course you can use our practices exactly as they are if you want to but you're also free to modify them if that means they enhance your relationship with the Gods and Goddesses.

Similarly, your High Priest/ess or your teacher don't have the right to tell you how you must *be* a Wiccan. That's the same as me telling you that you *must* eat breakfast at 7:30 every morning because that's what I believe as a Wiccan is appropriate. (That might be the case through the week by the way but weekend sleep-ins chuck 7:30am right out the window!)

Look, the simple truth is that what I think is the best way to talk with the Gods and Goddesses is the right way, but only for me. Your way is also right, but only for you. So everyone has the right way for them and that's Ok. We'll probably all share very similar ways of 'doing' that relationship but ultimately even if I teach you a way to have that relationship, it's *your* relationship and *your* responsibility to care for it the best way for you.

That means that this tradition will teach you the basics, will teach you about Wicca and will show you ways you can *be* Wiccan, but in the end you always have the right to make your Wiccan religion your own by changing things to suit your own needs.

This principle also means something else though as well and that is that pretty much every form of Wicca is Ok for that particular Wiccan. It doesn't matter if you're Alexandrian, a British Traditional Wiccan, a Dianic or an Eclectic, it's all valid. Each tradition might be different and have different viewpoints on this topic (goodness knows this is a volatile argument within the broader Wiccan community) but if the Wiccan hat fits, then wear it and allow others to wear theirs with dignity and respect too. Just because one tradition might disagree and define that any other tradition is null and void, doesn't mean you have to jump on the same bandwagon. Our viewpoint within this tradition is that everyone has a right to their religious experience and that means that while you might not agree with a particular point of view of another tradition, that doesn't mean that you have the right to say theirs is wrong and yours is right. As I mentioned earlier, what's right for them is right for them and what's right for you is right for you. Let's respect everyone's right to their own religion, be it Wicca or anything else.

Wicca is a Religion, Philosophy, Practice and a Way of Life - It is not a Dogma

Knowing now that you have the right to your own religious experience, just as everyone else does, it also means that we need to remember that religion should be flexible, open and understanding.

Democracy isn't just for politics, it's also relevant to Wicca. The Inclusive tradition takes the last point another step further by saying that not only do you have the right and responsibility to your religion and relationship with the Divine but you also have the right to do that without being confined inside someone else's demands. If you work within a coven or even as a solitary who might occasionally celebrate the festivals as a guest of a coven, you have the right to do so in flexibility.

We determine within this tradition that the development of rituals, coven charters and by-laws, group practices, coven operational processes and anything else related to Wiccan practice is democratically contributed to by all members. So within an Inclusive coven, the charter and coven agendas, the festivals and so on can all have shared contribution. They don't have to be written and 'policed' by the coven leader. Even more, the coven leadership can be rotated through suitably qualified priest/esses too where that might work for the coven members.

What this means is that as an Inclusive Wiccan you have much more control over how you and your coven brothers and sisters work together. You can't be dictated to by an autocratic, power tripping leader or indeed even by the dogma of a particular tradition come to that. You can be supported, cared for and taught by a democratic, empathic and Inclusive teacher and priest/ess but they can't make you do anything you don't feel comfortable doing. That means if you don't want to do rituals skyclad (in the nude) then you don't have to even if that particular tradition deems skyclad rituals as the 'only' way. That's not the Inclusive way. Similarly, if you don't want to take part in certain ritual practices, then you don't have to. Remember, this is *your* religion too so you have a democratic right to be involved in how it's conducted.

Tradition Members Deserve to be Honoured, Respected and Cared for

Wicca is about honouring the Gods and Goddesses, nature and people, and that doesn't mean just in ritual. In this tradition we honour all people both those who are our members and those who are not. We care about people and we show we care about people. Inclusive covens will usually support their community through appropriate charities and will often devote some of their collective and individual time to services and activities they feel will benefit causes or people in need. Oak and Mistletoe for example sponsors a Guide Dog puppy's training each year, the Animal Welfare League and The Ancient Ways Incorporation. This is one way we can support our community and show we care.

Inclusive Wiccans respect each other, respect the rights of others but more importantly they honour and support each other. Inclusive covens are a spiritual family and members become very close with one another offering understanding, empathy, friendship and love. Wicca, like most religions sees love and caring for each other as ultimately important and so Inclusive Wiccans see caring for others as well as themselves as being the best way to also honour the Gods and Goddesses.

The Real Religion of Wicca is More Important Than the Fluffy Bunny Stuff Around it

Whilst Inclusive Wicca can be seen as tolerant and flexible, one thing we don't see as being important is all the fluffy, peripheral, new-age stuff that many people think is Wicca. The religion honours its Gods and Goddesses, the cycles of nature and each other and conducts rituals that do exactly that. But Wicca is *not* tarot cards, crystal healing, chakra clearing, numerology, astrology or any other 'ology'.

Wicca is a religion where some practitioners also use these systems and methods of divination and this is often appropriate because they're usually very earth centred, natural and non invasive. However, of themselves they're not Wicca and you don't need to know about numerology, be an expert reiki practitioner, understand the complexities of astrology or know how to use the myriad of herbs available to us to be Wiccan. If you do some of these things, good on you but you don't have to in order to be Wiccan.

Let's talk quickly about Wiccan tools here too while we're at it. Many, in fact most, Wiccans have a bunch of Wiccan tools that enhance their practice and help them focus. They have athames, wands, chalices, censors, quarter candles and of rituals tools and artefacts. These are wonderful implements and a good teacher will always teach you what each tool is used for, what correspondences relate to which tool and how and when to use them all. The danger comes however when your Wiccan practice becomes dependent on tools to the point where you can't work without them. This is not good!

So why do we have tools then if we can end up dependent on them? Tools are objects that help us focus our ritual and magickal intent. They enhance our ability to get into the spiritual 'zone' and they help us to identify as Wiccan. After continued use, they often become infused with power and can become very special, valued and honoured artefacts that are precious to us. But Wicca is still a religion, not a devotion to a set of tools so in the Inclusive tradition, we'll always teach you how to develop your personal relationship with the Divine without tools first so that they become enhancers rather than dependencies.

The Wiccan Rede and Law of Return are our Prescriptions for Appropriate Behaviour and Consequences
We explored these two underpinning principles in the first lesson so you should already be familiar with and fully understand these concepts. The Rede defines the morals under which we should conduct our lives and the Law of Return tells us what will happen to us dependent on how we behave. It's as simple as that. These two principles are the cornerstones to Wicca regardless of the tradition and for us in the Inclusive tradition, they're pivotal to the way we conduct our religious and mundane lives. That's why you'll see them constantly referred to throughout this program and the tradition at large.

Wicca can be Eclectic and Flexible and Still be Wicca.
Inclusive's final principle is that of the legitimacy of eclectic flexibility within Wicca. That's not to say that Wiccan practitioners can go way

off in different directions and still call themselves Wiccan but where they modify practices or adopt slightly different ways of doing things to suit their own needs, that's still Wicca regardless of what anyone says.

Let's just explore this for a while because it's important, particularly where an inexperienced eclectic student is confronted with the fundamentalist approach of some traditions and isn't comfortable defending his or her position. Wicca includes a basic set of principles that you were introduced to in the first lesson. We've just expanded on that here by discussing Inclusive Wicca and showing that the principles this tradition adheres to support those of the fundamental principles of Wicca. However, let's meet the hypothetical Jane Doe and see if she's Wiccan or something else.

Jane calls herself Wiccan and in fact was initiated into an oath bound tradition many years ago. As such, according to Gardnerian, Alexandrian and several other traditions she could potentially claim legitimate Wiccan status. Now, Jane lives in a country in which the original and traditional peoples still live. She quite likes some of the practices they use which are of course native to them and she's watched what they do with Talking Sticks and Smoking Rituals. She's also very keen on some of the beliefs of Buddhism and has chosen to adopt a couple of the Buddhist ritual practices into her work. She now uses a prayer wheel and also celebrates the festival of Vesak alongside the Wiccan Wheel of the Year.

Now let's think this through together. Jane calls herself Wiccan so one could argue that this is exactly what she is. However, she's modified her practice so that now she actually has some extra festivals in her Wheel of the Year which aren't Wiccan and she also conducts her rituals without some of the traditional Wiccan inclusions but she's swapped them with some native options instead. Is she still Wiccan or is she now practicing 'Jane Doeism'? What do you think? Personally I'd have to fall on the side of Doeism rather than Wicca largely because her practice has become so different from Wicca and now also includes things native to her country people but not native to Wicca.

Let me make one thing clear here. There's nothing wrong with Doeism, nothing at all... for Jane. Anyone can create their own religion using the ingredients of a variety of religions, a sort of 'buffet' religion, but the trick is then to recognise that and call it a personalised religion rather than try and mould a square peg into a round hole.

This tradition is all for modification and very supportive of personalising one's religious experience but there needs to be a sensible balance. By all means develop your Wiccan experience into something that's meaningful for you but when it morphs into a different religion altogether, then that needs to be recognised. Perhaps that new religion can be classified as a Pagan religion, perhaps Shamanic but honesty about the family of religion in which it sits is important because your religion becomes an identifier of who you are and what you stand for.

Popular Coven Structures

Ok, so it's time to move away from our own tradition and go back into the big wide Wiccan world again as we take a look at how covens typically structure themselves. Most traditional, teaching covens are set up with two main groups of membership, the Outer Court and the Inner Court. Nice, quaint language but essentially that means those people who haven't been initiated into the coven and those who have. Let's start with the Outer Court first.

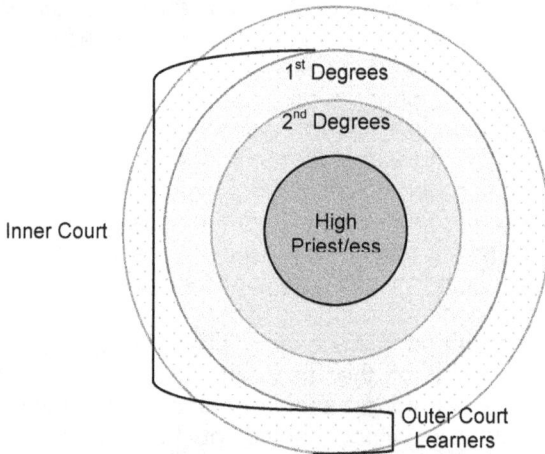

This group of people, and if you're reading this then you're probably a member of Oak and Mistletoe's Outer Court, are usually still learning about Wicca or they might well have been initiated but have moved from one coven/tradition to another and are going through the learning process for their move into their new coven. Outer Court is therefore the 'school' for each coven.

The most popular length of time for training in the Outer Court is a year and a day and this is quite valid for a number of reasons. Part of the Outer Court teaching process asks students to observe nature around them, record that in their diary and to begin to recognise how their behaviour is affected by seasonal changes. You've already been asked to do this from lesson one as part of your Wiccan learning experience with Oak and Mistletoe. If you can do this over a whole year you then have an entire seasonal cycle to look at and consider. A year is also a sufficient period of time for the teacher to work out if you need any extra help in any one area and if you've learnt enough to undertake an initiation. It gives the learner time to get to know their fellow students and also the Inner Court members so after a year, everyone pretty much should have had enough time to work out if they'll all be able to do magickal workings and rituals together.

Admission to the Inner Court usually happens only after initiation and just because you've reached the end of the training program, even if you met all the requirements, doesn't mean you'll automatically be accepted for initiation. The process of initiation karmically links both the initiator and the student together so whoever is conducting the initiation rite has to be absolutely sure that the student is ready and able to take on a new life as a Wiccan. Moreover, initiation to first degree and the Inner Court is *never* offered. It *must* be asked for by the student.

Once a student has asked for and undertaken their initiation rite, they then enter the Inner court membership of the coven as a first degree Wiccan. The training wheels aren't off though because now, during the rituals of the coven membership, the student really learns *how* to be a Wiccan. Outer Court is largely theory and background information while the practical, hands on learning generally takes place after initiation and once a first degree participates in the coven's rites and rituals.

First degrees spend at least another year, usually more learning how to cast circles, work with the elements, write rituals, work magick and focus and sharpen their skills. Many covens have a specific training program for first degrees to enter that trains them toward second degree status and the content of this is designed to really sharpen their capabilities and prepare them for a teaching and leadership role. As with first degree initiation, the practitioner must ask for a second degree initiation and like the first degree rite, this is not automatic. Becoming a second degree means taking on more responsibility which usually includes shared coven leadership, teaching, ritual writing, festival planning and general coven duties. The coven leadership need to be sure that the practitioner is ready for such a challenge.

There may also be specific roles that the practitioner needs to take on dependent on their age and gender. Covens frequently have coven office bearers such as the Treasurer and Secretary but they also have ceremonial and ritual roles such the Maiden, the Man in Black and the Crone. Second degree status usually means that the practitioner is prepared to accept their share of responsibility and leadership and so like the first degree decision, it's made after considerable discussion and consideration.

Having become a second degree, the more senior practitioner now teaches the Outer Courters (this is often also done by more advanced first degrees as well) and can if they so choose just remain at that degree. In fact, anyone can remain at whatever stage they choose to, even Outer Court. There is never any pressure for anyone to move through the degree process. However, having worked their way through to a second degree often indicates the practitioner would eventually like to move into the High Priest/ess role eventually. Unlike the first and second degree initiation, the third degree is the only rite that *is* offered to anyone and in fact it's rather bad manners for a second degree to ask for third degree initiation. This rite of passage is usually offered only after substantial experience as a second degree and can in fact take ten years or more before it's offered.

The major consequence of taking the third degree initiation is that the practitioner now takes on the title of High Priest/ess (as opposed to simply Priest/ess in lower degrees) and is encouraged to hive off and form their own coven. Their new coven, the daughter coven, may sometimes take Outer Court members from the mother coven with it and the High Priest/ess of the mother coven will usually offer support and coaching for a year or so as the new High Priest/ess finds their leadership feet. Thereafter those two covens, and any others that might also hive off, will often share festivals together and even look after each other's coven membership if the High Priest/ess goes on holidays or is ill.

This model is fairly universal across most traditions but many of the more flexible and eclectic covens have flattened the hierarchical structure and have moved toward a more democratic model of leadership rather than one based on seniority. Inclusive covens like Oak and Mistletoe sit somewhere in between.

The Structure of Inclusive Covens

We're back in our own tradition again so let's compare what Inclusive does with the popular model described above. Essentially we do things in a very similar fashion but we inject a little more flexibility, a lot more personalised, tailor-made leniency and we gear our training up to be student centred and not dogma centred. We do conduct initiations into the coven (not the tradition) for the physical coven membership but for those people who learn about our tradition via the internet or through supported distance training, we suggest self dedication. Let me explain what the difference between dedication and initiation is to make that a little clearer.

We've already determined earlier on that initiation is a three part, mystery rite that forces a person to first strip themselves of their current identity, that then introduces them to the Gods and

Goddesses who will give to the initiate some personal insights, and finally that provides them with a new Wiccan spirituality with which to live their life. Given it's a mystery rite, the student obviously can't conduct their own initiation if they already know what it involves! Where's the mystery if you already know it?

What they can do though is conduct their own self dedication before the Gods and Goddesses. This dedication ritual helps the practitioner to ritually, physically and emotionally dedicate their lives to the Divine and to see themselves as a true Wiccan and Witch. It's as powerful as an initiation and gets around the problem of living life as a Wiccan for solitaries who aren't able to be initiated into a coven.

For those students who are learning in an Outer Court with an Inclusive coven, if they ask and are accepted, they have the opportunity to undertake the mystery rite of initiation into that coven. We don't initiate into the tradition, only into the coven and we do so deliberately because we don't want to set up an elitist hierarchy of those who've been tradition initiated and those who haven't.

One of the other differences for the Inclusive tradition is that we're much more open during the training process. Most oath bound traditions will not allow a student to witness the circle casting rite until after they've been initiated but in Inclusive, we believe you can't make the very important and life changing decision to dedicate and live your life as a Wiccan unless you've experienced a little of it first. So our Outer Court students are encouraged to attend Full Moon Esbats, normally out of bounds for non initiates, and are asked to get involved in ritual writing from about half way through their Outer Court training program. We believe that only after you've really understood what you're getting into, can you ask to get into it!

Another quite fundamental difference between Inclusive and more long standing traditions is our principle of earlier hiving off and taking charge of your coven. For traditions such as Gardnerian and Alexandrian, the likelihood of you eventually leading your own coven really only begins to be reality after about eight to ten years and one could argue that even this is not sufficient time to take on the responsibility of teaching others something as personal as a religion. However in Inclusive, we believe that after a year or so as a second degree and if you've shown a willingness to lead a coven democratically, empathically and with enough knowledge and skill, then there's no reason why we can't support you to do that. We all live in the 21st century and we're big, grown up people now, not constrained by the post war reality that was apparent during the years when Wicca was first developed. This training, which is very comprehensive, thorough and well supported even for distance learners, does a great job of preparing you for coven leadership.

31

Read
So that you're really familiar with and can fully understand the training and degree structure of the Inclusive tradition, please now go to the Oak and Mistletoe website to read through their charter and bylaws. These are a pretty good descriptor for Inclusive covens and as an Outer Court member of that coven (if you're going through this book as a student of Oak and Mistletoe), you need to be familiar with its expectations.
http://www.oakandmistletoe.org.au/our-charter/

Your Second Visualisation

This month we want to extend the visualisation process and stretch you just a little more. Each month we'll take this visualisation process, grow it a little further and ask you to practice it repeatedly so you become comfortable with letting yourself 'see' and experience different planes of reality.

This time we're going to start working on the energisation visualisation that Oak and Mistletoe uses with all its students and practitioners to help them connect to the pure energy of the Earth and the Goddess of the planet. The purest forms of energy come from the planet below our feet and so in order to cleanse ourselves, refresh our energy levels and the purity of our soul based essence, we need to draw it from a suitable source. What better place than where it's most pure, the ground below us! In addition, this is the visualisation that Oak and Mistletoe practitioners use prior to conducting magickal workings so that they're cleansed and don't contaminate their work, and so they can direct the pure energy they're drawing in straight into the spell-work or ritual they're conducting.

A note of warning here for you. Please read through both the visualisation activity below and the grounding section that follows it *before* you conduct this visualisation.

Remember to prepare as instructed in the first lesson and make sure that you're comfortable and won't be disturbed.

Activity
Close your eyes, breathe deeply and slowly for a few seconds feeling the breath draw into your lungs and slowly back out again. Imagine a tap root growing from the base of your spine,your base chakra, downward toward the ground. It's a nice strong tap root and it slowly, gently but deliberately grows down through your chair, through the floor covering, on through the floor structure and

then down toward the ground below. See your tap root forcing its way into the earth below you and remaining strong and willing. Keep it growing, further and further. Push it further still, right down into the planet, right down into the dirt, the rocks and the substrata below your feet. Your tap root is strong and it's now anchoring you safely to the Earth. You're comfortable, you're connected to the planet and you're safe.

Now ask the glorious Goddess Gaia if she would allow you to draw into your tap root some of her pure, white, clean, fresh energy. She willingly gives you this energy. She always does because it's your pure white light too. See the pure white light, the cleansing, energising light being sucked up through your tap root and coming up closer and closer toward you. Draw it up toward you. Pull the energy up towards the base of your spine.

As it comes up through the tap root and enters your body, see it begin to tumble around at the base of your torso and then begin falling down your legs towards your feet. See the energy fill your toes up and any dark patches of negative energy are washed away as you breathe out. The energy just keeps streaming up through your tap root and flooding into your legs. Your lower legs, your thighs are now flooded with pure, white, clean, fresh light. Your legs feel cleansed and revitalised.

The energy keeps coming in and now it fills your lower torso, forcing away any dark and negative patches as you breathe out. Keep drawing up the energy, lots more yet, so much more yet. Your whole tummy area is now filled with white light and you feel comfortable, rested and calm. More white light, this time tumbling up into your chest and shoulders. The pure, white, cleansing light rolls down your arms and into your hands and fingers filling them with light. Yet more light, still coming into your body and now it fills your lower and upper arms and your shoulders feel relaxed and you feel safe and calm and peaceful. The white light then reaches up into your neck and as the light fills your body, it pushes any negative patches of old, faded, worn out, dirty energy away with each breath. Your head is filling with white light and so is your face and now, as you scan your body, you see all the parts of it are filled to the brim with wonderful, refreshing, rejuvenating, pure white energy. You feel alive, you feel calm, you feel peaceful and happy. Check your body for any last remaining patches of old, dark energy you don't need and breathe them away.

Spend a few moments luxuriating in the bliss of being bathed in pure, clean energy from the Goddess. When you're ready and have had your fill, honour Gaia by thanking her for her generosity and love and then slowly bring your attention back to the room you're in and gradually open your eyes. When you're ready (take your time) slowly look around you and come back to the here and now.

Grounding

While this energising visualisation is powerful and helps cleanse your body of old, residual, rubbish energy that's been hanging off you and recharges you with some of nature's most purest white light, it's really important that you don't just get up and go about your daily business fully charged like this. All that energy, locked inside your body can send you into a bit of a 'buzzy' state and it can be quite dangerous especially if you drive a car or do anything else that needs distinct concentration or safety. You absolutely must ground yourself again before you drive, before you care for children or do anything that might endanger yourself or anyone.

In addition storing all that energy up inside you can actually make you ill. It's a bit like being dosed up with mega powerful vitamins but not exercising them off again. If you don't ground again, you can end up with headaches, you can begin to feel quite nauseous and generally off colour. You're also are at greater risk of attracting other energies and sprits who might not be the friendliest of creatures and without adequate training in shielding and self protection, it's just plain silly to keep yourself dosed up like that. So once you've done that energising visualisation, if you're not going to use the energy up with magickal workings or ritual events, then let the excess drain back to the Earth again. You'll still feel recharged, calm, healthy, happy and pure but you won't feel quite so 'spaced out'. You can always do the visualisation exercise again at any time and draw fresh new light up whenever you want.

Activity
To release the excess energy back to the Earth, you can do one (or both) of two things. Eating crunchy food like carrots or apples is a great way to use up some of the excess, bubbling over energy you've drawn up. So find some nice fresh, raw carrots and make like a rabbit!
Alternatively, bend or kneel down on the ground, preferably outside on the grass or dirt, and place the palms of your
hands flat on the ground. Imagine some of the excess energy you drew up flowing smoothly back into the ground below you through your open palms. Not all that precious white light energy has to leave your body but you should imagine enough of it passing back home to the Earth so that you don't feel 'spaced out'.

Your Homework This Month

This month, your task is to really focus heavily on the very important skill of visualisation. Seeing and feeling different planes of existence is vital to your success in circle casting and magickal workings so it's well worth making the effort.

So for the next month ahead;

* Keep practicing the energisation visualisation. Make sure you prepare first and calm yourself. Really try and see and feel the pure white light streaming into your body and flushing out any dark and dirty patches. The more you practice it, the easier it becomes. Write the results in your Learning Journal.
* Write regularly in your diary and include any significant dreams you had, any meditations that offered you insights and look at what's happening around you in nature and write that down too.

Second month in and your skills are developing already! Keep it up, the more time and energy you devote to it, the more benefits and successes you'll see for yourself.

The Third Lesson
The Sacred Circle

Well, here we are at the start of your third month of training. By now you should have a fairly detailed feel for the big wide Wiccan world out there (an alternative meaning for the 'www' prefix!) and a firm understanding of the Inclusive tradition. It's time to start moving away from theory and move into the 'how' of Wicca. Here's where you begin to put theory into practice and really start 'doing' Wicca instead of just 'knowing about' Wicca.

By the time you've finished this third lesson you should be able to;

🕯 Explain what a circle is,
🕯 Describe the different types of circle,
🕯 Talk through why Inclusive's circle casting process is set up the way it is,
🕯 Be ready to develop and conduct your own personal circle casting 'script',
🕯 Behave appropriately inside your own or someone else's circle,
🕯 Set up your altar.

What is a Circle?

The first and most important question for this whole lesson is this first one really. What is a circle? Circle casting is fundamental to the practice of Wicca and so a thorough understanding of what you're doing and why is absolutely paramount to getting the best out of your rituals.

A circle is simply a temple or church without the physical walls and roof. It's a sacred place of honour, respect and appreciation and a cleansed and pure area in which to conduct magickal workings and honour the Divine. Your circle can in fact be created within a designated physical space and many Wiccans and Witches choose to have a dedicated room or a pergola in the garden just used for circle and ritual work. Having such an area is fantastic because it gives you a clearly defined physical location in which you can meditate and talk with the Gods and Goddesses. But the circle itself is not actually that space. It's not the walls of that room or the structure of the pergola. The circle itself is a temporary sphere, a circular envelope or shell of pure energy that you build and erect. That shell helps to keep in magickal energies, until you want them released and it helps keep out any unwanted intruders or negative energies you don't want hanging around.

The spherical shell you create, which we now understand is the circle, is created from the elemental and spiritual energies all around us, but it also gradually disintegrates, almost immediately, after being cast and those energies you drew together to form the circle shell slowly filter back to the surrounding environment. What many people find though is that when a circle is cast at the same location repeatedly, there tends to end up being some residual energy slowly building up there. It's as though each time you cast a circle, just a little part of it remains in that location as a spiritual footprint and the more times a circle is cast, the more spiritual footprints remain. Eventually, you can feel the residual energy in these sorts of locations.

Activity
Go into a really old church and just sit quietly and tune yourself into the building and the space within it. What do you feel? Do you feel peaceful, relaxed, maybe calm? Can you sense the thousands of people who have come here before you?
Go into the ruins or remains of an old jail, perhaps a courthouse or mental hospital if you can, maybe even somewhere still functioning in that capacity, somewhere where there's been considerable trauma, anger, frustration and hurt and do the same thing. What do you feel? Can you sense the hurt, the pain, the anguish of some of the thousands of people who have been there before you?

Ok, so now we know that our circle is simply a virtual, temporary ethereal space, supported by an elemental and spiritual shell that keeps what we want in and keeps what we don't want out. It's your portable church, able to be erected anywhere, anytime, even inside your head. This is really useful if you want to do some quick ritual or magickal working and you feel you need a circle to do it in. After all, it could be a little inconvenient, or even embarrassing, to cast the circle publically for instance in the local McDonalds, at work or in the stands at a football match!

How Different Circle Types Evolved

People have been working in circular spaces for thousands of years so erecting a spiritual circle is not new by any stretch of the imagination. Places like Stonehenge and Avebury for example, are surviving examples of how ancient peoples used the formation of a circle for sacred spaces of worship and ritual.

Research
Spend a few minutes exploring the internet for stone circles in England and Europe. You may be surprised by how prevalent, yet hidden, they really   are!
Try these sites and also do a search for your own sources too.

http://www.stonepages.com/
http://www.stonehenge.co.uk/
http://www.megalith.ukf.net/bigmap.htm

However, during the last couple of centuries, not everyone went down to the local stone shop, brought a few megaliths and set them up in their back garden! Practitioners of magick and esoteric studies developed ways of erecting magickal places without the need for physical parameters and in Europe, particularly England, historical records show that the circles we cast today were born from those that have been used for at least the last four hundred years. We'll do a detour now and look at a few people and systems that influenced how we cast Wiccan circles now.

Our first and probably most important historical influence was John Dee (1527-1608) who was a fairly well noted mathematician and scientist. So much so that he often acted as an advisor to the court of Queen Elizabeth 1st and indeed personally tutored her on several occasions. While Witchcraft was outlawed at that time, there was very little distinction between science and religion and of course the Elizabethan era was a time of healing after the religious and political turmoil brought about by

John Dee: Artist unknown

Elizabeth's father, Henry 8th and his tumultuous dissolution of the Roman Catholic Church in England. Religion and politics were so closely intertwined that the church was virtually the prime leader of the country at that time and it wasn't till the full establishment of the joint English/Scottish parliament in 1707 that leadership of England moved deliberately and noticeably from one of religion to one of democratic politics.

Science at that time was of course rudimentary but flourishing. The Elizabethans were avid scientists, desperate to learn all they could about their world and to search for foreign lands.

John Dee saw very little distinction between science and religion and he devoted the last part of his life almost solely to communicating with angels and trying to discover the magic of creation and spirituality. He worked with, and paid, Edward Kelly for seven years after he met him in 1582 and together they drew up what they believed were channels of communication to the supernatural. With the strong influences of the Catholic and Protestant churches at that time, Dee and Kelly felt it necessary to cleanse and protect themselves from sorcery and evil spirits as they attempted to commune with the angels and it was from these studies that their protectionist circle was developed.

Dee and Kelly's Protection Circle: Artist unknown

The circle they defined was one they cast around themselves, so they were inside it and its purpose was to protect them from any nasty spirits and ghosts who might be lurking around outside. From the safety of that circle they could talk with the angels while being safely tucked away inside a shell of pure energy. It's worth remembering that John Dee was a pious Christian and devoted to the teachings of the church but he came at it from a Hermetic viewpoint which was quite intensive at that time.

Dee was also a member of the Rosicrucian Order and it's been suggested that his influence was significant in its esoteric and philosophical development. Rosicrucian ritual practices, many of which built further on the work of Dee and Kelly, had a profound impact on Gerald Gardner several hundred years later and the circle rituals he developed were built in part on Rosicrucian principles.

The Enochian Magic system was one that was a comprehensive ceremonial magical system that Dee and Kelly claimed was given to them by the angels and which they then wrote down and tested. Sceptics have since claimed that due to Kelly's suspect reputation, it may well have just been a ploy to get more money from Dee and some of the content is strangely similar to that found in earlier grimoiric texts. The fact remains however, that contemporary Wiccan circles are born from Dee and Kelly's Enochian system and many Wiccans and Witches today study this complex and powerful system of connection with other planes.

While Dee and Kelly worked on the protection circle principle in which they stood inside and the nasties roamed around outside, the other, equally as important influence on Gardner and how he built the Wiccan circle was that of the containment circle. In this example, the magician stands outside the circle and the nasties are locked inside it. Alternatively, and certainly more popularly, the containment circle is used to hold magickal energies until the magician is ready to release them in a focused and targeted fashion. This is currently how Wiccans understand the principles of the containment circle.

One of the earliest examples of combining both the protection and containment circles was the Solomonic version in which the practitioner marked out his protection and containment vessels on the floor with chalk and then conducted the evocation. In this example, the person stood inside the marked out protection circle and evoked a spirit or the un-dead into the containment triangle shape on the eastern perimeter of the circle. This example was a sophisticated means of engaging in both protection from the undesirables and also containing them so they weren't just roaming unchecked.

Solomonic Circle

In developing the Wiccan circle casting ritual, Gardner also decided to combine both the containment and protection circle and of course, while he claims his circle was reconstructed from the fragments of information handed down to him, scrutiny and research shows that much of the content comes from other sources.

His original circle scripting from 1949 shows a remarkable resemblance to many other, already published circle rites including the Hermetic, Rosicrucian, Thelemic and Freemasonry systems. These systems incorporate either protectionist or containment rites and have some very old, often medieval elements to them. Honest research and appraisal however, leads us to the conclusion that in developing his initial circle rite, Gardner used various different 'ingredients' from across those available to him and cobbled them together into his then "Wica", later "Wiccan" version.

Read
Read the extract below which is supposedly straight out of Gardner's 1949 version of the circle casting rite. It's published quite extensively in various different locations both in hardcopy and on the internet but it's reproduced her to save you searching for it.

It is most convenient to mark the circle with chalk, paint or otherwise, to show where it is; but marks on the carpet may be utilized. Furniture may be placed to indicate the bounds. The only circle that matters is the one drawn before every ceremony with either a duly consecrated Magic Sword or an Athame. The circle is usually nine feet in diameter, unless made for some very special purpose. There are two outer circles, each six inches apart, so the third circle has a diameter of eleven feet.

[1] Having chosen a place proper, take the sickle or scimitar of Art or a Witch's Athame, if thou mayest obtain it, and stick it into the center, then take a cord, and 'twere well to use the Cable Tow for this, and loop it over the Instrument, four and one half feet, and so trace out the circumference of the circle, which must be traced either with the Sword, or the knife with the black hilt, or it be of little avail, but ever leave open a door towards the North.

Make in all 3 circles, one within the other, and write names of power between these.

[2] First draw circle with Magic Sword or Athame.

[3] Consecrate Salt and Water: Touch water with Athame, saying, "I exorcise thee, O creature of Water, that thou cast out from Thee all the impurities and uncleanlyness of the Spirits of the World of Phantasm, so they may harm me not, in the names of Aradia and Cernunnos."

[4] Touching Salt with Athame, say, "The Blessings of Aradia and Cernunnos be upon this creature of Salt, and let all malignity and hindrance be cast forth hence from, and let all good enter herein, for without Thee man cannot live, wherefore I bless thee and invoke thee, that thou mayest aid me."

[5] Then put the Salt into the water.

[6] Sprinkle with exorcised water.

[7] Light candles; say, "I exorcise thee, O Creature of Fire, that every kind of Phantasm may retire from thee, and be unable to harm or deceive in any way, in the names of Aradia and Cernunnos."

[8] Caution initiate (if any); warn companions; enter circle and close doors with 3 pentagrams.

[9] Proclaim object of working

[10] Circumambulate 3 times or more before commencing work.

[11] Summon: "I summon, stir, and Call thee up, thou Mighty Ones of the East, South, West, and North." Salute and draw pentacle with Magic Sword or Athame, the first stroke being from the top down to the left.

By Gerald Gardner (1949)

Gardner's intent with his original version, albeit a clumsy one, was to cast a circle that both contained the magic he intended to create at point 9 and to protect himself from any of the potential nasties that might comes from the quarters at point 11. This needs some further explanation so let's check out some more on point 11.

Bear in mind that Gardner was using parts of rites that were themselves written during some puritanical and pious Christian periods. The calling in of the elemental quarters from the East, South, West and North was originally built on the Christian concept of the watchtowers that were guarded by archangels. You see, apparently the Christians in earlier times decided that God felt mankind couldn't really be trusted to live nicely so he created the watchtowers and installed the archangels in them to keep an eye on us. The towers also act as prisons for Cain, Judas, Herod and Herodias's daughter and just to top it all off, they also hold the really nasty Four Horsemen of the Apocalypse as well as a whole bunch of very nasty spirits. When us mortals finally tip the balance and prove how bad we supposedly really are and when the archangels decide we've gone too far, they'll let God know and with that, he'll release the Four Horsemen, all the really nasty prisoners in each of the towers and those buildings will come tumbling down. Generally speaking at that time, mankind is pretty much screwed! So if Gardner, John Dee, Kelly and all the other esoteric practitioners for the last thousand years were faced with that kind of a threat, it's no wonder they wanted to protect themselves from the pretty awful things lurking inside those towers at the four quarters of the Earth!

What's amazing, and certainly ironic, if you think about it is that Gardner drew on rites and rituals that were hundreds of years old that were built on Christian views of the world and turned them into a brand new religion which those same Christians would have seen as being Witchcraft and anti what they believed! Silly really eh?

The other point that I think is worth noting here is the obvious hypocrisy of some fundamentalist Wiccans who yell loud and long that Wicca must remain 'pure' and that the eclectic Wiccans are 'bastardising' their faith. What rubbish! The truth is that Gardner created a new religion in the late 1940s and cobbled it together from all manner of sources, Abrahamic, Thelemic, Hermetic, Rosicrucian and a fair sprinkling of his own creativity. Wicca was the mongrel off spring of all those different approaches so is born from flexibility and eclecticism. That we should have contemporary Wiccans denying our right to do exactly what the religion's founder did is hypocritical and shows a blatant disregard for the eclectic historical input and journey our current religion has taken.

I'll jump off my soapbox now but I'll conclude this particular conversation by asking you to consider that although Wicca comes from a broad range of sources, the absolute fact is that it works. Every religion has to start somewhere and the fact that the Wiccan population has mushroomed is testament not only to global communication techniques but to the simple observation that Wicca works. It's a valid, legitimate religion which offers hundreds of thousands of people a way to connect with their Gods and Goddesses and whilst Gardner might have slightly 'fudged' the truth, there's no denying he created a wonderful religion.

With all that said, and humans being what they are, there were bound to be changes and Gardner's first attempt at a circle casting rite was no exception. While he definitely created the foundation, different people took the basic rite and moulded it into something more useable. As a result we now have a massive number of variations on the same original version that meet different needs for individuals, for traditions and for covens.

Research
Spend an hour or so exploring the internet for circle casting rites that have been published. You'll find thousands! Read through a few and see if you can see any recurring themes. Are there similarities between them? Are there any that do things completely differently or do they all pretty much do the same type of thing but maybe say it slightly differently?

How Do Inclusivists Cast a Circle?

So you've seen the history of circles and by now you should have looked at a few examples of circle casting available on the internet. Hopefully you'll have found that there are recurring themes throughout the differing examples. Different people and covens might say slightly different things, maybe even do things in a different order on occasions, but essentially they're all casting a combination containment and protection circle.

The Inclusive tradition of course has its own way, just like every other tradition does, but while I'll give you our circle casting model, and later one of our actual circle casting scripts, you'll also be expected to modify that and develop your own later on. There's some basic building blocks to the circle casting rite of course that help us define and order what we do and no matter what your own personal circle rite actually looks like, it'll work much better if it follows this basic framework so that you cover all the requirements.

The Composition and Order of the Circle
1. Preparing the Circle Area
Your circle will be easier to cast if you actually have a visible perimeter or circle edge within which to work. Using chalk, ribbon, string, candles or any other suitable means, mark out the circle boundary on the ground so you can see it throughout the rite. Place your altar either in the eastern quarter on the inside edge of the marked circle or in the centre. You can also use candles to mark the quarter points as well.

If necessary sweep the area clean of any residual, negative energies and prepare the altar with everything required. Purify and cleanse yourself and just before beginning the rite, light the incense.
2. Casting Announcement
The High Priest/ess or ritual leader lets everyone present know that the circle is about to be cast.
3. Circle Boundary Creation
The circle boundary is created and set with the elements of Water and Salt, then Fire and Air and finally with the fifth element of Spirit.
4. Welcome and Consecration of any Visitors
Some traditions bring visitors in at this time. We prefer to have them in the circle area already so the boundary remains strong.
5. Calling in the Elements
The four elements of Air, Fire, Water and Earth are called in with elemental invoking pentagrams.
6. Welcoming the Lord and Lady
With the circle cast, the elements present and everything ready, the Gods and Goddesses can now be welcomed in to the circle space.
7. Casting Completion Announcement
The High Priest/ess or ritual leader lets everyone present know that the circle casting has been completed.
8. Magickal or Ritual Workings
Any workings are conducted now.
9. Drawing Down the Moon
The High Priest draws the moon down into the High Priestess and she either delivers to the coveners the messages received or recites The Charge of the Goddess.
10.Cakes and Ale

The cakes and ale are consecrated and shared with coveners.
11.Closing the Circle
The circle is dismantled.

Now you have the very basic order and inclusions of the circle casting rite that Inclusive uses, it's time to just look at some of the underpinning principles that hold this all up. We need to look more closely at the elements, the correspondences and the symbology. While the 'script' for casting a circle is one thing, the words spoken, the symbols used, the intent within the phrases and actions are the real techniques of circle casting.

The Wiccan elements are a curious conglomerate of both 'representations' and 'states' and to complicate it even further, we use the 'state' of the elements to cast the circle boundary but call in the 'representation' of the elements at the four compass points of East, South, West and North.

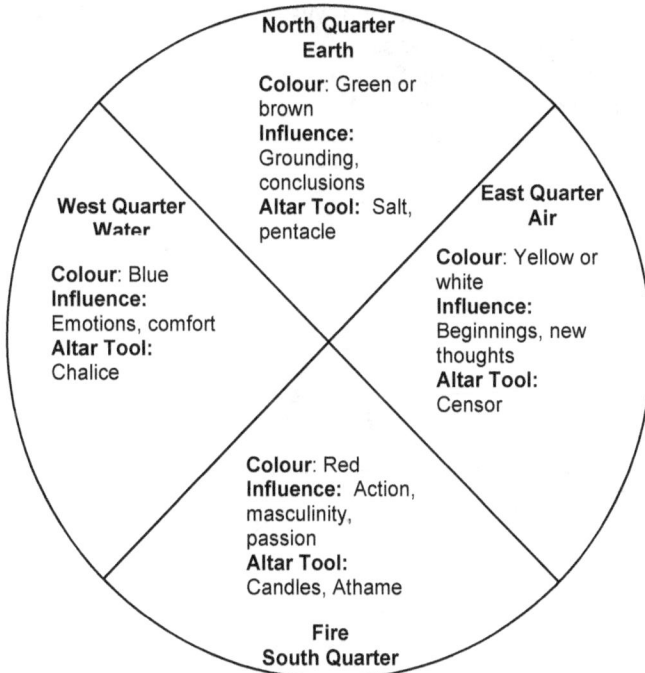

Elemental Quarters and their
Correspondences

The Wiccan elements are therefore a fluid and dynamic interpretation and a symbolic representation of the four states that make up our universe, Air, Fire, Water and Earth. This is a European concept of course because the Chinese have five elements which include the same Fire, Water and Earth but then also include Wood and Metal and omit Air. The figure on the previous page shows how they fit together and what other things, compass directions and aspects correspond, or relate to each of the four elements.

Now that I've just given you four lots of correspondences related to the four elemental quarters, I'm going to complicate it even more and tell you there are actually five elements in the Wiccan faith. The fifth and less definable element is that of Spirit. This element doesn't correspond necessarily with a compass point like the other four do but is instead something more ethereal and all encompassing. A bit like oxygen that you can't see, can't feel but you know it's everywhere around you. The fifth element though is used in the circle casting ritual because the formation of the boundaries is done with the four compass elements but also with Sprit. So in other words, the boundary of the circle is built in five layers, first with Spirit as the circle is cast using the athame and then it's layered with Salt and Water mixed, then Air and Fire together in the form of incense.

The fifth element of Spirit is also seen very clearly on the pentagram which of course is Wicca's most primary symbol, just as the Christians use the symbol of the cross.

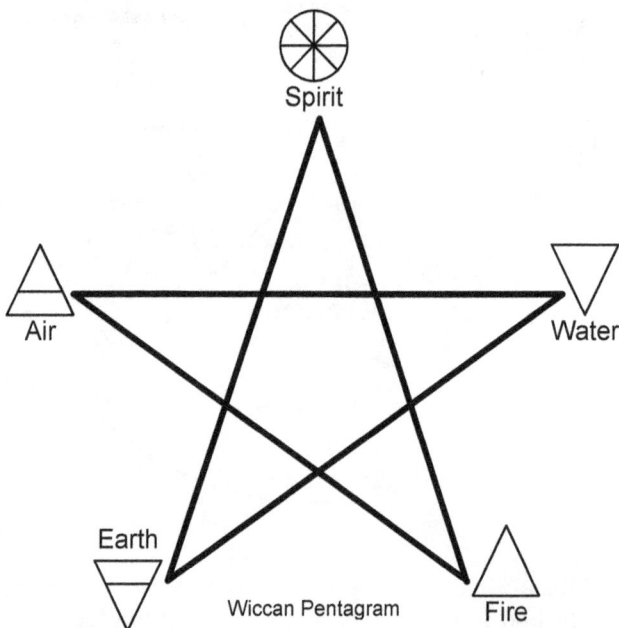

Wiccan Pentagram

The format and placement of the five elements against the five pentagram points is the same across virtually all Wiccan traditions. Some traditions might use slightly different symbols to represent the elements but the placements are usually the same. Notice that if you were to transpose the pentagram over the circle, the elemental placements in the pentagram won't line up with the compass points or the compass placed elementals either. What this results in then is a multi-dimensional circle with the elements being called in at the compass quarters, with their states being used to layer the circle circumference shell and then also being layered again in the use of the pentagram. Many traditions mark the pentagram out on the ground inside their circle with the five points just touching the edge of the circle and Spirit pointing directly north similar to the diagram below but personally I find this confusing so I choose not to do this.

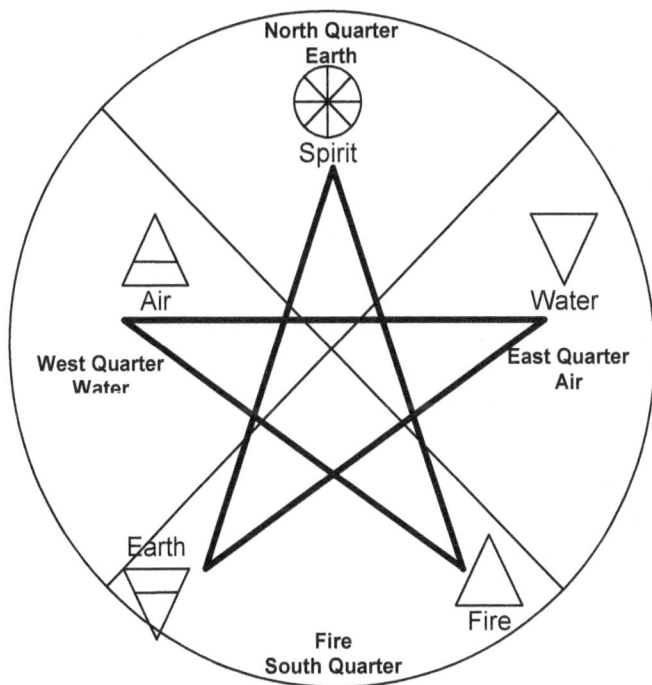

Circle and Pentagram

So with all the universal technicalities out the way, let's now move into one of the actual Inclusive circle casting 'scripts'. We have both the old fashioned and the more contemporary version and we use either/or depending on whether it's a Sabbat or an Esbat or whether we have guests or not. The one given here is our contemporary version and I've included this one deliberately because it's an easier version to understand and to modify in order to meet your own needs. It's been put together, and comes from a variety of sources, just as Gardner's and most other covens do and can be used by a solitary or by a group. Remember that whilst this is the ritual that Oak and Mistletoe uses for many circle castings, it's given here only for you to have a hands-on idea for the how it all comes together. I'll be encouraging you to develop it into something that works for your own practice over the next few months.

Read
Over the next few pages, you'll find the detailed version of Oak and Mistletoe's contemporary circle casting ritual. Read through it several times so that you get a feel for the language and then try and work out which actions and words fit into the 11 components under "The Composition and Order of the Circle" subtitle as discussed earlier in this chapter.

Esbat Circle Casting
Required
On the altar in the East quarter: Athame, wand, God and Goddess candles, solar candle, censor with incense, pentacle, water chalice, salt in the salt dish, bell, dish of anointing oil, dish of cakes and wine chalice with wine (or juice), tapers, tissues or cloth to wipe athame tip, libation dish, candle snuffer.

Elsewhere: A quarter candle at each of the four quarters, balefire candle if desired set in the centre of the circle, additional candles marking the circle boundary if required, magickal or ritual materials if required for circle workings.

Prior to the Ritual
Cleanse the circle space with a broom or smudge stick.
Prepare the altar and circle area.
Mark a circle area out with chalk, ribbon or similar material.
Purify and cleanse self.
Light the incense just prior to the commencement of the ritual.

Ritual Opening
Ring the bell three times.
The ritual leader stands before the altar and lights the solar candle saying; "I kindle this flame like the fires of the sun. The bell has been rung and the circle begun."

The 'East Person' or ritual leader lights a taper from the solar candle and lights the East quarter candle saying; "Here do I bring light and air in at the East, to illuminate our temple and bring it the breath of life."

The 'East Person' walks toward the 'South Person', they bow to each other and the 'East Person' hands the taper to the 'South Person'; (Or the ritual leader takes the taper to the South quarter candle) saying; "Here do I bring light and fire in at the South, to illuminate our temple and bring it warmth."

The 'South Person' walks toward the 'West Person', they bow to each other and the 'South Person' hands the taper to the 'West Person'; (Or the ritual leader takes the taper to the West quarter candle) saying; "Here do I bring light and water in at the West, to illuminate our temple and wash it clean."

The 'West Person' walks toward the 'North Person', they bow to each other and the 'West Person' hands the taper to the 'North Person'; (Or the ritual leader takes the taper to the North quarter candle) saying; "Here do I bring light and earth in at the North, to illuminate our temple and build it in strength."

The 'North Person' or the ritual leader walks toward the altar and extinguishes the taper and lays it on the ground.

Casting the Circle

The ritual leader takes the athame from the altar, continues to face East, raises the athame toward the sky in salutation to the Gods then kisses it. They then spend a minute drawing power from the earth into themselves and concentrate it into the athame. They then walk slowly round the circle, deosil, pointing the athame toward the marked circle and sending the power into the circle marked on the floor, through the athame. Once back at the Eastern quarter in front of the altar, they raise the athame to the sky and lower and kiss it.

The Ritual leader places the point of their athame into the salt saying; "As salt is life, let it purify us in all ways we may use it. Let it cleanse our bodies and spirits as we dedicate ourselves to these rites, to the glory of the Lord and Lady."

The ritual leader uses their athame tip to scoop up a few grains of salt and drops these into the water chalice three times. Stirring the salted water, the ritual leader says; "Let this sacred salt drive out any impurities in the water, that we may use it throughout these rites."

The ritual leader wipes the tip of their athame blade with the cloth or tissues (to stop the salt from eventually corroding the blade) takes the salted water within the water chalice, raises it toward the sky in the East, lowers and kisses it, then moving deosil, sprinkles the salted water along the line of the circle. Once back at the East quarter before the altar, the ritual leader raises the chalice again to the sky, kisses it and returns it to the altar.

The ritual leader then takes the censor, raises it toward the sky in the East, lowers it, then moves deosil, passing the censor along the line of the circle. Once back at the East quarter before the altar, they raise the censor to the sky, and then return it to the altar.

Welcoming the Visitors
The ritual leader then uses the tip of their athame to take a few grains of salt that they then drop into the dish of anointing oil. Again they wipe the blade tip. Having stirred the salted oil with their finger, they anoint any visitors by marking a pentagram on their forehead with their forefinger and saying; "I consecrate thee in the names of the Lord and Lady. Welcome to this sacred space. Merry meet." The person being anointed says; "Merry meet."

Once any visitors have been anointed the ritual leader says; "May each one of you be here in love and peace."

Elemental Invitation
The 'East Person' or the ritual leader, stands before the altar, facing outward and raises their wand to the sky in salute, and then draws an Air invoking pentagram saying;

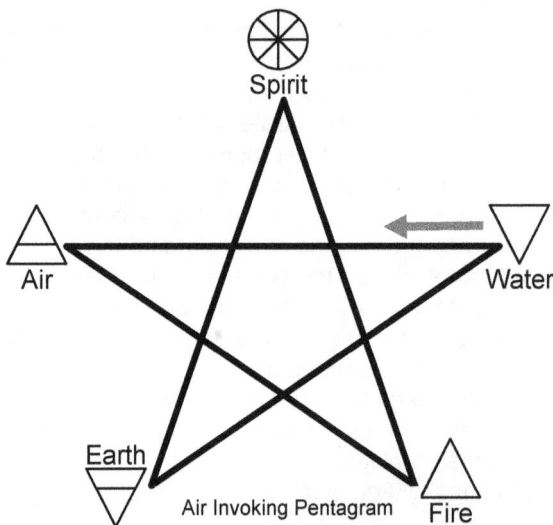

Air Invoking Pentagram

"We welcome and honour the mighty element of Air. May your winds refresh and revive us always."

The 'East Person' or ritual leader kisses their wand and turns back to the circle. The 'East Person' bows to the 'South Person' (or the ritual leader moves to the South), who then faces outward toward the South, raises their wand to the sky in salute, and then draws a Fire invoking pentagram saying; "We welcome and honour the mighty element of Fire. May your light temper and warm us always."

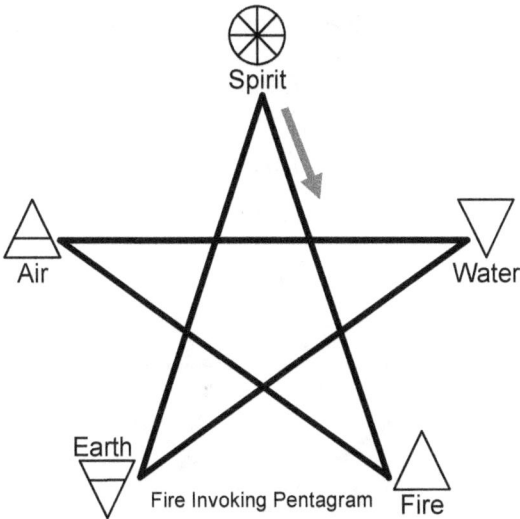

Fire Invoking Pentagram

The 'South Person' or ritual leader kisses their wand and turns back to the circle. The 'South Person' bows to the 'West Person' (or the ritual leader moves to the West), who then faces outward toward the West raises their wand to the sky in salute, and then draws a Water invoking pentagram saying; "We welcome and honour the mighty element of Water. May your love nurture and cleanse us always."

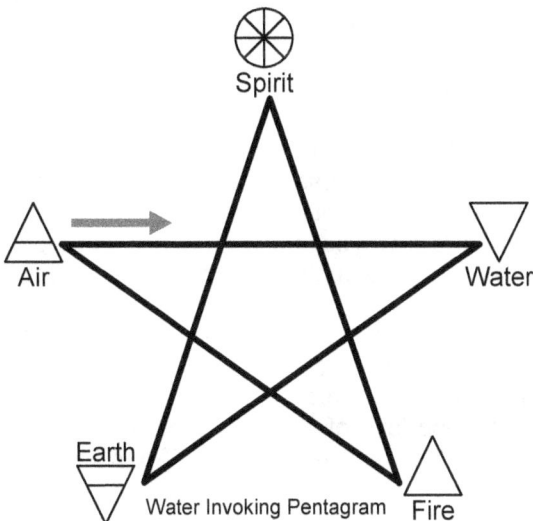

Water Invoking Pentagram

The 'West Person' or ritual leader kisses their wand and turns back to the circle. The 'West Person' bows to the 'North Person' (or the ritual leader moves to the North), who then faces outward toward the North raises their wand to the sky in salute, and then draws an Earth invoking pentagram saying; "We welcome and honour the mighty element of Earth. May your strength shelter and purify us always."

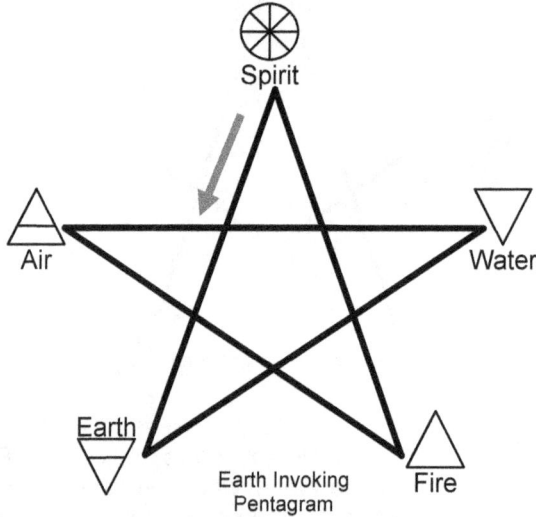

Earth Invoking Pentagram

The 'North Person' or ritual leader kisses their wand and turns back to the circle. The 'North Person' bows to the ritual leader who returns their wand to the altar. The ritual leader then faces the coveners and says; "We welcome the elemental quarters and offer our thanks for sharing this rite with us."

Invitation to the Gods
The ritual leader turns to face the altar, takes the solar candle and lights the God and Goddess candles. They turn to face the coveners again and say; "We light these candles as a reflection of the light and love we receive from our blessed Lord and Lady." (Looking skyward) "We ask that you honour us this day/night with your presence as we celebrate our love and dedication to you. To you we offer this rite."
(To the coveners) "To the Lord and Lady we say hail and welcome!"
Everyone says; "Hail and welcome!" and the ritual leader now announces that the circle is erected by saying;
"By the strength and love of all within, this circle is cast. Let each person here remain so in love and peace. So mote it be!" Everyone says; "So mote it be!"

Circle Business
Any magickal workings, meditations, path workings or ritual work/circle business may be conducted now.

Drawing Down the Moon
The Goddess is drawn down on the High Priestess. This should only be conducted by those with experience in invoking the Divine.

Cakes and Ale
The cakes and ale rite is then conducted at the end of any magickal workings or circle business. It should be the last rite prior to closing the circle although a discussion post cakes and ale about the events that occurred may be beneficial just before actually closing the circle.

This should ideally be done with two ritual leaders so that they may offer each other the wine and cakes but it can be modified so that it can be conducted alone.

Ritual leader A rings the bell once to signal the commencement of this rite. They face inward towards the coveners and hold up the main wine chalice with wine (or juice) toward the sky saying; "Gracious Goddess of abundance, bless this wine and infuse it with your love. In the name of the Lord and Lady, I bless this fruit of the earth. So mote it be!" Everyone says; "So mote it be!"

Ritual leader A then pours a small amount onto the ground or into the libation dish to be later left overnight outside as an offering of thanks saying; "To the Lord and Lady!" Everyone says; "To the Lord and Lady!"

Ritual leader A then offers the wine chalice to Ritual leader B saying; "May you never thirst. Blessed be." Ritual leader B thanks them saying; "Blessed be."

They take the chalice, then make a personal toast or prayer to their patron and matron, that may be silent or aloud, before sipping from the wine chalice.

Ritual leader B then offers the wine chalice back to Ritual leader A saying; "May you never thirst. Blessed be."
Ritual leader A thanks them saying; "Blessed be."

They take the chalice back, make a personal toast or prayer to their patron and matron, that may be silent or aloud, before sipping from the wine chalice.

With both leaders now having toasted their patron and matron and having sipped from the wine chalice, they now take it in turns to repeat the offer of the chalice to each person present as follows.

In turn ritual leader A or B offers the wine chalice to each person present saying; "May you never thirst. Blessed be." The recipient thanks them saying; "Blessed be."

They then take the chalice, make a personal toast or prayer to their patron and matron that may be silent or aloud, before sipping from the wine chalice and handing it back to the alternate ritual leader. After each person has sipped from the chalice, it is returned to the altar.

Ritual leader B faces inwards towards the coveners, holds up the plate of cakes to the sky and says; "Powerful God of the harvest, bless these cakes and infuse them with your love. In the name of the Lord and Lady, I bless this fruit of the earth. So mote it be!" Everyone says; "So mote it be!"

Ritual leader B then crumbles one cake onto the ground or adds one to the libation dish to be later left overnight outside as an offering of thanks saying; "To the Lord and Lady!" Everyone says; "To the Lord and Lady!"

Ritual leader B then offers the plate of cakes to Ritual leader A saying; "May you never hunger. Blessed be." Ritual leader A thanks them and takes a cake saying; "Blessed be."

They then make a personal prayer to their patron and matron, that may be silent or aloud, before eating the cake.

Ritual leader A then takes the plate of cakes, offers a cake back to Ritual leader B saying; "May you never hunger. Blessed be." Ritual leader B thanks them and takes a cake saying; "Blessed be."

They then make a personal prayer to their patron and matron, that may be silent or aloud, before eating their cake.

With both leaders now having offered their personal thanks to their patron and matron and having eaten their cake, they now take it in turns to repeat the offer of the plate of cakes to each person present as follows.

In turn ritual leader A or B offers the plate of cakes to each person present saying; "May you never hunger. Blessed be." The recipient thanks them and takes a cake them saying; "Blessed be."

They then make a personal prayer to their patron and matron that may be silent or aloud, before eating their cake. Once each person has taken their cake, the plate is returned to the altar.

One of the ritual leaders now closes this rite by saying;
"As we share in these fruits of the earth, let us remember those who cannot feast before the Lord and Lady, those that lack food, those that lack shelter, and those who lack the freedom to practice their faith in the open. Let us remember the persecuted, the executed and the frightened. All are welcome here who come in the spirit of peace and love. So mote it be!" Everyone says; "So mote it be!" There should now be a moment of silent contemplation.

Closing the Circle

The ritual leader says; "We met this day/night in love and peace and our rite was blessed by the light of all within this circle. May the goodness, energy and light within be reflected in our lives without. Blessed be the Lord and Lady in all the ways they were reflected today/tonight as hope, as promise, as healing and as the sacred mother and father to whom we owe our lives."

The ritual leader moves to the north or they bow to the 'North Person', who faces outward and says; "Earth that is life, brought from the North to shelter and purify us, to the North return. We thank you for attending." They snuff out the North quarter candle.

The ritual leader moves to the West or the 'North Person' turns, walks to the 'West Person', hands them the snuffer, bows and moves away. The 'West Person' then faces outward and says; "Water that is life, brought from the West to nurture and cleanse us, to the West return. We thank you for attending." They snuff out the West quarter candle.

The ritual leader moves to the South or the 'West Person' turns, walks to the 'South Person', hands them the snuffer, bows and moves away. The 'South Person' then faces outward and says; "Fire that is life, brought from the South to temper and warm us, to the South return. We thank you for attending." They snuff out the South quarter candle.

The ritual leader moves to the East or the 'South Person' turns, walks to the 'East Person', hands them the snuffer, bows and moves away. The 'East Person' then faces outward and says; "Air that is life, brought from the East to refresh and revive us, to the East return. We thank you for attending." They snuff out the East quarter candle.

The 'East Person' hands the snuffer to the ritual leader, bows and moves away. The ritual leader turns inwards and says; "Lord and Lady, sacred parents, sacred lovers, sacred children, may your light grow ever stronger, lifted into the heavens as moon and sun and reflected in the eyes of all who can gaze skyward with the light of the Law within them."

The ritual leader turns to the altar, snuffs out the solar candle and then the God and Goddess candles. They then turn back to the coveners and say; "Now our rite is complete. May the circle be open but never unbroken. Blessed be. Everyone says; "Blessed be."

Activity
It's now time to cast your own circle. Prepare your circle area and make sure you won't be disturbed. Take this book in with you so you have the words handy.

Conduct the ritual. Do NOT draw down the moon! You'll probably feel a little awkward about it at first but that's Ok. Circle casting is like riding a bike, the more you practice, the easier it gets and once you've learnt how to do it, you don't forget!

Casting Your Own Circles

This is where Wicca comes out of the classroom and starts demanding you become lots more hands-on. Wiccan students say that generally it takes at least a year to learn how to cast a strong circle without forgetting the words or the actions. It's hard to remember which invoking pentagram to do with which quarter and which direction to form each invoking pentagram in. Was that left to right or right to left? Was I supposed to face this way or that? Was I supposed to use the wand or the athame for that bit? Speaking of which, let's have a quick word about tools and the circle.

You don't need the athame, the wand, the robes, special water and wine chalices or anything big and fancy to cast a circle. In fact as you're learning how to do it all, I'd strongly encourage you cast with your fingers instead of an athame and wand. The Gods and Goddesses gave you two perfectly good arms with some very helpful fingers on the end of them and if you want to feel the power of a circle casting run through your body, then use it rather than tools. Point your fingers strongly and see the energy come streaming from the point of your finger instead of from the point of an athame.

You can use a coffee mug for your water chalice and the same for your wine chalice and you can wear ordinary street clothes when in circle. Eventually you're probably going to want special robes used only for ritual wear and a set of rituals tools especially for you including your own athame but for now, it's best to learn without all that paraphernalia. You don't need it and any Witch worth their salt can cast a circle with absolutely no tools at all.

Activity
Cast the circle again, making sure as usual that you won't be disturbed. Do NOT draw down the moon. This time after you've cast your circle, carefully move to the edge of your circle and put the palms of your hands out to the boundary and slowly and carefully feel it. Can you feel anything at the edge of the circle? If so, what? Don't be discouraged if you can't. With more practice it will eventually come. After a while, you should be able to feel a resistance at the circle edge, sort of like a force field. Sit on the floor in your circle, does the circle feel heavy or light, strong or weak. Does it have a sense of wishy washy water to it or perhaps an airy fairy feel, perhaps a passionate fiery feel or a very grounded earthy feel to it? Did you feel more comfortable invoking one element more than any other? Write your answers and thoughts into your Learning Journal while you're still in the circle then close it down. Ground again if necessary.

It's time now to start thinking about how you want your own circle casting words to sound. You can use the Inclusive circle ritual in its entirety if you want to but it will be much more powerful for you, and personal if it has your touches, your personality, your creativity in it. You've already seen some other circle casting rites (if you did the research activity on that earlier in this chapter) so you should be ready to write your own or modify Inclusive's to turn it into your own.

Activity
In your Learning Journal, draft out your own circle casting ritual. It doesn't matter if you make mistakes and have to cross parts out. You probably won't come up with your final version for several months yet and that's Ok. It can take months, even years to develop the circle you know is right. Your changes will help your creative juices flow. Be creative, have fun! Rhyme is much easier to remember than rambling text and so if you can put your words into a beat, it will roll off your tongue much better.

You don't have to use 'ancient' language either if you don't want to. You don't have to have 'thee's' and 'thou's'. This is your circle casting rite, you can do what you want. Borrow from other rites you've found if you want. Just make sure whatever you write fits into the 11 components as described in 'The Composition and Order of the Circle' earlier in this chapter. Then go right ahead and conduct it!

Change it again if you need or want to. Do NOT draw down the moon. That quite intense rite is not covered until second degree training. In the meantime, just play with your draft circle casting rite so that you gradually feel more comfortable with the process. Remember to say thank you to the Gods and Goddesses while in the circle. After all, that's really what you're there for!

Setting up Your Altar

The final piece in the jigsaw puzzle about circle casting is setting up your altar, including its location inside the relevant quarter and what to put on it. Some traditions prefer their altar in the North, some in the East and some in the centre so the end result for you is personal choice.

At Oak and Mistletoe we often have the altar in the Eastern quarter but on occasions, we occasionally site it in the centre or even in the North depending on what we're doing and which version of the circle casting script we're using. The altar should sit just inside the circle boundary so that everything sitting on it is within the shell of the sacred space.

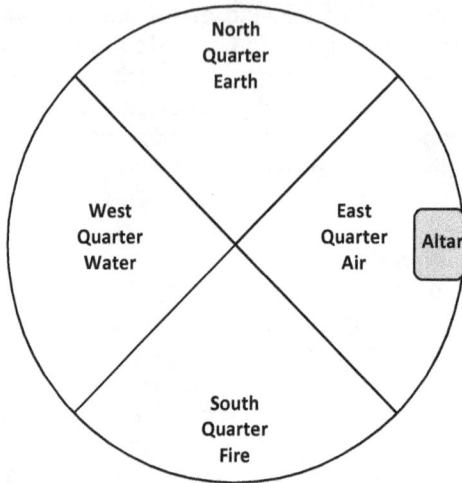

North
Quarter
Earth

West
Quarter
Water

East
Quarter
Air

Altar

South
Quarter
Fire

Altar Placement in the Circle

In terms of what sits on the altar, generally speaking there's a specific set of tools that sit there. These tools, their significance and use will be discussed later in chapter 5 so for now it's sufficient to just describe where they each sit on the altar. The picture below gives you a fairly crude but useful idea of where each tool sits and the positioning is usually related to their elemental correspondence.

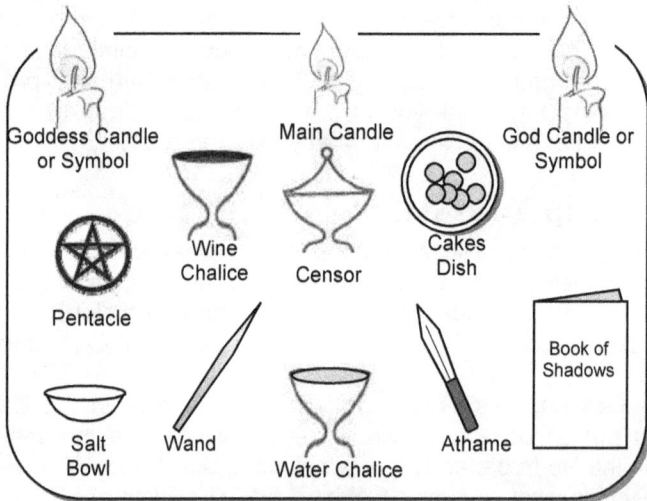

Goddess Candle
or Symbol

Main Candle

God Candle or
Symbol

Wine
Chalice

Censor

Cakes
Dish

Pentacle

Book of
Shadows

Salt
Bowl

Wand

Water Chalice

Athame

Altar Setup

Because every tool has a correspondence with a particular directional quarter of the circle, it's usually appropriate to sit each one of them on the altar to the East, South, West or North depending on their correspondence. Having said that, it's also important to be careful where you sit the candles and the censor because it's not much fun if you have to lean over them to get to something else and you burn yourself in the process! So try and place these further back behind the other tools if possible.

Circle Etiquette and Manners

While there are scripts and instructions and recipes and whatever else the myriad of Wiccan folks call their circle casting rites out there, there's also a set of expectations around behaviours, manners and etiquette in the circle. Now if you're working as a solitary, you could argue that it doesn't matter about manners because you're the only one in the circle. Well, let's blow that idea out of the water straight away. You're not the only one in the circle at all. The elemental quarters are there with you and even more importantly, so is the Lord and Lady. Would you be on your best behaviour if someone important came to share your home with you? Probably. Well that's exactly what the Gods and Goddesses are doing. They're sharing your circle with you and in fact the main reason you should have cast it in the first place was to honour them, and that means being on your best behaviour and minding your circle manners.

Manners are equally as important when you visit someone else's coven and work with them in their circle. The old adage 'When in Rome...' works really well here with the exception that if they expect you to do something you don't feel comfortable with, respectfully decline. So what are some of the manners and etiquette expectations you should be aware of?

The More Traditional Must Do's
- Wear robes of a certain colour dependent on your degree level,
- Go skyclad (naked) where the rites require it,
- Wear a single piece of jewellery significant with your degree level/rank,
- Walk only in a deosil (clockwise) direction around the circle,
- Always address people in the circle by their Craft or magickal name even if you usually use their 'everyday' name at other times.

The More Traditional Must Not's
- Do not wear a watch or any jewellery other than your consecrated piece in circle,

- Never turn your back to the altar,
- Do not leave the circle until it is dismantled,
- Do not walk in a widdershins (anti-clockwise) direction unless you are dismantling the circle,
- Never enter a circle if you have not been initiated or without first answering the challenge.

The More Contemporary Must Do's

- Wear whatever you would like in circle but most participants wear a simple robe used only for circle work,
- Show respect for the fact that you are in a sacred space,
- Respect and follow the ritual actions of the host coven. (When in Rome etc),
- Whenever the ritual leader says "Blessed Be" as part of a ritual, you repeat the same term,
- Whenever the ritual leader says "So Mote it Be" as part of a ritual, you repeat the same term,
- If you do not wish to sip from the wine chalice, kiss the front of it instead,
- It's quite acceptable to laugh when in the circle (except during meditations),
- Always address people in the circle by their Craft or magickal name even if you usually use their 'everyday' name at other times.

The More Contemporary Must Not's

- Never take a mobile phone into the circle,
- Do not enter the circle under the influence of illicit drugs or alcohol,
- Do not leave the circle until it has been dismantled unless absolutely necessary,
- Never bring guests with you to a circle without permission from the ritual leader,
- Do not enter the circle when you are angry or upset. (The negative energy can be quite destructive to others present),
- No smoking in the circle,
- No eating or drinking in the circle except for cakes and ale or magickal workings,
- Do not perform individual magickal workings for your own needs inside the circle unless you have first discussed this with your coven colleagues,
- Never feel pressured to participate in any activity that makes you feel uncomfortable or unsafe.

Your Third Visualisation

By now hopefully you'll be feeling much more relaxed and comfortable with the concept of visualisation and seeing and feeling different things. This month, we're going to take it one step further yet again as we develop your skills into what will eventually become your preparation for magickal work and also for drawing up energy to cast the circle which you should already have been practicing too.

Remember to prepare as instructed in the first lesson and make sure that you're comfortable and won't be disturbed. As usual, read the energisation visualisation below first, and also remember to ground again afterwards.

Activity

Close your eyes, breathe deeply and slowly for a few seconds feeling the breath draw into your lungs and slowly back out again. Imagine a tap root growing from the base of your spine,your base chakra, downward toward the ground. It's a nice strong tap root and it slowly, gently but deliberately grows down through your chair, through the floor covering, on through the floor structure and then down toward the ground below. See your tap root forcing its way into the earth below you and remaining strong and willing. Keep it growing, further and further. Push it further still, right down into the planet, right down into the dirt, the rocks and the substrata below your feet. Your tap root is strong and it's now anchoring you safely to the Earth. You're comfortable, you're connected to the planet and you're safe.

Now ask the glorious Goddess Gaia if she would allow you to draw into your tap root some of her pure, white, clean, fresh energy. She willingly gives you this energy. She always does because it's your pure white light too. See the pure white light, the cleansing, energising light being sucked up through your tap root and coming up closer and closer toward you. Draw it up toward you. Pull the energy up towards the base of your spine.

As it comes up through the tap root and enters your body, see it begin to tumble around at the base of your torso and then begin falling down your legs towards your feet. See the energy fill your toes up and any dark patches of negative energy are washed away as you breathe out. The energy just keeps streaming up through your tap root and flooding into your legs. Your lower legs, your thighs are now flooded with pure, white, clean, fresh light. Your legs feel cleansed and revitalised.

The energy keeps coming in and now it fills your lower torso, forcing away any dark and negative patches as you breathe out. Keep drawing up the energy, lots more yet, so much more yet. Your whole tummy area is now filled with white light and you feel comfortable, rested and calm. More white light, this time tumbling up into your chest and shoulders. The pure, white, cleansing light rolls down your arms and into your hands and fingers filling them with light. Yet more light, still coming into your body and now it fills your lower and upper arms and your shoulders feel relaxed and you feel safe and calm and peaceful. The white light then reaches up into your neck and as the light fills your body, it pushes any negative patches of old, faded, worn out, dirty energy away with each breath. Your head is filling with white light and so is your face and now, as you scan your body, you see all the parts of it are filled to the brim with wonderful, refreshing, rejuvenating, pure white energy. You feel alive, you feel calm, you feel peaceful and happy. Check your body for any last remaining patches of old, dark energy you don't need and breathe them away.

Spend a few moments luxuriating in the bliss of being bathed in pure, clean energy from the Goddess. Now draw up yet more pure, clean, white light and now see that extra energy flowing through from within your body, through the pores of your skin and gradually out into the air immediately around you. From head to toe, front and back the energy is wisping its way through your skin and into the area out to about eight inches around you. This is your aura. It's the energy field immediately around your body that radiates your emotions, health and thoughts in different colours, densities and depths and some people can see these auras. Let the wonderful clean and fresh, white light filter into your aura cleaning out any muddy, dirty patches of old, worn out energies. See the white light wisping through the pores of your skin and penetrating and washing clean your aura. Breathe away any dark patches of negativity from your aura, make it clean and fresh and bright and calm and peaceful. Spend a little more time just bathing in the luxury of pure cleanliness and peace.

When you're ready and have had your fill, honour Gaia by thanking her for her generosity and love and then slowly bring your attention back to the room you're in and gradually open your eyes. When you're ready (take your time) slowly look around you and come back to the here and now.

Ground yourself by bending or kneeling down on the ground, preferably outside on the grass or dirt, and place the palms of your hands flat on the ground. See the excess energy you drew up flowing smoothly back into the ground below you through your open palms.

Your Homework This Month

The 'real' work begins in earnest this month as you start to cast circles and really get to grips with the energisation visualisation. For the next month ahead;

- Practice circle casting using either the Inclusive version or your own if you prefer. If using your own, make sure it fits within the 11 components discussed and feel free to modify your version as often as you need to till it feels right. Do NOT draw down the moon.
- Keep practicing the energisation visualisation including the aura cleansing and the grounding. Write the results in your Learning Journal.
- Write regularly in your diary and include any significant dreams you had, any meditations that offered you insights and look at what's happening around you in nature and write that down too.

The visualisations and the circle casting are fundamental to well rounded, effective Wiccan practice. Focus on practicing these this month.

The Fourth Lesson
The Wheel of the Year

J ust like any other religion, Wicca has an annual calendar of festivals that celebrates its underpinning mythology. Our calendar, known as the Wheel of the Year also celebrates the seasonal changes and highpoints that happen each year and that help to connect us with the beauty of nature around us.

By the time you've finished this fourth lesson you should be able to;

- Explain the difference between an Esbat and a Sabbat,
- Appreciate the northern versus southern hemisphere issues and problems,
- Describe the festivals that make up the southern Wheel of the Year,
- Write your own Sabbat rituals,

Esbats and Sabbats

So many terms and unfamiliar names! Esbats and Sabbats, what are they exactly? Simple really, an Esbat is the name of the regular ritual that you're likely to conduct throughout the year, often on each full moon. In the last chapter you looked at the circle casting ritual which would open and close that Esbat.

A Sabbat by comparison is the celebratory festival that marks a particular time of the year, much like Christians celebrate Christmas and Easter. Many Wiccans celebrate the Esbats on the full moon for a variety of reasons but largely because the energy at that time of month is much more intense and acute by comparison to the new moon's, much lower and softer energy level. This means that any magic you conduct is likely to have more success. There are of course exceptions to this rule which will be covered in chapter 6.

If you can't celebrate your Esbat on the night of the full moon for whatever reason, it's best to conduct it on the night before rather than the night after. Your Esbat, in which you honour the Lord and Lady and possibly work magick, is much better worked while the energy levels are still rising with the waxing moon rather than when they're diminishing with the waning moon. The energy levels are important to the intensity of any ritual and they correspond to the cycle of the waxing and waning moon as shown below.

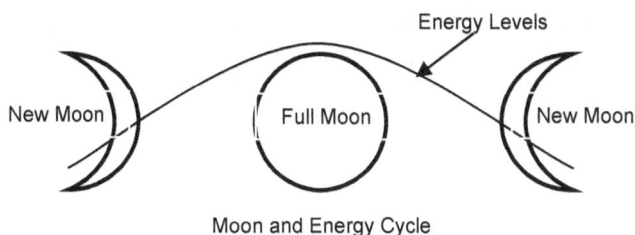

Moon and Energy Cycle

Activity
Have a look on the internet to find information on the lunar cycle. Find out the dates and times of the full and new moon for the next 12 months and write these in your Learning Journey. Make sure you're looking at geographically local times for your area. Some good sites are;

http://en.wikipedia.org/wiki/Lunar_phase
http://www.ga.gov.au/geodesy/astro/moonphases/moonphases.jsp
http://www.archaeoastronomy.com/almanac.html

The Dilemma of the Northern and Southern Hemisphere Calendar

Before we move into the Wheel of the Year in detail we also need to consider the problems that those of us in the southern hemisphere face because the problem has potential issues around circle casting, altar placement, elemental quarter locations, Sabbat dates as well as the way Sabbats are celebrated.

Back to a bit of history for a few minutes though and I'll simplify the problem a little at this point by not considering the underpinning mythology of each Sabbat and instead just focus on the seasonal factors which of course are fundamental to Wicca.

Wicca originated in England as you know by now (if you've been reading this book properly and done your own research!) and its Wheel of the Year is closely aligned to the natural seasonal cycle of that country. In England, summer is generally across May, June and July (notwithstanding that with global climate change the seasons are gradually moving later in the calendar year around the globe) and winter occurs around November, December and January. Now this means that for example on December 21st in the northern hemisphere they'll be celebrating Yule or Winter Solstice, the shortest day of the year. But here in the southern hemisphere we're experiencing Summer Solstice and the longest day of the year. It's cold, wet, maybe snowing and the plants are dormant and everyone's hiding from the freezing cold in the northern hemisphere but in the southern hemisphere, it's warm, maybe even really hot and our days are long. They're drinking warmed wine and burning Yule logs on a roaring fire over there and it just doesn't seem to fit for us to do the same in the southern half of the world when we're at the height of summer instead.

Similarly on 21st March for example, our northern hemisphere friends are enjoying their festivities celebrating their Spring Equinox. The flowers are beginning to bloom, new life is budding all around them, baby animals are being introduced to the world and all around they can see the new light of the sun after a dark and cold winter. But for us here in the bottom half of our planet we're seeing the autumn leaves coming out, plant life is beginning to go into its low growth season, the baby animals have all developed into teenagers and we're preparing for winter. How can we celebrate the birth of new life synonymous with the Spring Equinox of the northern hemisphere when all around us we're seeing nothing like that?

Let's take the problem one step further particularly for Wiccans in parts of Australia. England tends to have four very clearly defined seasons which of course are winter, spring, summer and autumn. The weather and plant and animal life follow predictable patterns through those seasons but Australia doesn't necessarily have four seasons that sit opposite to England. Depending on where someone in Australia might live, they might experience anything between two and eight seasons so they can't even swap the northern hemisphere Sabbats over from winter to summer and so on. Let me explain.

If you live in the temperate zones of Australia, then you'll probably enjoy similar experiences in the seasons albeit opposite to England but if you live in Darwin for example then you have two seasons, particularly if you have empathy with the traditional owners of that area. They pretty much have summer all year and then the wet season and that's about it. If you're in the middle of Western Australia, you have six seasons so it's not quite as simple as doing a straight swap. Let's push the envelope even further while we're here.

If you live in the very hot parts of Australia like the northern parts of Western Australia, then unlike England where summer is the growth season with blooming flowers and full blown life all around, the summer up there is the dead season. Plants don't grow, they hibernate from the heat. People don't celebrate the light and warmth, they hide in the air conditioning from the beating sun that burns their skin and makes them dehydrated. The rains come (hopefully) and at times the wet season floods the desert plains.

That's not much like the seasonal experiences of the northern hemisphere in their summer so how can you even swap the Sabbats over and still work with them? Not easy! And wait; there are more dilemmas yet...

Casting a circle is always done in a deosil (clockwise) direction in the northern hemisphere and that's because that's the direction in which the sun travels from dawn to dusk. So working in this direction is always regarded as being in sync with the natural cycle of the sun. You cast a circle in the same direction the sun travels and you dismantle it by working widdershins (anti-clockwise). So deosil creates energy for circle casting and widdershins diminishes it for closing the circle back down again.

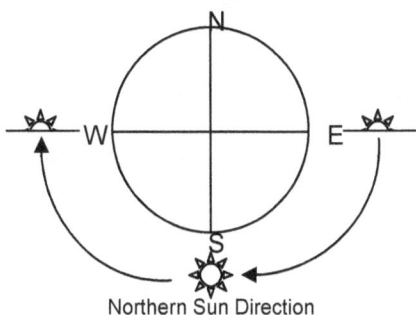

You can see the sun's clockwise or, deosil directional movement across the sky in the northern hemisphere in winter more so than in summer when the sun is low across the sky. It rises in the East (regardless of which hemisphere you're in) and moves toward the South and follows on to set in the West.

Northern Sun Direction

But down at the bottom of the planet in the southern hemisphere, while of courses it still rises in the East, it travels in a widdershins or an anticlockwise way. So if we follow the same principle that says we need to work in sync with the sun's direction, then we should be casting our circles in a widdershins or anti-clockwise direction. Confusing isn't it? But it doesn't stop there!

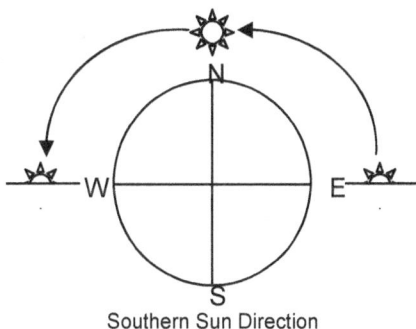

Southern Sun Direction

The original elemental correspondence to south is Fire and this is because in the northern hemisphere, a southerly direction will take you towards the heat and light of the equator. Makes sense doesn't it? But for those of us in the southern hemisphere, going in a southerly direction will take us to the ice and darkness of the South Pole, not to the heat and light of the equator. Does that mean that if we follow the same guidelines, we have to swap the north and south elemental quarters as well? It's getting complicated isn't it? So what do we do about it?

Well there are no definitive answers I'm afraid and virtually every coven does things slightly differently according to what they consider to be appropriate. This makes it really hard for solitaries who occasionally celebrate Sabbats with different covens because they all might do things differently, celebrate different festivals at different times, work in different directions and place their quarters at different compass points. Very confusing for a student! Remember the previous discussion on circle etiquette though when visiting other covens and politely work to their framework for that celebration even if you don't agree with it. You don't have to go back again if you don't want to!

Some covens in the southern hemisphere stick to the original northern framework working deosil, while others work widdershins to cast. Some keep the Sabbats to the northern calendar completely while others swap the names over but keep the content the same as the original. Some swap the names and content of the Sabbats over. Some covens keep their Fire and Earth elementals at the original compass points while others swap them over. East and West always stay the same because regardless of where you live, the sun always still rises in the East. So that's one saving simplicity at least.

Some eclectic covens try to match their Sabbats with what's happening around their geographic location and have moved away from the Wiccan Year of the Wheel altogether and they've copped some serious criticism about whether they're still Wiccan or not. So you never really know how a coven in the southern hemisphere works until you share a Sabbat or Esbat with them. It's a serious dilemma for southern hemisphere practitioners and a real challenge for students.

For Oak and Mistletoe, we prefer to follow the original notion of working deosil and to be honest, this is simply because as the founder, I brought the training with me that I was provided with but even more so because I can trace my family back to its Celtic origins in Cornwall and Brittany in the 6th century. I was born in England and still feel my cellular and soul roots there so for me, sticking with some of the original concepts work.

However, just to complicate things a little (what a surprise!) Oak and Mistletoe swaps the names and content of the Sabbats over so unlike our northern hemisphere cousins who celebrate Yule and Winter Solstice on December 21st, we celebrate it in June. We've also chosen to keep the element of Fire in the south. All the information given in this chapter about the Sabbats is what Oak and Mistletoe uses in terms of dates and content. It works for us and it's quite similar to many processes used by other southern hemisphere covens.

However, as part of the Inclusive tradition, which encourages you to find an expression of Wicca that suits you, we suggest that you do a bit of experimenting to see what works for you personally. It may be that you were born and raised in the Simpson Desert of Australia and you feel the need to swap the Sabbats and even your circle casting direction. Perhaps you were born in the beautiful South Island of New Zealand and for you it feels more comfortable to have your Fire element in the northern quarter. Maybe you were born in the USA and, like me, you still connect strongly with your homeland even though you now live in the southern hemisphere. That might mean you want to keep more of the original concepts. Remember that this is *your* relationship with the Lord and Lady and you have the right and responsibility to make it work for you. As long as you continue to work within the fundamental concepts and practices of Wicca, you'll still be a Wiccan but with a tailor-made approach to your practice.

The Sabbats in the Wheel of the Year for the Southern Hemisphere

First of all, we need to make some more clear distinctions between an Esbat and a Sabbat. Esbats are akin to going to Church on a Sunday for a Christian where you attend to the regular business of honouring deity, doing magickal work and generally revelling in your religion. You cast a circle to create a sacred space and you honour the Gods and Goddesses. Sabbats by comparisons are much more akin to celebrations, fun and festivities where you honour the time of year, the relevant mythological underpinnings and you can join together in celebration with other members of Wiccan community. Buddhists have fun and celebrate Vesak, Hindus celebrate Diwali with fun and Christians all get together and spend Christmas and Easter with the ones they love and have special meals together. That's what Sabbats are too.

You can cast a circle first before you do a Sabbat but you don't have to and in many cases, where non initiates are present or where you're celebrating with oath bound Wiccans and someone isn't initiated, a circle won't be cast first. You don't conduct magick at a Sabbat, that's personal or coven business and it's generally reserved for Esbats instead. At Sabbats you have fun, you get together with others and really celebrate with laughter, shared meals, special activities and conduct little traditions like turning pumpkins into lanterns, making Brigid's Crosses and re-enacting mythological stories. You write and/or participate in specific Sabbat rituals and these can be different every year if you like. So now we're clear on the difference between Esbats and Sabbats, let's talk

The Wheel of the Year

a little more about what and when each Sabbat is, what they each mean and how you celebrate them.

Research
Spend an hour or so exploring the internet to learn about the terms 'Sabbat' and 'Esbat'. Don't worry too much at this time about finding out about particular Sabbats but instead focus on learning what else you can that differentiates an Esbat from a Sabbat.

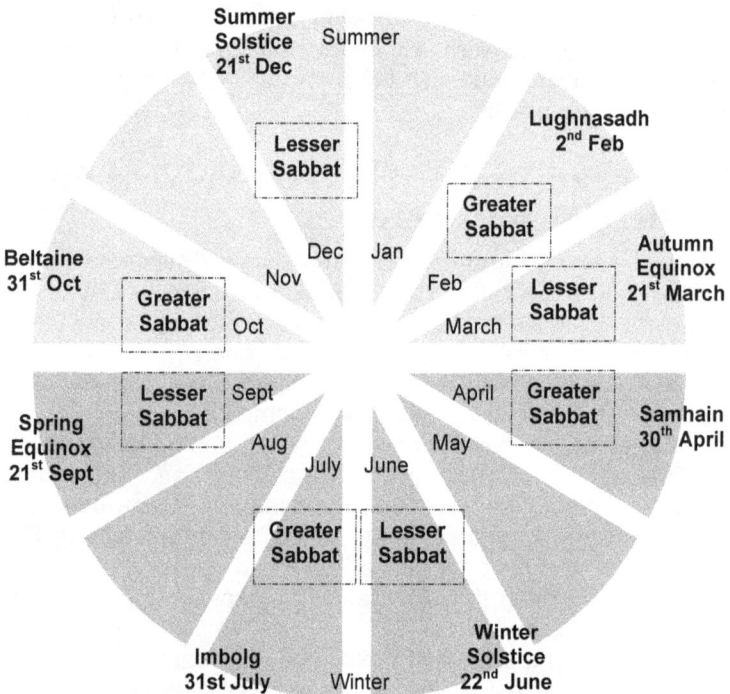

Oak and Mistletoe Wheel of the Year

Sabbats fall into two major categories, Greater and Lesser. The Greater Sabbats fall on days of very high, natural seasonal energy and the Lesser Sabbats mark the passage of the sun through the equinoxes and solstices. For each Sabbat we focus on two things; the seasonal relevance of the date and the underpinning mythological stories synonymous with that celebration. To celebrate those two factors, we participate in rituals and practices that symbolise both the seasonal relevance and mythological stories so

70

that we can better understand how important each Sabbat really is for us as Wiccans.

Samhain/All Hallows
A Greater Sabbat and an Earth Cross-Quarter Day
April 30th
Seasonal Relevancy

Summer's already losing its power and people are preparing for the long winter ahead by making preserves from the harvest like jams and pickles and chutneys. They're also slaughtering all but the animals which will be used for breeding next season's stock because in the harsher earlier times, many of the weaker animals wouldn't have survived the chill of winter and there wasn't usually enough food to keep them all alive anyway. This is the time of the final harvest of the crops, the root and surface vegetables and the last of the fruit.

Mythological Relevancy

Samhain (pronounced Sow-ayne) is without doubt the most important Sabbat of the Wiccan faith. While some covens might celebrate other festivals on the closest weekend to the date, this Sabbat is usually always celebrated on the actual date even if coveners have to get up for work the next morning!

It's a sombre festival that celebrates the dead and marks the time when the veil between the world of the mundane and that of the Spirit is at its thinnest. This is the Wiccan New Year and at sunset, when neither the old nor new year exist and thus when time stands still, humans can commune with their ancestors and loved ones who've passed over.

Popular Traditions

While this Sabbat celebrates our relationship with our ancestors and with the dead, it's not a frightening or sad occasion. It is a time to feast on the last of the harvest foods and to make ready for the cold times ahead. Many Wiccans lay an extra place or two at the feast table so that their departed ancestors and spirits can share in the festivities.

You can carve jack-o-lanterns from pumpkins to honour the Witches and other religious practitioners who've been persecuted for their faith over the centuries. Pay any debts, settle your quarrels and prepare for a few weeks of quiet solitude and meditation.

An Oak and Mistletoe Samhain Ritual

Decorate the circle perimeter with flowers and lay seasonal fruits and vegetables on a black cloth on the altar. These traditionally include apples, pomegranates, pumpkins, nuts and seeds. For the cakes and ale have apple cider and gingerbread. Ensure there's sufficient for those present as well as for absent friends and loved ones who may join us from the spirit world.

Have a piece of paper and a pen available for each person present.

Have a knife available to slice an apple.

Have a bonfire at the centre of the circle or a cauldron with a candle inside it.

Cast the circle as normal if there are no visitors present, otherwise, omit the circle casting.

Have a discussion about Samhain and its meaning with those present. When that's concluded, begin the ritual by standing before the altar and saying; "Now is the time of change between the passing of the seasons. At this time of year the gates between the worlds are open. We call upon our ancestors and our loved ones, to pass through and join with us at this time. We invite them to delight in celebration with those they love."

Take an apple from the altar and slice it in half across the middle so that the star of the pips and core is evident. Place the two halves on the pentacle and hold it aloft over the altar saying; "This is the fruit of life, which is also death".

Slice the apple into pieces, one for each person present plus one for visiting spirits. Go round the circle and offer a piece to each person. Ask them as they eat the apple to think of loved ones including pets who have passed on.

If using a candle in a cauldron instead of the central bonfire, light the candle using a lit taper from the spirit candle. Offer each person a piece of paper and a pen and ask them to think about an aspect of themselves they are uncomfortable with. This might be a bad habit, perhaps they get angry too quickly, upset too easily or spend money unwisely. It might be a behaviour or a thought pattern which does them a disservice and that they would like to eradicate. Ask them to write this on their paper and then fold it closed with a single fold.

In turn, each person offers their unwanted aspect to the flame. Ask them to consider that as the flame burns the paper away, they are offering this unwanted aspect to the Goddess so that it can be changed and removed. This is a way of recognising issues of self detriment and deciding to let that issue leave and be replaced instead with something more productive.

Consecrate and then have the cakes and ale and then close the circle. Have a Samhain feast that includes the traditional foods from the altar. Ensure there's a fully set place at the feast table for any spirit visitors. When the feast is over, lay a spare plate of food (not leftovers) outside the front door overnight to bring sustenance to any passing spirits.

Winter Solstice/Midwinter/Yule
A Lesser Sabbat and a Sun Quarter Day
June 21/22nd
Seasonal Relevancy
This is the longest night of the year and the shortest day and winter's at its peak. It's cold and dark and animals are hibernating, the birds are silent and the plants are all dormant.

Mythological Relevancy
This festival marks the re-birth of the sun with the cyclic story of the death of the Holly King (the king of the waning year) and the re-birth of his son the Oak King (the king of the waxing year).

Popular Traditions
Yule is a time to look forward to the return of the light of the sun and the warmth that it brings. Although it's still cold, this time of year brings hope for a brighter future as we quietly celebrate the forthcoming warmth and prepare for the growth season to come.

Find a good size Oak log and decorate it with Ivy, (traditionally also with Holly and Mistletoe; Holly because it's an evergreen and symbolises ongoing life while the seeds of Mistletoe, prevalent at this time of year, symbolise the sacred seed of new life). Light the log with an unburnt piece of last year's Yule log to symbolise the kindling light of the re-born sun. Save a small piece of this year's log from burning to use to light next year's log and spread the ashes of the burnt log on the garden.

An Oak and Mistletoe Winter Solstice - Yule Ritual
Decorate the altar and the circle perimeter with Holly and Ivy leaves, golden garlands and lots of candles. There should also be a crown made from Oak leaves (these should be gathered in the previous summer, pressed and lacquered ready for Yule). Light a balefire in the centre of the circle and beside it, lay this year's new Oak Yule log and the piece from last year with which to light this year's log.

Cast the circle as normal if there are no visitors present, otherwise, omit the circle casting. The Oak King lays down in a foetal position in the Eastern quarter of the circle. The High Priestess then opens the rite by saying; "This festival marks both the rebirth of the sun at the midpoint of winter and the rebirth of the Oak King as he returns to us each year. The Goddess, in all her glory, gives birth to the light of the sun above us and her son the Oak King before us. (Pointing to the baby Oak King laying on the floor in the east of the circle). The Holly King must die to make way for his son and the return of the light. We celebrate this night with the joyous birth of the Oak King!"

The maiden takes the Oak leaf crown from the altar and kneels before the baby Oak King saying; "We honour thee, our newborn God". The Oak King rises to face her and she places the crown on his head. He stands before those gathered and says; "I am reborn once more, and with me comes the light of the sun. I honour my father, the Holly King, the King of the waning year."

The High Priestess says; "All hail the Sun God!" Everyone says; "All hail the Sun God".

The High Priestess picks up last year's Yule log and hands it to the Oak King saying; "As we honour the reborn Sun God, let us also remember that life is but a cycle of death and life. Here is the last of the bounty from the year before that we saved to honour this year's bounty. Oak King, Lord of the waxing year, rekindle the light of the sun".

The Oak King uses last year's log to light the new Oak log in the balefire. When the new Yule log is burning, he says; "All hail the Sun God!" Everyone says; "All hail the Sun God"

Consecrate and then have the cakes and ale and then close the circle. Follow up with a feast and games beside the Yule balefire.

Imbolg/Candlemas
A Greater Sabbat and an Earth Cross-Quarter Day
July 31st
Seasonal Relevancy
Spring is on its way at last and we can very clearly see that the days have become longer and the warmth and light of the sun is returning. Imbolg comes from the ancient word meaning 'ewe's milk' and reminds us that this is lambing season. In addition, the grass is beginning to grow again and the spring flowers are just beginning to burst forth from the ground.

Mythological Relevancy
Imbolg is the time of the quickening. The baby Oak King is growing and the Goddess is a maiden once more. This Sabbat belongs to the fire Goddess Brigid, who presides over healing, the well springs and the hearth.

Popular Traditions
Because this time of year is synonymous with new life, new ideas and new beginnings it's particularly relevant for initiations and dedications. Even more, it is a purifying time of year when we should clear out the old things that have held us back and make room for brighter and healthier behaviours and actions for the growing season ahead.

74

Make a Brigid's Cross from straw, hang it on your front door as a protective charm and burn the old one from last year. Conduct rituals with candles to invoke the fire Goddess Brigid, and to symbolise the light of the longer days.

An Oak and Mistletoe Imbolg Ritual
The altar is prepared as usual. A cauldron with at least one stone in it for each person present sits in front of the altar. Each covener should previously have been asked to bring a food donation of one tin or packet of non perishable food item with them. Also have a space, box or bag in front of the altar for people to offer this food donation. Cast the circle as normal if there are no visitors present, otherwise, omit the circle casting.

The ritual leader addresses those gathered; "Welcome to all those who have gathered here today to celebrate the festival of Imbolg. Traditionally this is a time of year when we should be spring cleaning our homes and repaying old debts in preparation for the coming light of spring. Making sure we have completed these tasks allows us to be more emotionally free and prepared to take on the new challenges of the growing season ahead and thus develop ourselves along with the new light of spring."

"In these modern days of isolation where we don't always know, let alone see, our neighbours, today we will be focusing on community and how you can contribute to the people around you as you prepare to bring in that light of Spring."

"The "Stone Soup" fable is a simple story that shows how a group of people can work together to support each other and bring joy and a sense of belonging to one another. The story goes like this..."

Some one reads the following fable out to the group.

A weary traveller, in the depths of winter, came into a dark village. His feet were sore and his stomach was empty. He walked, door to door, with nothing but a single copper coin to his name, and asked the villagers if he could buy some of their food. At each door, a gaunt villager told him that they were starving, unable to spare even a morsel of their winter stores.

Finally, the young man sat down in the centre of the square, aware of the eyes peeking at him from shuttered windows. He reached down, brushed some snow from a small rock beneath his feet, and lifted it. With a start, he leapt to his feet, looked up to the shuttered windows, cleared his throat and made an announcement. "You silly, starving people! How can you hide behind your walls, desperate for food when you have perfectly good stones like this laying all around you? Does but one of the women here have a good kettle she can loan me? I promise enough stone soup to feed her whole family if she loans it to me for the day!"

The Wheel of the Year

The washerwoman had a kettle frozen behind her house, a large kettle last used for stew at Christmas time, too large to use for her family's meagre meals and too small for laundry. She volunteered it, and the young man dragged it, full of snow, from the outdoor hearth it had occupied for a month to the centre of the square. Villagers, bored in the dark winter, gathered around to help the man start a fire and melt the snow and ice in the pot. They were all convinced he was nuts, but helped him nonetheless. It was a sleepy village, and his obvious lunacy was worth a few cold feet to observe.

Once the snow had melted, he lifted the stone high for all of the villagers to see and plopped it into the pot. "Stewus blueus magic rock," he chanted, "give us soup within this crock!" He walked three times around the pot and took a spoon someone handed him and dipped it in. Ever the diligent cook, he tasted the water and its mild aftertaste of Christmas stew and shook his head. "It's bland," he told them, "If only I had a bit of salt."

The butcher told him he had salt sitting in his salting pot, the remnants of salting the midwinter's catch, which had run out the week before. It was brown and hardened into one lump, but he'd give it to the man for free.

The man took his offer gladly, and added the brown lump to the pot. He again took a sip. "the magic is working" he told his audience, and, indeed, there was a faint smell of food coming from the pot. He sipped the soup again, and made a face. "It's too sweet!" he said. "If only I had the ends of some turnips, or some radishes to give it some bite!"

Two women looked about and then went into their houses, coming out with half-rotten vegetables. The man carefully cut the rotted parts away and added the vegetables, greens and all.

There was no mistaking that it smelled like food now. The man tasted the soup, and said "It's missing something" and handed the spoon to the brewman's wife, who nodded, then scurried into the closed tavern, returning with a small burlap bag of barley. As she dumped it in, the wife of the mayor objected. "You can't have barley in soup without parsnips!" she declared, and produced a bunch of limp, greying parsnips, which she handed to the man, who skinned them, chopped them and plopped them in.

Another woman objected as well, adding a fat, dry onion to the broth, and another, and still another, each adding the small secret ingredient that made the soups they made at home 'perfect'.

Within an hour, the smell of the soup filled the square, and the people came from every crevice and corner with a bowl. The mayor of the town hailed the wanderer as their saviour and put him up in his own house after he and the villagers had filled their bellies with delicious, if odd-tasting, stone soup.

76

At this point, the ritual leader begins a discussion by suggesting that listening to that story leads us to consider a whole bunch of things. What might that story be teaching us? Perhaps it teaches us about community contribution, a spirit of togetherness, compassion, and that each little bit helps. Sometimes we need one person to start the chain of events off and it's often easier to ignore someone in need than to provide help.

The ritual leader asks those gathered; "Who or what is community? Is the community the people around where you live? Is it your work mates? Is the community your coven or your spiritual group of friends? Is it the Pagan community? Maybe it's your social group?"

The ritual leader addresses those gathered; "Like the kettle of stone soup in the story, here you will find a cauldron loaded with different stones. Stones and rocks are bounty from our Earth and each stone brings with it different Earth memories and contributions from Gaia. Each stone here is therefore a gift from Gaia and these gifts are yours to use wisely and appropriately. Each stone here represents a contribution that you can make to your community."

"Take a moment now to think about who your community is and what contribution you can make to it. It may be that your contribution is; to mow your elderly neighbour's lawn, to wash your friend's/partner's/parents' car, to visit that friend in hospital, to make the time to bring morning tea in for your colleagues at work, to donate a rug to a charity".

"When you have decided who your community is and what you can contribute to it, take a stone. Then spend a few moments to send your thoughts of contribution into that gift from Gaia."

"Now that you have all sent your thoughts into your stones. What do you think we need to do now? We need to enact the thoughts we just created."

Someone else addresses those gathered; "Gaia, Mother Goddess of our planet, let these stones before us be the catalyst that brings about our intention. We ask that you hear our thoughts and help us create the reality. Help us donate our energies, our actions, ourselves to those around us, who mean so much to us and who help make us who we are. Let these stones remind us of our pledge to our community and ensure that we live up to our pledge. So mote it be."

Yet someone else addresses those gathered; "As we go home to our families, to our friends, our work and our lives, let each of these stones remind us that we pledged here today to make a contribution. We pledged to offer something of who we are to help someone else be who they are. So mote it be."

The ritual leader addresses those gathered again; "Imbolg comes from the ancient word meaning 'ewe's milk' and reminds us that this is lambing season. Ewes provide us with warm woollen clothing and with food. To honour Imbolg's ancient link with food and to further honour our commitment to community as in the Stone Soup fable, we have elected to donate some of our food to the larder of those less fortunate than ourselves. In sharing our food with others, we honour the Gods and Goddesses and the community of which we are part."

"Please take a moment now to place your food offering before the altar. As you do so, take a moment to remember those who are not always able to provide food for their own families".

Consecrate and have the cakes and ale then close the circle. Follow up with a feast during which everyone considers those less fortunate than themselves who may be unable to feast. Maybe have some toasts to acknowledge those people less fortunate than us.

Spring Equinox/Ostara/Eostre
A Lesser Sabbat and a Sun Quarter Day
Sept 21st
Seasonal Relevancy
Spring has arrived and there's an equal balance of light and dark. The flowers are all blooming again, the birds are nesting and all around, new life is bursting forth.

Mythological Relevancy
This Sabbat is named after the Saxon Goddess Ostara and the festival specifically marks an equal balance between male and female energies which coincides perfectly with the fact that the days and nights are of equal length. Thus there is balance in all universal elements. The young Oak King, who's grown to a young man, now courts the maiden Goddess.

Popular Traditions
Eggs are symbolic of new life and Wiccans use painted eggs to celebrate the wonderful eruption of new life all around them. Throw hard boiled, painted eggs high into the sky and as you do make a wish for the summer months ahead. The higher the egg goes, the more likely your wish will come true. Bury the fallen eggs to cement your wish. Bake and eat Hot Cross Buns marked with an equilateral cross to symbolise all things equal.

An Oak and Mistletoe Spring Equinox- Ostara Ritual
Hold the ritual in a park or cheerful, open garden area. Decorate the altar with bright yellow daffodils and other spring flowers. Mark the perimeter of the circle with spring flowers so that it looks happy and colourful.
On the altar have:

Yellow card cut into the shape of big sunflowers with petal sections that can eventually fold up so that the flower shape becomes a bowl (1 sunflower for each person present).
A pen for each person to use.
A pot of parrot or bird seed.

Cast the circle as normal if there are no visitors present, otherwise, omit the circle casting.

The ritual leader says to the group; "The Spring Equinox is a both a time of balance and a time of renewal. It is a time of balance because this event marks one of two points in the year when the days are the same length as the nights. Thus there is balance in light and darkness".

"It is also a time of renewal and rebirth as Spring provides the warmth and light for new plants to grow, for young animals to grow healthy and fit, and for life to blossom around us. So as the caretakers of our precious planet and as the architects of our own life balance and renewal, we can use this time to refocus on those things that are important to us."

Give each person a sunflower card and a pen saying; "Each of you now have before you a symbolic sunflower, one of the flowers that erupts at this time of year and grows toward full bloom in Summer. Take a few moments now to consider what parts of your life are out of balance. Are you spending too much time and too much effort on one part of your life at the expense of other, equally or more important parts? Are you spending too much time on things and not on people? Do you use one set of behaviours instead of spreading your wings and trying better ways to cope? Are you ignoring parts of your life, parts of who you are when you should be balancing your life and being a whole person?"

"When you are ready, take your pen and write in the centre of your sunflower one way you will rebalance your life. Write down one behaviour or one aspect of your life you will change to bring your life back into balance".

"Now take your sunflower and bend the petals up so that you form a bowl with your committed behaviour change written in the middle".

When all participants have done this, have someone take the pot of bird seed and pour some seed into each of the sunflower bowls. The ritual leader then says; "Your commitments to rebalance your lives are now nestled beneath seed, which is the icon of new life, of rebirth and of renewal. Please take your sunflower bowls home. Each bowl signifies both life balance and rebirth. At home, place your bowl out in the garden to feed the local birds and to give to the Earth your commitment to rebalance your life."

Consecrate and then have the cakes and ale, then close the circle. Follow up with a feast.

Beltaine
A Greater Sabbat and an Earth Cross-Quarter Day
Oct 31st
Seasonal Relevancy
The summer begins at this point and the days are warm and balmy. The nights are getting shorter and growth is all around.

Mythological Relevancy
This is a time of great fertility and is a fun filled time in marked contrast to the sober and sombre Sabbat of Samhain. It celebrates the sacred marriage of the Oak King and the Goddess and the consummation of that union. The fire God Baal is celebrated at this time as the God of light or 'The Bright One' while the Goddess Maya is also celebrated.

Popular Traditions
This is a true fertility festival with dancing round the Maypole (an ancient phallic symbol) to symbolise the sexual union between male and female energies.

Light a balefire with nine different types of wood (three pieces of each wood type) for the God Baal. Leap over the purifying flames and let them cleanse you of unwanted behaviours or openly state your desire and as you jump, let the flames take those desires to the skies to be fulfilled.

An Oak and Mistletoe Beltaine Ritual
Decorate the perimeter of the circle with flowers. A Maypole should be set up in the east quarter with ribbons tied to it at the top. There should be at least one ribbon for each person present. There should be a balefire set in the north quarter. This should be a festival of fun, frivolity, dancing and laughter. It is not a sombre affair at all.

Cast the circle as normal if there are no visitors present, otherwise, omit the circle casting. A covener shouts; "Hast, haste! No time to wait! We're off to the Sabbat, so don't be late!" The Priestess shouts; "To the Sabbat!" and everyone shouts; "To the Sabbat!"

The High Priestess leads the coveners in a dance around the circle with everyone singing and chanting. The music of "The Lord of the Dance" is particularly good for this especially using the following words adapted from the original lyrics of Sydney B Carter by Spiral Child.

She danced on the water, and the wind was Her horn, The Lady laughed, and everything was born,
And when She lit the sun and its' light gave Him birth, The Lord of the Dance first appeared on the Earth.

The Wheel of the Year

(Chorus): Dance, dance, where ever you may be,
I am the Lord of the Dance, you see!
I live in you, and you live in Me,
And I lead you all in the Dance, said He!

I danced in the morning when the World was begun,
I danced in the Moon and the Stars and the Sun.
I was called from the Darkness by the Song of the Earth,
I joined in the Song, and She gave Me the Birth!

I dance in the Circle when the flames leap up high,
I dance in the Fire, and I never, ever, die.
I dance in the waves of the bright summer sea,
For I am the Lord of the wave's mystery.

I sleep in the kernel, and I dance in the rain,
I dance in the wind, and thru the waving grain.
And when you cut me down, I care nothing for the pain.
In the Spring I'm the Lord of the Dance once again!

I dance at the Sabbat when you dance out the Spell,
I dance and sing that everyone be well.
And when the dancing's over do not think that I am gone,
To live is to Dance! So I dance on, and on!

I see the Maidens laughing as they dance in the Sun,
And I count the fruits of the Harvest, one by one.
I know the Storm is coming, but the Grain is all stored,
So I sing of the Dance of the Lady, and Her Lord.

The Horn of the Lady cast its' sound 'cross the Plain,
The birds took the notes, and gave them back again,
Till the sound of Her music was a Song in the sky,
And to that Song there is only one reply.

The moon in her phases, and the tides of the sea,
The movement of the Earth, and the Seasons that will be, Are the
rhythm for the dancing, and a promise thru the years,
That the Dance goes on thru all our joy, and tears.

We dance ever slower as the leaves fall and spin,
And the sound of the Horn is the wailing of the wind.
The Earth is wrapped in stillness, and we move in a trance, But we
hold on fast to our faith in the Dance!

The Wheel of the Year

The sun is in the southland and the days grow chill,
And the sound of the horn is fading on the hill,
'Tis the horn of the Hunter, as he rides across the plain,
And the Lady sleeps 'til the Spring comes again.

The Sun is in the Southland and the days lengthen fast,
And soon we will sing for the Winter that is past,
Now we light the candles and rejoice as they burn,
And we dance the Dance of the Sun's return!

They danced in the darkness and they danced in the night. They
danced on the Earth, and everything was light.
They danced out the Darkness and they danced in the dawn,
And the Day of that Dancing is still going on!

I gaze on the Heavens and I gaze on the Earth,
And I feel the pain of dying, and re-birth,
And I lift my head in gladness, and in praise,
For the Dance of the Lord, and His Lady gay.

I dance in the stars as they whirl throughout space,
And I dance in the pulse of the veins in your face,
No dance is too great, no dance is too small,
You can look anywhere, for I dance in them all!

Everyone gathers around the Maypole and takes a ribbon. The High Priestess says; "Beltaine is a time of fertility. The Maypole and ribbons symbolise the sacred union between male and female and the creation of new life for the year ahead". Everyone then dances around the pole holding their ribbons, intertwining them as they go until they are all tied around the pole.

Everyone then moves to the north quarter where the balefire is set and burning. The maiden says; "Jumping the balefire is an old fertility tradition often done together by couples who would like to be blessed with the seed and creation of children. For those of you who have a beloved partner, the balefire wish is often one of long lived health and happiness in your sacred union together. Today we honour the Lord and Lady with our rite and ask that they bestow upon us their blessings for fertility, perhaps not of children, but of good luck and happiness. I invite you all now to jump the balefire and send your wishes for good fortune up to the Lord and Lady in the rising smoke from this balefire. Consider your good luck wish, offer it to the rising smoke and set it with your jump!"

Everyone has as many turns at jumping the balefire as they wish. Couples can jump together if they wish to honour their marriage. Consecrate and then have the cakes and ale then close the circle. Follow up with a feast.

Summer Solstice/Midsummer's Eve/Litha
A Lesser Sabbat and a Sun Quarter Day
Dec 21st
Seasonal Relevancy
Litha marks the longest day of the year and the zenith of summer. The sun blazes down, the ground below us holds its heat, the grass is rampant and the baby birds are now flying on their own.

Mythological Relevancy
The Holly King is born of the Goddess and the Oak King (his father) dies. This symbolic cycle is repeated each year as new life takes over from old.

In synopsis, the King marries the Goddess (who is his mother) fathers his own child, then dies in sacrifice so that his son might take over.

Popular Traditions
With the sun at its zenith, this is traditionally the time when magic is at its full strength. Many rituals incorporate some form of magic at this time.

Because the sun has reached its peak and will be slowly growing dim from this point on, this is also a great time of year for banishing magic. Banish away the behaviours or the issues and situations you have that no longer serve you.

An Oak and Mistletoe Summer Solstice - Litha Ritual
Decorate the altar and mark the circle perimeter with summer flowers. Have on the altar a prepared daisy (or other weed) chain, an orange candle and some bergamot oil. Have a cauldron in the centre of the circle. Ideally this ritual should be conducted at midday on the year's longest day. Cast the circle as normal if there are no visitors present, otherwise, omit the circle casting.

The High Priestess moves to the South and says; "We gather here before you, the blazing God of summer's sun, to honour you and bathe under the strength and light that is yours. The Wheel of the Year is turning again, as it does year after year. From the time of Yule when you were reborn of the Goddess, through Ostara you grew and now you light the days with your full strength. Tomorrow we will see you slowly wane toward the Autumn Equinox to once again be sacrificed to the darkness of winter. But as the Wheel of the Year turns, we know you will return. As you blaze in the skies before us now, may our lives blaze in glory below."

The High Priestess dresses the candle with the bergamot oil saying; "As the zenith of the sun God's power reaches its height so too does our magickal will. And as the sun God's power wanes from this point, so too do our misfortunes. I infuse this candle with the power of the sun God at the height of his reign and command that as it burns, any misfortune and unhappiness we bare will burn away."

The High Priestess places the candle in the cauldron and lights its flame saying; "May the power of the sun God above be as the power of the flame below".

The maiden takes the daisy chain from the altar saying; "As this daisy chain symbolises the weeds of summer, may it also hold the bad habits, the misfortunes and the wrong doings of our summer. As you take the weeds of summer amongst you, let them hold all that you want banished from your lives".

She spends a moment pushing any of her own banishment requirements into the weed chain and then passes it to the person on her right (so that it will travel around the coveners in a widdershins fashion). As each person takes the weed chain, they too send anything they want banished into it. When the weed chain reaches the maiden again, she holds it up to the sky in the south saying; "Weeds of summer, weeds of misfortune, weeds of poor judgement, as the summer's zenith passes and the light slowly dies, may our sadness and misfortune die with the fading sun."

She turns and throws the weed chain on the candle flame in the cauldron letting it burn away. As it burns she says; "Summer fades now, weeds die now, misfortune be gone now. So mote it be!" Everyone says; "So mote it be!"

Consecrate and then have the cakes and ale then close the circle. Follow up with a feast.

Lughnasadh/Lammas
A Greater Sabbat and an Earth Cross-Quarter Day
Feb 2nd
Seasonal Relevancy
Some of the flowers are already beginning to fade while the late bloomers are coming into their fullness. The new life that came in spring is fast developing toward adulthood and we're beginning to see the outcomes of the fertile energies sewn earlier in the seasonal year.

This festival celebrates the first harvest being brought in from the fields and from the fruit trees and so rituals tend to focus on the theme of harvest.

Mythological Relevancy
Lughnasadh (pronounced 'Loo-nar-sar) is in honour of the Celtic Sun God Lugh and marks how he sacrifices his life so that the fruits can ripen and the crops can grow toward their harvests. Lugh is a God of harvest and light.

Popular Rituals
Bake bread from many different grains to honour the harvest and celebrate the food of the Gods. Drink red wine and toast to the glory of the Gods and Goddeses.

An Oak and Mistletoe Lughnasadh/Lammas Ritual
Everyone should begin gathering at the ritual site late in the afternoon so that the ritual can commence close to sunset. The circle is to be is to be marked out with a trail of grain. The altar is to be decorated with the flowers that are currently in season (Iris, Lilies, Frangipani, Lavender, Jasmine etc) and with the bread rolls that each person has been asked to bring with them. Cakes and ale should be small bread rolls and red wine.
Each person is to bring with them their ingredients for Summer Pudding (see below).

Cast the circle as normal if there are no visitors present, otherwise, omit the circle casting.

The ritual leader commences by explaining Lammas; "Lammas is an ancient Celtic Fire festival that celebrates the first grain harvest of the season and also marks the turning point between summer and the commencement of autumn. In times gone by, people would have used this opportunity to give thanks for the bounty of the harvest and to begin the preparations for the coming dark, winter months. Winter was a harsh time when many animals and people did not survive either because of the cold, through hunger or through illness. The harvest was therefore extremely important because the grain helped ensure adequate supplies of food through those coming months".

"Lammas comes from the Anglo Saxon word, "Hlafmas" or loaf-mass and shows us that a thousand years ago, the grain crops were of immense importance to the ongoing survival of village life. "Many cultures across the globe celebrate a similar concept at this time. The Irish honour the solar God Lugh with their Lughnasadh festival. Lugh was the King of the Tuatha de Danann, the God of light and of the harvest and this festival marks the point at which he begins to die in sacrifice to ensure an abundant crop. The Scots call this event Lunasduinn, the French honour the God Lugus while even the Christians adopted this festival to celebrate St Peter's release from prison."

"As a celebration of the grain harvest that delivers increased opportunity to survive the coming months, bread is the icon of Lammas. Bread is the product of the grain and thus the embodiment of continued life. Christians see bread as the body of Christ while Greek mythology sees bread as a symbol of mortality. Bread, like wine, is a food substance that undergoes a fermentation process and as such bread, and wine, are separated from the usual fruits of the harvest which need little preparation before consumption. Apples, oranges, nuts, berries, vegetables and many other fruits of the land can be eaten almost straight from the tree, the vine, the bush or the ground. They may require washing or even simple cooking but grain and grapes undergo a process of modification in order to become the revered produce they are and this process symbolises civilisation, community and the intellectualisation of man."

"Bread is thus the symbol of life, of man's ability to survive but also of the separation between the immortal world of the Gods and the mundane and harsh world of mortal man."

"As we celebrate this festival, let us each consider what we have to be grateful for today. What are the things you are reaping now that you began last year? What are the bounties that you are grateful for? What are the blessings that have enriched your life? Moreover, what are the things you need to do now in order to prepare for the darkness of winter? What are the things you must think about that will bring you happiness and peace during the next six months? What processes do you need to start right now that will help you reach your goals?"

At this point each person present is given a bread roll from those that were placed on the altar prior to the commencement of the ritual.

The ritual leader says; "Each of you has brought to this rite some bread which is a symbol of enduring life. The bread you hold in your hand is like the bread that came from the grain harvests which enabled our ancestors to live through the extremes of winter. The Irish-Gaelic God Lugh gave his life for the harvest so that the cycle of life could continue. Break your bread in half now and before you take a bite, consider the bounty that you have for which you can be grateful. If you would like, please share your thoughts of thanks."

Each person can then share what they are grateful for with the group and take a bite of their bread roll.

The ritual leader now continues; "While each of us has issues of concern and problems that we face, the likelihood that we will die from starvation or cold through the winter is not strong. We are blessed to be part of a community that has bread, that has heating, supermarkets, jobs, money, transport. It may not always be a bed of roses, but we are blessed more than many others. Take one more bite of your bread and as you do, give thoughts to those who do not share in your blessings."

Each person can take one more bite in silent contemplation.

The ritual leader completes this ritual task by asking the group to place their left over bread roll pieces back in the altar bowl and explains that these left over pieces will go to feed the local chickens and birds so contributing to the continued cycle of life.

Consecrate and then have the cakes and ale then close the circle. Follow up by making Summer Puddings together.

The ritual leader says; "While grains are abundant now, so too are berries in Australia. The supermarkets are awash with blueberries, mulberries, blackberries, strawberries and so on. The season is brief and the fruits are so yummy that it would be a shame not to incorporate these into our Lammas event. So each person is going to make a Summer Pudding using the berries, bread and bowls they brought with them. (A recipe is included below).

The ritual leader explains how to make the pudding and why it is significant; "The berries are abundant now but the season will be over within the month. The redcurrants, strawberries, raspberries and so on are the colour of dark fire, the colour of the fire Gods, the colour of blood which is the universal liquid of life. The bread that surrounds the berries within the pudding bowl incorporates the bread aspect of this festival and envelops the berry red blood of life within a symbolic bread shell of enduring life. The Summer Pudding is thus our symbol of survival."

"Once made, the pudding will then chill in the fridge overnight so that it becomes solid and edible and this storage reflects how the grain of our ancestors was stored to be consumed later. Our Summer Pudding is thus a tribute to our past and a way to connect with the fruits of our harvest."

This should be a joyous and fun filled occasion given the abundance of life around us and the promise of enough food through winter so as everyone makes the Summer Puddings, they can sing along with the old Celtic folksongs that so often told the stories of these times.

Summer Pudding recipe (Courtesy of Delia Smith)
Serves 6

* 8 oz (225 g) redcurrants
* 4 oz (110 g) blackcurrants
  1 lb (450 g) raspberries
  5 oz (150 g) caster sugar
  7-8 medium slices white bread from a large loaf
* You will also need a 1½ pint (850 ml) pudding basin, lightly buttered.

Separate the redcurrants and blackcurrants from their stalks by holding the tip of each stalk firmly between finger and thumb and sliding it between the prongs of a fork pushing the fork downwards, so pulling off the berries as it goes. Rinse all the fruits, picking out any raspberries that look at all musty.

Place the fruits with the sugar in a large saucepan over a medium heat and let them cook for about 3-5 minutes, only until the sugar has dissolved and the juices begin to run – don't overcook and so spoil the fresh flavour. Now remove the fruit from the heat, and line the pudding basin with the slices of bread, overlapping them and sealing well by pressing the edges together. Fill in any gaps with small pieces of bread, so that no juice can get through when you add the fruit.

Pour the fruit and juice in (except for about two thirds of a cupful which will be used later), then cover the pudding with another slice of bread. Then place a small plate or saucer (one that will fit exactly inside the rim of the bowl) on top, and on top of that place a 3 lb or 4 lb (1.3 kg or 1.8 kg) weight, and leave in the fridge overnight. This ensures the pudding is compressed and soaks up the fruit juice.

Just before serving the pudding, turn it out on to a large serving dish and spoon the reserved juice all over, to soak into any bits of bread that still appear to look white. Serve the pudding cut into wedges, along with a bowl of whipped, thickened cream on the table. Leftovers can be refrigerated for later use and will last several days when stored appropriately.

Autumn Equinox/Mabon
A Lesser Sabbat and a Sun Quarter Day
March 21st
Seasonal Relevancy
At this time of year, there's an equal balance of light and dark, summer and winter, male and female. The second grain harvest is brought in, the fruits are ready and the hunt begins.

Mythological Relevancy
There's equilibrium between male and female energies again so this festival honours the balance between good and bad, light and dark, male and female.

Popular Traditions
Save some ears of corn or grain from the current harvest to make into a Brigid's Cross at Imbolg and keep the ears safe within your home till then.

An Oak and Mistletoe Autumn Equinox - Mabon Ritual

The altar should be decorated with different fruits and vegetables. There should be a basket of apples with one apple for every two people present and a knife. An empty cauldron sits in the circle centre.

Cast the circle as normal if there are no visitors present, otherwise, omit the circle casting.

The High Priestess opens the ritual saying; "The Autumn Equinox signals the midpoint in the journey of the sun across the seasons. As we celebrate this day, let us remember that there is balance in all things, day and night, light and dark, life and death, good fortune and misfortune. Let this rite be one of honour for the balance in seasons and in life."

The maiden takes the basket of apples from before the altar and cuts them in half across its middle saying; "The apple is a sacred fruit and contains the five pointed star. The points of the star herein mark the balance of the elements Air, Fire, Water, Earth and Spirit in all things." She hands a half apple to the first covener saying; "Blessed and thankful are we for the balance of our lives". The covener replies; "Blessed be." She repeats this for each covener until everyone has an apple.

The High Priest says; "Each of you have one half of a whole. For balance to continue there must always be a joining of dark and light, good and bad for nothing sits alone."

The High Priest and High Priestess come together and press the two halves of their apples together. She says; "We come together in harmony and balance as the Lord and Lady come together through the seasons." Together they raise their apple pressed together to the sky and the High Priest says; "May we give thanks for the balance of the Lord and Lady above and for the balance in our lives below".

The maiden asks the coveners; "come together with your partner, loved one or friend and join your apple halves together with the other. Let each half become the balance of the other so that all are whole. Take a moment to give silent thanks for the balance in your life." The coveners pair up and press their apple halves together to make a whole. They take a moment in silent thanks.

The High Priestess says; "As the apple seeds form the pentagram, the symbol of our faith and the seed of life that has brought us to this point of balance, let us now eat of the fruit given for us". Everyone can sit round now and eat their apples and talk through amongst themselves what they see as having balance in their lives. The apple cores can be put into the cauldron and buried after the circle has been dismantled.

Consecrate and then have the cakes and ale then close the circle. Follow up with a feast.

Writing Your Own Sabbat (and Other) Rituals

You now have a set of rituals you can use for the Sabbats and these will keep you in good stead for the next year ahead as you gradually find your own feet. But find your own feet you must and that's what this section of the chapter is about.

While it's nice to learn using the rituals of others who've gone before you, the test of a good Wiccan and Witch is their ability to tune into nature, to the Lord and Lady and to themselves and create their own rituals. Writing rituals takes practice and it might take a while till you feel comfortable with what you come up with but there are some ways to make things easier.

Like the Esbats circle casting ritual, there are given steps in designing a ritual that guide how it can be developed and if you follow these steps, tune in to your natural connection with nature and understand the principles of the underpinning mythology, then you're half way there. Let's take a look at the various parts that make up most simple Wiccan rituals.

- Preparing the ritual space (cleansing it, setting up the altar, the ritual perimeter and any equipment and requirements),
- Preparing yourself which may include bathing, centering and anointing,
- Casting the circle and creating the sacred space. (This part can be omitted or removed where there are people present who may not have been initiated or where it might be inappropriate.)
- Stating the reason for the ritual. This might a simple explanation or an introduction to the ritual's purpose,
- Creating an environment where people can shed their current identity and lose their ties to the mundane. This can be done through by introducing an 'ordeal' or challenge which helps people to understand that their life in the mundane world is not the most important aspect of their life. Technically speaking this is a state of liminality in which they lose their identity and become 'blanks' ready to seek new meaning from the Divine,

🕮   Providing a means of connecting people with the Lord and Lady so they're better able to receive the messages and insight waiting for them. At this point, the people present are between two worlds with their everyday, mundane world and what that means on one side and their new, hopefully more meaningful world on the other side,

🕮   Bringing the coveners back to the here and now with their new found wisdom and insight,

🕮   Cakes and Ale,

🕮   Dismantling the circle if it was cast.

Now essentially what all this means is that when you're creating a ritual or rite of passage regardless of whether it's conducted alongside the circle casting ritual or otherwise, the main aim of most rituals is to bring you closer to the Divine and to better understand your true self. In order to do that, you need to strip away the shell of your 'normal' self so that you can get to the real 'you' underneath and allow the insights from the God and Goddess to reach you directly.

If we try and connect with the God and Goddess while we're still in normal, everyday mode, we're still hampered, even if don't realise it, by the woes of our daily lives. In the back of our minds sit the concerns we have like, when will that damn washing machine get fixed, who broke the photocopier this time, why did that bill have to turn up today and what shall I cook for dinner tomorrow! It's as though the God and Goddess have to fight their way through this whole fog of thoughts, concerns, worries and so on to get to the real you underneath. So a good ritual helps people strip away all that mundane stuff so we have a direct connection with the Lord and Lady. A bit like stripping out all the interference in a radio conversation so we hear just the words and not all that white noise crackle.

This might happen through centering ourselves with a guided mediation, perhaps through conducting a doorway exercise, maybe through a challenge that helps someone get closer to their soul. It might even be as simple as telling a story, conducting a play acting of a mythological story or even asking people to recall a particular event that connects them with each other and the Divine.

Once all the mundane, daily rubbish has been stripped away, people are much more open and available to connect with the Lord and Lady at a much deeper and more emotional level. It's as though the Gods and Goddesses can touch our hearts deep within us now and not be filtered through or hampered by our over active brains.

These insights can come as a part of the meditation, the pathway exercise or they can come from a separate activity specifically designed for that purpose.

Finally, charged with new insight, renewed vigour, determination, even simply just a purpose, the ritual participants can be given the opportunity to commit to and live that new life, create that outcome they were told was important by the Divine and work toward whatever it was that their connection with the Lord and Lady gave them.

Writing ritual is actually every simple but the true measure of ritual is how much it moves and motivates people. Ritual is a powerful tool for influencing and pushing people to achieve their true potential and to honour their Gods and Goddesses, their universe and themselves. Successful ritual can be fun, can be sombre, can be exciting, can be calm but it should always be moving and motivating.

A simple trick in making any ritual even more effective is using both rhyme and rhythm. We remember complex things much more easily if we can see a predictable tempo in the words. That's partly why we remember songs so easily because they follow a repeatable pattern and the pattern of words and music locks the song in our brain. If you learnt The Lord's Prayer in school, can you still remember parts of it even though you might not have recited it for many years? Ritual can have the same longevity in our memories if it's written to a pattern or a beat or a rhyme. This is why so many rituals that have lasted many years continue to be used and it's not just because of their beauty, but because rhyme and rhythm make them easy to remember.

One other thing to remember is simplicity. A complex ritual like the old Rosicrucian, Hermetic or Thelemic rites might have a sense of wonder and awe around them but they're not very easy to conduct, much less remember! People more easily recall a simple but powerful ritual, something that touched their hearts much more than a complex, long winded routine that tested their patience and left them confused. Using simple tools to help people connect with nature is one easy way to keep things grounded and sensible. Things like seeds to signify fertility and new life, flower petals to signify unity, feathers to connect with the Air element or perhaps candles to help us focus. All these tools and objects are simple items that help us focus on the ritual content and intent and the simplicity enables us to get straight to the heart and point of the ritual.

In many of the Oak and Mistletoe rituals, we use the simple tools of nature like seeds, flowers, feathers, stones, crystals, cotton string, shells, twigs and branches and so on, as metaphors and bridges for meaning. Nature supplies so many iconic symbols that with a bit of imagination and meditation, you can easily use them to develop a memorable ritual that's inspiring and effective.

Activity
Now it's time for you to give it a go. Wicca is a 'doing' religion that not only expects you to know 'about' it, but to also engage 'with' it and 'be' it.
Think of a significant event in your life which has or is about to occurr. Perhaps it's the birth of a child or grandchild, perhaps it's getting a new job, perhaps moving house. Choose an event that has significant meaning for you and write a ritual to celebrate that. Make sure it has each of the steps described above and that you're comfortable with the words you've written. When you've written it, go and conduct it! Write it up in your Learning Journal and describe how you feel it went.

Your Fourth Visualisation

After several months of practice, this visualisation should be second nature to you now. This month, we're going to take it yet another step further and actually move into the generation of energy for magickal workings.

Remember to prepare as instructed in the first lesson and make sure that you're comfortable and won't be disturbed. As usual, read the energisation visualisation below first, take some time to consider what area of your body you'll focus on and also remember to ground again afterwards.

This is especially important this month as you'll be generating lots more energy than you have been up to now. While this visualisation is quite powerful, it really is the framework and basis for all personal magick. With this particular visualisation well practiced, you can adapt it to generate any ethical outcome you desire so it's well worth spending time really practicing this one.

Before you begin, take a few moments to consider if there is anything in your physical health or wellbeing that you'd like to improve. Perhaps you've had sore muscles of late or your feet have been aching. Consider one part of your body that may need healing as you're going to send it some energy for improvement.

Activity
Remember to prepare as instructed in the first lesson and make sure that you're comfortable and won't be disturbed. As usual, read the energisation visualisation below first, and also remember to ground again afterwards.

Close your eyes, breathe deeply and slowly for a few seconds feeling the breath draw into your lungs and slowly back out again. Imagine a tap root growing from the base of your spine, your base chakra, downward toward the ground. It's a nice strong tap root and it slowly, gently but deliberately grows down through your chair, through the floor covering, on through the floor structure and then down toward the ground below. See your tap root forcing its way into the earth below you and remaining strong and willing. Keep it growing, further and further. Push it further still, right down into the planet, right down into the dirt, the rocks and the substrata below your feet. Your tap root is strong and it's now anchoring you safely to the Earth. You're comfortable, you're connected to the planet and you're safe.

Now ask the glorious Goddess Gaia if she would allow you to draw into your tap root some of her pure, white, clean, fresh energy. She willingly gives you this energy. She always does because it's your pure white light too. See the pure white light, the cleansing, energising light being sucked up through your tap root and coming up closer and closer toward you. Draw it up toward you. Pull the energy up towards the base of your spine.

As it comes up through the tap root and enters your body, see it begin to tumble around at the base of your torso and then begin falling down your legs towards your feet. See the energy fill your toes up and any dark patches of negative energy are washed away as you breathe out. The energy just keeps streaming up through your tap root and flooding into your legs. Your lower legs, your thighs are now flooded with pure, white, clean, fresh light. Your legs feel cleansed and revitalised.

The energy keeps coming in and now it fills your lower torso, forcing away any dark and negative patches as you breathe out. Keep drawing up the energy, lots more yet, so much more yet. Your whole tummy area is now filled with white light and you feel comfortable, rested and calm. More white light, this time tumbling up into your chest and shoulders. The pure, white, cleansing light rolls down your arms and into your hands and fingers filling them with light. Yet more light, still coming into your body and now it fills your lower and upper arms and your shoulders feel relaxed and you feel safe and calm and peaceful. The white light then reaches up into your neck and as the light fills your body, it pushes any negative patches of old, faded, worn out, dirty energy away with each breath. Your head is filling with white light and so is your face and now, as you scan your body, you see all the parts of it are filled to the brim with wonderful, refreshing, rejuvenating, pure white energy. You feel alive, you feel calm, you feel peaceful and happy. Check your body for any last remaining patches of old, dark energy you don't need and breathe them away.

Spend a few moments luxuriating in the bliss of being bathed in pure, clean energy from the Goddess.

Now draw up yet more pure, clean, white light and now see that extra energy flowing through from within your body, through the pores of your skin and gradually out into the air immediately around you. From head to toe, front and back the energy is wisping its way through your skin and into the area out to about eight inches around you. This is your aura. It's the energy field immediately around your body that radiates your emotions, health and thoughts in different colours, densities and depths and some people can see these auras. Let the wonderful clean and fresh, white light filter into your aura cleaning out any muddy, dirty patches of old, worn out energies. See the white light wisping through the pores of your skin and penetrating and washing clean your aura. Breathe away any dark patches of negativity from your aura, make it clean and fresh and bright and calm and peaceful.

As you sit and bathe in the peaceful, regenerative energy, hold your arms out before you and point ahead. Draw up even more light than before and let it course through your arms, down into the palms of your hands and through your finger tips. See the white light streaming from your fingertips into the space before you. See the light before you grow into a ball of pure energy that glows and shimmers. Draw more light up and push it into that ball. See the ball grow bigger and bigger before you, glowing and shimmering with its power. Keep the ball growing till it reaches about a foot or two in diameter.

Take a short moment now to think of the part of your body you want to heal or improve. See it healthy, pain free and strong. Now look back to your glowing, shimmering ball of pure, clean, rejuvenating light and all at once, suddenly, send it straight to that chosen body part. See the white light ball suddenly dart straight to the very part of your body you want healed or improved. Feel the energy ball surge into your body and weld with your cells. Sit for a few moments and absorb the excess energy you created just for your own healing.

When you're ready, honour Gaia by thanking her for her generosity and love and then slowly bring your attention back to the room you're in and gradually open your eyes. When you're ready (take your time) slowly look around you and come back to the here and now.

This month, grounding is very important as you've absorbed a considerable amount of energy. Ground yourself by bending or kneeling down on the ground, preferably outside on the grass or dirt, and place the palms of your hands flat on the ground. See the excess energy you drew up flowing smoothly back into the ground below you through your open palms.

Your Homework This Month

You're now almost half way through your Outer Court training and your practice should be starting to get stronger as you grow more confident. For the next month ahead;

- Using the steps provided to you in this chapter, write a ritual that you can conduct for the next Sabbat on the calendar. Record it in your Learning Journal.
- Continue doing the energisation visualisations including the aura cleansing, the magickal ball of light and the grounding. Write the results in your Learning Journal.
- Write regularly in your diary and include any significant dreams you had, any meditations that offered you insights and look at what's happening around you in nature and write that down too.

Well done on getting this far! Your tenacity and dedication should be serving you well. Now's the time to go back over the book and see if there are any research, reading or activities boxes you've missed. If so, complete them this month as well.

The Fifth Lesson
The Tools of Wicca

Itches and Wiccans love their tools and while you've already learnt how to cast a circle without the tools, now you can learn more about them and what they're used for. It's important to know how to practice without tools though because they're simply props and enhancers and are *not* the basis of your practice.

By the time you've finished this fifth lesson you should be able to;

* Describe the importance, or otherwise, of tools,
* Explain what each tool is used for, why and when,
* List the correspondences for each tool,
* Consecrate your tools.

Are Tools Important?

I know we've talked about this briefly in previous chapters but it's important and well worth reiterating. It saddens me that one of the first things apprentice Wiccans and Witches are often taught or are exposed to is the range of tools available. Very often people tend to think that tools are what identify a Wiccan or Witch. In other words, that you can't be a Wiccan or a Witch without them. Nothing could be further from the truth. Tools are simply that, tools and they are *not* what identify you as a Witch. The Gods and Goddesses don't really give a rats if you have tools or not. They're far more interested in how you connect with them and the world around you than if you have a great looking athame or a special set of ritual robes.

Now, don't get me wrong, tools are wonderful assets to your practice and they most definitely have a place as we honour the Lord and Lady but you just mustn't get to the point where you can't practice without them. You need to know how to cast a circle, how to honour the Divine and how to connect with nature without the paraphernalia. So why have tools then if we don't need them?

While being Wiccan means connecting with the Divine, with nature around you and with a deeper part of who you are, sometimes tools can enhance that. They can give the edge, the ability to go just a little deeper into your practice and gain just that bit more.

In addition, after a period of time in use, tools begin to retain sacred energy and almost take on a life of their own in conjunction with you. They become sacred objects that can transfer and contain power at your will and this can be really useful. The tools become an extension of who you are because the power you generate surges through the tools and they lock into some of that and keep hold of it. So they become batteries of your own power.

It's partly for this reason that it's bad form to touch another practitioner's tools without permission. Because each one of us has a different 'signature' of power, a different way of holding and using that power, we eventually infuse our tools with our own brand of power. If you touch someone else's tools, you take a little bit of their power and you 'infect' their tool with a little bit of yours. Your tools should hold *your* power, not someone else's and this is especially so if the person touching your tools has had a bad day and is infecting your tool with some bad vibes! It's for this reason that your tools should be protected from the hands of others who may not understand how precious and sacred they've become. If you can leave them out on a private altar without fear of them being touched by others, so much the better. Otherwise keep them safely locked away so they can hold your power and be an accessory to your practice and not someone else's.

Another important factor about tools worth noting is that using them can become a signal to the brain that you're about to go into a sacred space and connect with the Divine. It's a bit like a habit forming technique that instills into your brain that you're about to do something important or special. A simple example of this is that after years of practice and reinforcement, it's now virtually a habit that you put your seatbelt on when you get in the car isn't it? You probably don't even realise you're doing it anymore and it's become so ingrained into the process of starting your car journey that you do it automatically. Using tools can be the same. Wearing your ritual robes every time you do a ritual is a really good comparison to the seat belt example. If you always wear robes for a ritual, eventually your brain cottons on that when you're putting your robes on, you're preparing to enter a sacred space and connect with the Divine. It then gears your mind and body up for that experience.

Now let's go back to the original discussion for a brief moment where I said tools weren't necessary for you to be a Wiccan or Witch so I can show you even better what I mean now that you have the example of the robes. You don't *need* robes to be Wiccan. You can just as easily do a ritual without them as with them. It makes only a little difference to the potential success of your work but, if you do have them and put them on before each ritual, then you're using those robes to enhance your Wiccan and Craft practice. So you see, you don't have to have robes but they're helpful, just like all the other tools.

I'll just mention one other thing about the usefulness of tools while we're here. Over the last fifty years of Wiccan development and international growth, a universally accepted set of tools has developed. This is a base set of tools that many Wiccans and Witches use which we'll go through in a moment but one of the benefits of having these tools is that they've become a universal shared language within the Pagan community. When conducting or sharing rituals across different groups, many rituals call for the use of tools, particularly the athame, and given that many Wiccans have the same set of tools, we've created a point of connection that helps bind us together as one. It's nice, it's a feeling of spiritual family, it's a joyous event when Wiccans get together and share in similar practices, using similar tools and artefacts because it gives a sense of shared identity and community. I mentioned earlier that the tools don't define you as a Witch but as a collective, they do help to bring us together with shared language, shared understanding and shared practice.

The Tools Explained

Just before we jump into the tools and look at them more closely, let's just talk through the 'personality' of your tools as you acquire them. I mentioned earlier in the chapter how tools take on and store the energy of their owner and this includes a sense of your personality. A tool will 'speak' to you if it's yours and you'll know when you see it if it belongs to you. Different styles of tools suit different people. I have a friend whose athame is very dainty and feminine and it reflects her personality very much. Another friend's athame is large and chunky and perfect for him so feel free to choose what feels right for you.

If you can make your own tools, so much the better. The process of making them will infuse them with your energy, your personality and your brand of Divine dedication. It's not always easy to do that though so if instead you purchase a tool, try to personalise it somehow by attaching crystals to it, engraving it or adding parts to it that come from your own creativity.

Read
So that you get a rounded Wiccan education and not just my own point of view, I'd like you to read the thoughts on tools that others have offered students. Please take some time now to read these articles by other well educated and well known Wiccan teachers.

The Tools of Wicca

So let's now look at each of the tools in turn and we'll do so in the order of importance that I give them which, of course, is not necessarily what another Wiccan or Witch might feel. However, generally speaking the sequence of the tool discussions here are pretty much a reflection of general ratings across the broader Wiccan community. Remember as you read through this list, that the tools are 'nice to haves' and you don't have to have them in order to be Wiccan or a Witch. Notice also that I haven't included every tool, partly because the list is endless and partly because there are some, like the scourge for instance, that I prefer not to use.

Athame

The athame (pronounced a-tha-may) is probably the most important tool for any Wiccan and certainly the most sacred tool in their collection. Traditionally, it's a black handled, double edged dagger, usually no more than about 12 inches long and it often has runes or Craft related symbols burnt into the wooden handle or engraved on the blade.

The athame is a ritual tool only so while the blade edges can be sharp, the tip should be dulled so no unintentional accidents mar ritual practice. It's never used to cut anything and is used to mark out the spirit circle during the circle casting rite or cut open a doorway to let someone in and out of the circle. It has a masculine energy and corresponds to either air or fire depending on the Wiccan tradition in which the owner operates.

Gardner was a recognised expert on the Malay Kris or Kerris which is a ritual, double edged blade, said to have magical powers and used by people from Thailand through Indonesia and Malaysia. It's been suggested that Gardner realised that knives such as the Kris could bring additional strength to magical work and so he added it to Wicca as its primary tool. It's interesting that he chose a knife rather than a wand as the Wiccan primary tool given that historically the wand has become synonymous with Witchcraft and the esoteric arts.

Making your own athame can be quite difficult unless you're a blacksmith but you can buy a readymade athame or knife and modify that. Wrap leather round the handle, glue a crystal to the handle or blade, paint the handle black and then mark it with gold designs. There's a myriad of ways of personalising a pre-made athame so that it reflects your personality and your creativity. My first athame was a beautiful ceremonial knife, the handle of which I wrapped in leather and to the blade I attached some amethysts. That athame served me for many years until the time felt right to move on to my next athame.

Research
Given this tool is probably the most prevalent and certainly the most important, it's worth spending some time looking at the types of athames available and where you can locate one.
Take a few minutes to look on the internet at athames and what's available. Look in your local new-age shop or Pagan supplies shop to see if they have athames. Look at as many as you can from a variety of sources before you commit to buying one so that you can get exactly what you want rather than just buying the first thing you see.

An important point to note with knives is that while there are several places you can buy athames online, in many states and countries, double edged blades are illegal and can't be imported. Before you buy any athame online, check your local laws to find out if you can import it.

Book of Shadows
I have a soft spot for the Book of Shadows, affectionately known as the BOS. Maybe it's because I write lots or have done a considerable amount of tertiary and academic research and recording but the fact remains that for me, after my athame, this is my number 2 tool. There's nothing like seeing a well loved and used book sitting there holding its secrets for you and waiting to be opened once more.

The Book of Shadows is something that virtually every Wiccan and Witch has and while it might double up as a diary, a recipe book and a record of ritual and spell-work, it is without doubt probably the most useful tool in the Wiccan broom cupboard. Even after only a year of practice, you'd be hard pressed to remember what you did, what worked and what didn't work so you'd be at a loss if you wanted to repeat a magickal working, a ritual or verify that insight you got from a path working last year to see if it came to fruition. I hate to use the term and I do so with no reference to Christianity, but your Book of Shadows should become your 'bible'. If you record everything in there that you do, it will reward you years later with a truly beautiful and sacred record of everything you've done.

There are tonnes of different types of Books of Shadows out there for you to use and at first, I recommend every student just use a simple exercise book or a loose leaf binder. The Oak and Mistletoe shop has a Book of Shadows you can use for a very reasonable price and it's a great starter book till you really know what you do want. You can write directly into your book with pen or you can write your rituals on your computer, print them and stick them in the book. Alternatively, you can just print them off straight into your Book of Shadows binder if you choose that option. Many Wiccans print their rituals off from their computer and then add to it with little stick-on symbols or drawings so the work has a more personal touch.

It will probably take you a year or two to work out exactly what you want to record and how and it's a great pity to see a beautiful leather bound book, written in one style, then changed halfway through because you decided to do things differently. In addition, some books are lifelong investments and can cost several hundred dollars for the more elaborate tomes that could almost be classified as works of art.

My own Book of Shadows is a truly beautiful handmade, leather book of 600 hand-torn parchment pages. It truly is a wonderful piece of art as well as a functioning book that I adore. It has the Green Man's eyes looking at me from its cover and marker ribbons to keep my place. As I'm clearly not a bookmaking artisan I had my wonderful book made by some very clever people in America at Witches Moon (http://www.witchesmoon.net) and while it may have cost just a little extra to have a personally designed, handmade book created for me, it will last many, many years and become a sacred record and guide of all things Oak and Mistletoe.

Robes

I've put robes third in order of importance deliberately, not because I think it's cool to dress up and look Witchy but because as mentioned earlier, donning your robes is a great signal to the brain to get into sacred gear.

Originally many Witches and Wiccans worked naked or 'skyclad' and working without clothes ensured that no one was seen as higher or lower than anyone else through the quality of their clothes. In addition, when you worked naked, you were presenting yourself before the Gods and Goddesses in your natural form and beauty. Having said all that, a growing number of Witches, Wiccans and Pagans generally prefer to work clothed now and that's certainly understandable when you're shivering outside in the freezing temperatures of winter or sheltering from sunburn in the summer!

So robes have become very popular with Witches to keep them warm, to keep them protected from the harsh rays of the sun and to offer some protection for those of us who are a little shyer about our bodies than our predecessors. Most Witches choose to wear robes at both Esbats and Sabbats and while they might have one set of warm robes for winter and a cooler set for summer, in fact most Witches have one set of robes with a separate cloak for added warmth in winter.

Your robes can be as plain or as decorated as you choose. Traditionally robes are very simple and are pulled in at the waist with a corded belt that's tied in a particular fashion with the ends left to hang down, much like monks still do now. In terms of colour you can have pretty much anything you like with a couple of provisos. Your robes should be a single colour and not multicoloured so choose a plain coloured fabric. Secondly, it's probably unwise to choose black or white fabric for your robes. Black has a little too much public misconception about Satanism while white might be rather impractical given you may well be sitting on the ground during some rituals.

Different traditions also require different robe (or cord belt) colours dependent on the degree you belong to within the tradition but outside that, you can really choose whatever you want. Popular colours are purple, green and blue and many Witches like medieval type patterns for their robes. I've included a very simple pattern here for you follow as a starter.

Robe Materials
2 yards (3 metres) of chosen material that's at least 1 yard (150 cm wide)
Matching thread
Matching bias binding
Scissors
Sewing machine

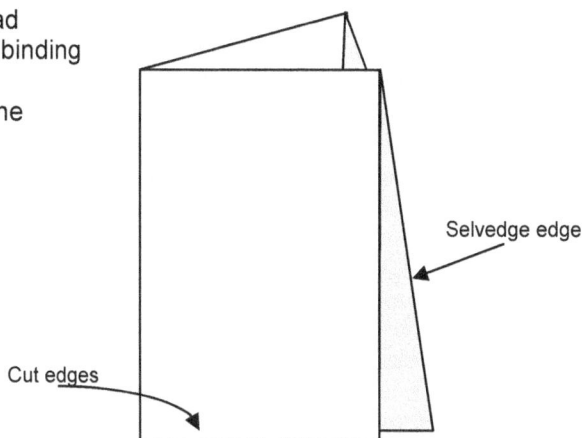

Selvedge edge

Cut edges

Fold the material inside out, selvedge edge to selvedge edge. Fold it in half again, this time from left to right. All selvedge edges should now be on one side with a fold on the other as in the previous diagram

From the bottom, selvedge edge/cut edge corner, mark a diagonal line up to within 13 inches of the top fold of the laid out material so that the diagonal line ends at about 15 inches from the selvedge edge. Now mark a line back down the selvedge edge again. You've now marked out the body and sleeve shape.

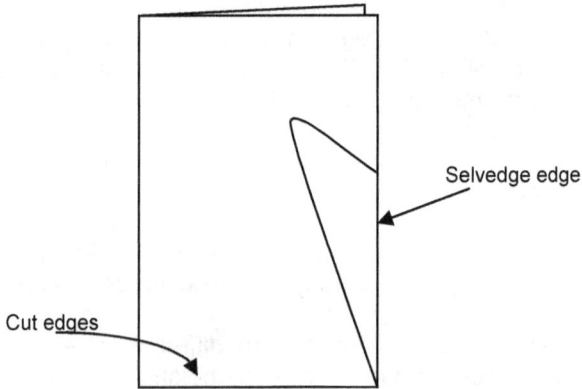

Selvedge edge

Cut edges

Now on the opposite side, the folded side at the top, mark out a small quarter circle for the neck opening. You should end up with a rectangular shape of folded material with a V shaped marked out on the lower right hand corner and a quarter circle marked out on the top opposite corner.

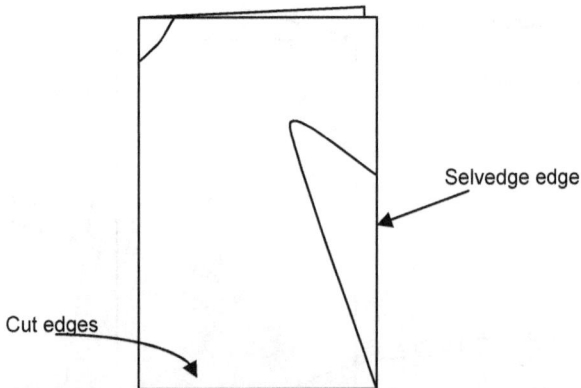

Selvedge edge

Cut edges

Cut the body and sleeve shape out but not the neck marking yet and unfold it. Transfer the quarter circle shape to the other half and cut out just the front half of the neck circle. You should have a T shape with that flares out at the bottom and a circular neck shape in the middle at the top.

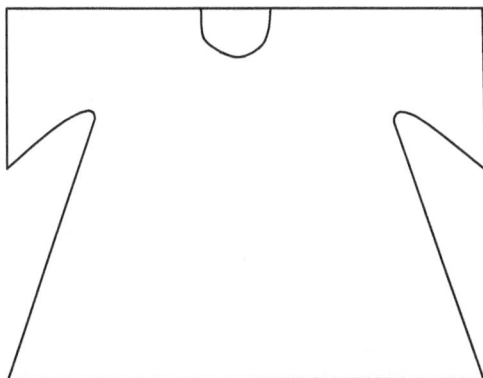

All you need to do now is sew the side seams from the armpit down to the hem, right side inside, then sew the sleeve seam from the armpit to the wrist, also right side inside.

Now take the bias binding and cut enough of it to match the circumference of the neck opening plus one inch. Sew one edge of the bias binding to the right side edge of the neck opening and sew over the 1 inch overlap. Fold the binding over so that the neck opening now has a neat finish. Finally sew up the robe hem.

This is of course a very simple design and more elaborate robes can be developed from this simple pattern. For those people who find sewing a little on the challenging side, you can also quite easily buy a ready-made smock, dress or ritual robe from the internet and simply add your own personal touches to it. With your robes already made, buy some silver embroidery thread and mark out a pentagram or other symbol with pen somewhere on the robe (shoulder, sleeve or chest maybe) and then embroider over the mark with chain stitch.

Another simple idea is to paint small symbols on to the fabric with fabric paint. This is very easy to do and as long as you follow the instructions on the product bottle, the design should stay permanent even after several washes.

Something just a little more complex is to cut two rows of tiny holes perhaps down a sleeve or the back of the robe and then sew around the edge of each hole to neaten them and make sure they don't spread and run. Then thread some contrasting colour of ribbon or leather through the holes in a crisscross pattern to add some more unique elements of your personality.

While you can make your robe from any material, many Witches prefer natural fibres such as cotton or wool. If you do use these materials, remember that wool itches next to skin and that cotton will constantly require ironing!

Now that you've got your robes, if you visit a host coven for an open festival, check with them first about the robe protocol. Some covens do not expect robes for Sabbats while others do. Some covens expect skyclad attendance and if you'd prefer to wear robes, negotiate before you arrive.

Wand

While I do use a wand during my circle casting rite, it's certainly not essential and in fact many Wiccans choose not to use a wand at all. Wands have far more association with Craft practices than with Wiccan in fact and there's been a blurring between the two for many years. They've been used for thousands of years by all manner of energy based practitioners though and examples of that include dowsing tools and staffs.

Wooden wands were originally the preferred option and some traditionalists would suggest a wand must be cut from a virgin hazel tree and that it must be twenty one inches long. Others argue that it should be Rowan while others prefer ash or willow and suggest that it should be the same length as that from your elbow to the tip of your fingers. With so much contention around this, my suggestion is to go for what feels right for you regardless of what others might say.

To complicate it further, there's now a host of crystal wands available or wands of wood with crystal tips so in the end, given that the power comes from the Earth, through you and then through your wand and doesn't come from the wand itself, the choice is yours. Let the wand speak to you and if it does, it's yours.

Again I prefer a handmade wand rather than a pre-purchased one because it holds much more of your own personality within it. I have a wand I brought in a cute little crystal shop in England which is turned wood with a crystal on the end and while it looks nice, it holds no power whatsoever. By comparison, my most treasured wand is from a piece of Sheoak I found waiting for me in a park and which I hand whittled and sanded into its beautiful current form.

Wands are used to focus energy and to invoke the Gods and Goddesses as well as the elementals. They're used to point and direct energy to a particular spot much like a magnifying glass focuses light on one spot. They correspond with Air for most Wiccans and having been used frequently, they'll often store as much energy within them as the athame.

Altar

I'd hazard a guess that just about every Wiccan has an altar of some description even if it's the lounge coffee table or a garden bench by day. Many Wiccans have a personal altar which often doubles as the lounge sideboard or bookshelf and covens will often have an altar set up permanently within a defined circle space. But before we get caught up on the details, let's just explore what we mean by the term 'altar".

It's important to remember that when we talk about altars, we're not referring to the sort of heavy, ornately carved wood or stone structures you might see in a church. You know the ones I mean. The big tables that sit at the 'business' end of church, often draped with beautifully worked and complex tapestries or embroidered linens, weighed down by brass, silver or gold candelabras, bowls and other donated antiquities and artefacts. No, nothing quite so grand for a home grown Wiccan.

While a circle altar might in fact be quite formal and reflect the requirements of both the Wiccan tradition in which it's being used and the festival or event that's occurring, home altars are much less formal, much more relaxed and friendly. Your home altar is really a place where you can sit your Wiccan ornaments and any pieces that represent your Gods and Goddesses. You might also have a candle or two there to honour the fire element, perhaps a shell you found when on the beach to represent water, some nice incense or a feather for air and maybe a bowl of salt for the earth element. Your altar can sit on an East or North facing wall (depending on your preference) but in fact it can be anywhere that feels right for you.

There are some real gains in having a readymade altar, always available. With a personal altar you can go to regularly;

* you strengthen your relationship with the Divine because you'll usually remember to take a few moments, more often to talk with her,
* You have a central place of honour where you can position your Wiccan objects,
* You have a focal point for any meditative practice,
* You have a readymade place to conduct any magickal workings and hold magickal tools or equipment,

☙ You'll more than likely have the benefit of warm, comforting residual energy that builds in the location of your altar the more you use it.

Altars are more often than not made from natural substances like wood or stone largely because they will hold residual energy like your tools do. Natural substances, as gifts from the planet retain energy far better than factory made, plastic goods. While it might be cheaper to buy a plastic picnic table from the hardware store, it won't 'feel' quite as special as a wooden table.

Make sure whatever table you buy or make is big enough to hold your altar tools and any other items that will be going there for ritual. For example, at a Spring Equinox Sabbat, you might want to decorate the altar with flowers from the garden so you need enough room for those to be there as well as your athame, censor, chalice and so on.

An important point to remember with personal altars inside the home is safety. While a personal, permanent altar at home is a wonderful way to keep your Wiccan practice constant, please remember safety. If you have sharp objects (like an athame for instance) or candles and incense burning on your altar, always remember that while the Gods and Goddesses will be attracted to your place of honour and respect, so will small children and your pets. Never leave candles and incense to burn when you're not there and always make sure your altar items are safe from small children, animals and even non Wiccan prying eyes who may not understand or appreciate how much you value your tools.

Water and Wine Chalices

Virtually all circle casting rituals require you to use a water chalice at some point. Depending on the tradition, you might need to use it to sprinkle the coveners as part of the cleansing process but more often than not, you'll need a water chalice to sprinkle salted water around the circle perimeter as part of the elemental circle building.

You can of course use a kitchen coffee mug is there's nothing else available. After all, a chalice is just an elaborate cup when all's said and done! Some people use a clean shell they found on the beach and for many years I used exactly that. I still keep that same shell on my personal altar as a sacred representation of the water element. It's become a very special memento of my Wiccan journey.

The chalice of course corresponds with the water element and because it also holds salt as part of the circle building process, I prefer to see chalices made from clay or glass rather than from silver or pewter. Salt can have rather damaging properties after a while and can eat at metals, especially where for instance the silver is just plated.

The Tools of Wicca

There are two chalices on the altar however and both have a specific role. The water chalice as mentioned holds the salted and consecrated water that then is sprinkled around the circle perimeter to build the salt and water elemental walls. But the other chalice, the wine chalice is almost equally as important. In the chapters on circle casting and the Wheel of the Year, you would no doubt have noticed the prevalence of the Cakes and Ale rite.

Cakes and Ale is an ancient rite which has been performed by virtually every religion the world over for thousands of years albeit with different names and done slightly differently. Many Christians take Holy Communion where they eat the body of Christ as a mark of honour, respect and worship. The wedding feast, long a tradition of the celebration of marriage, is a way for people to share food and wine together in celebration and in honour of the sacred union of marriage.

For Wiccans, the rite of Cakes and Ale is an opportunity to give thanks to the Lord and Lady for the wonderful bounties they provide for us. It's a ritual of respect, of thanks and of community. The wine chalice is then a very sacred tool. Having said that, like the water chalice you can use a coffee mug if needs be!

There's no hard and fast rule about what your wine chalice has to look like or be made from but it is worth remembering that if you're going to be sharing ritual with people and you're responsible for supplying the wine chalice, then it needs to be big enough for everyone to sip from. Many covens use pewter or silver goblets but because I don't like the taste of metal, like my water chalice, I prefer ceramic, glass or pottery. This is personal choice only of course and everyone is free to make their own decision on chalice design and construction.

With the often irrational fear of AIDS and quite rightly the hygiene warnings to avoid communicable diseases like colds and gastroenteritis, many covens now ask each covener to have their own wine chalice. They have a coven one which holds the wine and is used for the consecration but then a little wine is poured from that chalice into each covener's own chalice and they drink from that. While this certainly helps avoid spreading disease, particularly where a covener has a cold or perhaps a cold sore, there's also considerable evidence that says wine is a wonderful disinfectant that can kill most germs. I leave the choice of individual versus coven chalice to you.

Activity
Have a look around in your kitchen or that cupboard that holds all the stuff you never use, to see if you might have a chalice or two hanging around you could use for ritual work. Do you have any shells big

enough to use for your water chalice? Is there a beach nearby where you could stumble over one? Are there any nice goblets hidden away, perhaps a special wine glass you've forgotten about that you could use as your wine chalice?

Incense and Incense Burners/Censor

Like the water chalice, the censor, or to be more precise, the incense inside it, is fundamental to casting a circle. As the water chalice corresponds with Water and holds the salt (Earth) and water mix for casting the circle, the Incense corresponds with Air and is used as a marriage between the elements of Air and Fire to cast the circle.

It's fair to say that you don't actually need a censor and you could instead just use incense sticks. Many people use a fire proof dish, fill it with sand and then use charcoal blocks and powered incense. From my own experience I've found this way of using incense messy and I can never time the incense to be in full swing when I need it so I prefer incense cones inside my censor.

I'd advise against getting cheap incense for three reasons. The first is that much of the cheap incense sold is made using slave or very poorly paid labour in countries where there are minimal rules and support mechanisms for people in need. I prefer to know that my incense was made ethically and that people were paid for their labours appropriately. The second reason is that cheap incense often simply burns too quickly or doesn't burn at all. It's a nuisance when you're in the middle of a ritual and at the point where you need the incense only to find that it won't light or has already burnt out! Finally, the third reason is simply that cheap incense very often smells cheap and there's nothing more off putting in the middle of a ritual than being overcome by foul aromas!

Historically, incense was used in churches for three main reasons. The first was that until a couple of hundred years ago, most of the peasant class in England, all of whom had to go to church or face being fined, often didn't have a bath more than once a year so you can imagine what the BO was like when they all got together in church! This is actually how bridal bouquets came to be. All those hundreds of years ago, a sweet smelling bunch of flowers was helpful in disguising the rising body odour especially when you're facing the person you're about to become intimate with in the marriage bed!

But not only can incense mask smells, it also purifies the air. Many faiths use incense for this reason including the Jewish, Hindu and Buddhist faiths.

Incense also has another much more important function and that is that the body responds to certain smells with certain responses. Aromatherapy practices use this valid notion by influencing the body's reactions through using perfumed oils. Citrus smells wake us up, while the smell of lavender soothes and helps us relax. Church leaders have known this for centuries and they've created different types of incense from plants and oils that help the body go into states of deep concentration. Frankincense and Myrrh are used extensively in incense production for their qualities to soothe the mind and let it more freely wander into the realm of meditation and spiritual connection. Nag Champa is a very popular incense for spiritual work but I'd encourage everyone to try different fragrances to see what works for them. I've found that it's helpful to have a range of incense fragrances on hand because different rituals will often benefit from different smells. Personally I love Jasmine in my incense but it's not for everyone.

Just a point of warning before we talk more about censors. An increasing number of people are allergic to, or are troubled by incense. With the air heavy with fragranced smoke, people with asthma often have trouble breathing. If you're an asthmatic or someone in your coven is, then please stay away from the incense smoke. I've found that when I have a cold and my chest is feeling heavy, incense does nothing to help that!

While it's the incense itself that's important in ritual work, for safety sake, it's important to have a receptacle of some sort to hold both the burning incense and the ash. If you use incense sticks as many people do, you can push the stick into a blob of blu-tak and that will work very well. You do still have to clean up the ash afterward but it does keep the incense safe in one place.

A very simple option is the incense holder which is either an upright holder or just a long slice of wood with a hole in one end to secure the incense stick. The ash falls onto the wooden base and you just pick it up and empty it. These holders are very cheap and easy to come by and a practical, easy solution to keeping incense safe.

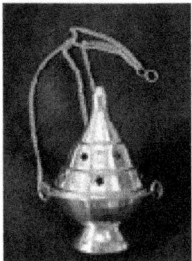

A much more elaborate option is that of a censor. To all intents and purposes, the censor is really just a dish with holes in the top to let the smoke out and it has a set of chains so that you can hang the container from a hook. The chains are really handy for hanging and swinging (gently!) the incense around the circle perimeter when you're circle casting and having the incense away from your hands makes sure you don't burn yourself either.

The Tools of Wicca

Salt and Salt Dish

Salt is the Wiccan representation of the element of Earth and as such it's also an important factor in ritual work. As the ground below us the home of the purest energy possible, salt that comes from the earth is a crystallised form of the Earth's sacred purity. Make sure you're using rock salt and not seas salt in your ritual work because sea salt comes from the sea of course rather than the earth.

Research
Up until this point you may have thought that salt was salt and that's all there was to it. Well, salt is not quite that simple. Spend just a few moments looking at the different types of salt available on the internet. You may be surprised! This is a great reference site;
http://www.saltworks.us/salt_info/si_gourmet_reference.asp

Altar Pentacle

There's often confusion between the pentacle and the pentagram. Let's clear that up first. A pentagram is a five pointed star and of course this is the predominant symbol of Wicca. The uppermost point represent Spirit, the upper right point is Water, the lower right point is Fire, the lower left point is Earth and the upper left point is Air

A pentacle by comparison is that same five pointed star but now enclosed within a circle. It's called a closed pentagram and many Wiccans wear a silver or gold version of this around their necks just as Christians might wear a cross.

However, there's another way we Wiccans describe the pentacle. As well as a symbol, it's also an altar tool. The pentacle altar tool is a round plate, about six inches wide, often made of copper, wood or wax and marked with a pentagram. In many cases, particularly for the more traditional forms of Wicca, the original Gardnerian symbols are engraved into the pentacle as shown on this copper example.

The pentacle is an Earth corresponded tool and its use is primarily to hold things that are to be consecrated during ritual. Given it's usually only about six inches across though, it doesn't

The Tools of Wicca

always hold everything you need so many people use the pentacle to hold their salt because both items are Earth bound.

Cords

A plaited length of cord has been used by Wiccans since Gardner first promoted his new religion. Essentially the cord is a braided length of thread or rope, often worn as a belt around the waist to tidy your robes and to hang any bags and your athame from. It has other uses as well which I'll explain shortly.

Your cords should be nine feet long and made from three lengths of natural fibres with silk the preferred option. Three is a very magickal number in Wicca and Witchcraft and crops up repeatedly. Nine foot long cords, three times three, that are made from three separate lengths are thus very powerful tools. When braided together, the thickness only needs to about half an inch, enough so you can comfortably tie them. Both ends should be knotted or bound so the braids don't come undone.

One of the reasons for the nine feet is that you can use your cords to mark out your circle. Traditionally, the circle is nine feet in diameter so if you place a small stake in the ground, fold your cords in half around the stake, you can trace out a nine foot circle around the stake.

The colours of your cords are important if you choose to focus on Alexandrian and Gardnerian approaches. In those older traditions, white signifies a first degree Wiccan, red for second degrees and third degrees can wear blue. Keep in mind however, that even though you may choose to wear the colours of the oath bound Gardnerian or Alexandrian traditions, unless you're trained and initiated by an initiated member of that tradition, your cord colours will still be seen as meaningless by those practitioners.

In more eclectic traditions, the cord colour has become irrelevant and while many covens maintain the more traditional approach to coven colours signifying degree status, many others choose whatever colours they feel comfortable with.

Cords are also used for magick in a number of ways. They can be knotted a certain number of times to hold power within the knots or to bind problems within the knots. Coveners can also stand round in a circle, remove their cords and hold one end while some else holds the other so that a spider's web of cords is created across the circle space. Then magickal energy is generated and pushed through the cords to the centre of the circle where it's eventually released for its intended purpose.

So your cords aren't just a convenient belt to hang your athame sheath and a bag from. They also have very practical applications in magick.

Read
The importance and historical significance of cords is often forgotten. There are some wonderful web sites which talk about cords, their history and what they're used for in various traditions. Please take some time to read the information on the following sites;
http://cardiffpagan.co.uk/magazine/issues/4/articles/cord-magic.html
http://www.angelfire.com/de2/newconcepts/wicca/cord.html

Cauldron

What a versatile tool the cauldron is! Like the chalice, it's a feminine aspect and while originally it was simply a cooking pot, it can be used for so much more than that. Ideally, if you decide to get a cauldron, try for a cast iron one on three legs. There are a few antique ones around although they're rare and with a bit of tender loving care, they can be restored if you can find one. There are also new ones available to buy now as they're returning to popularity.

Mine was given to me by a dear friend and has been used for so many different purposes. When the fire bans are on during summer, I use it to hold a candle so that we minimise the likelihood of setting the surrounding area on fire. I also use it for candle and fire magick so that if anything has to be burnt, it can be contained in the cauldron and cleaned out when cool.

It's also a great scrying tool if you fill it with water. Because it's black inside, the water remains dark and that's exactly what you need for any scrying and divination work.

So with all these uses, it's no wonder that the cauldron becomes a focal point in the centre of your circle area especially when you need to hold anything or even jump the balefire. It's one of those 'Witchy' type tools that are not in the slightest bit necessary but so useful and so much fun.

Besom

The besom, or straw/twig broom, is by no means a required tool but it is one of my favourites. Originally made from birch twigs its function is to psychically sweep the area clean before creating a sacred space. My own broom has ribbons and some silver pentagram trinkets hanging from it which make it look a little more like a magickal tool and less like a functional housekeeping instrument but that's my choice.

Traditionally, the sweeping broom end of the besom should never touch the floor and so it should be stored with the twigs upright. When

using it to sweep an area before casting the circle, again never let the twigs touch the ground. Start in the centre of the area and move around in a spiral, sweeping the area clean of any negative energy and unwanted feelings that may still be hanging around.

One of the fun traditions with this tool is jumping the besom which occurs when a couple handfast. Handfasting is the traditional equivalent of a wedding and dependent on the couple's wishes and the official status of the celebrant, the handfasting can also be a legal wedding. Many hundreds of years ago, a couple were not considered married until they'd jumped over the besom. This signified their leap from one stage of life as single people to the next stage of life as a couple joined in the sacred union of marriage. Handfasting besoms are decorated with ribbons, tinsel and all manner of wedding type decorations and remain a memory for the couple of a very special day.

Activity
Now that you have more of an idea of tools, list in your Learning Journal what tools you think are necessary for your own practice. Which tools would you make or buy first and why? How will you begin to acquire those tools and where will you keep them?

Consecrating Tools

Ok, after all that discussion, you've decided what tools you want and you've gone out and made/found/bought yourself some. That's great, but what now?

Before you go using those tools, it's a really good idea to cleanse and consecrate them. You need to do this to rid them of any inappropriate energy that might be hanging around in or on them from the manufacturing process or from whoever owned them previously. You want them 'blank' and ready to absorb your energies and your intent rather than them holding on to some previous, quite unrelated energy.

When you've cleansed and consecrated them, the tools are truly yours and you can use them knowing they're more able to absorb your creativity and your energy. Try not to let anyone else touch them after that because you don't want your connection with them contaminated by the residual energy that someone else might leave on them, no matter how positive and happy they might be. Also, don't use the tools for anything else other than ritual work. So for example, don't use your athame as a screwdriver when you can't find the real deal.

Ok, so how do we cleanse and consecrate your precious ritual objects? There are a number of ways and you can pretty much take your pick from a list of options depending on the tool. In terms of cleansing first and ridding the tool of any old associations, there are two very good ways to do this that will work with just about anything. The first is to bury the object in the ground for a few days. This will allow the Earth to absorb old energies and leave the item 'blank' and ready to be dedicated. The other option is to plunge the object into water, preferably natural, running water like a stream but the sea or a lake will do. Your bathtub will do at a pinch as well, especially if you run it and add some salt to it.

Be careful with both these options and think about what method suits the tool itself. For instance, it may not be wise to plunge a wooden wand in water but burying for a day or two won't hurt it. By comparison, leaving a crystal in water will probably be much more effective for it than burying it.

Once the tool has been stripped of old energy, you're ready to rededicate it to its new service with you through the consecration process. You can pretty much say or do what feels right for you in this process so these ideas here are simply a platform. You do however need to make sure that you purify the tool with all four elements and then go through a dedication rite with them so the consecration is in fact a two-step process.

First of all lay your new tools on the altar and then cast your circle in the normal way. With your circle cast, have a candle (the God and Goddess candles will do) and some incense burning on the altar alongside you cup of salted water. Pick up your tool, or the first tool if you're doing more than one on this occasion, hold it up toward the sky as though you're showing it to the Lord and Lady saying; "I offer this (name of tool) in service to the Lord and Lady".

Now pass the tool through the smoke of the incense making sure that the smoke touches all parts of it saying; "May the power of the element of Air, the glory of the East, purify and protect this (name of tool)".

Now pass the tool through over the flame of the candle making sure that all the parts of the tool have 'felt' the candle flame without being burnt of course saying; "May the power of the element of Fire, the glory of the South, purify and protect this (name of tool)".

This time, with your fingers, sprinkle some of the salted water that you used during the circle casting rite from the water chalice over the tool. This action combines both Air and Water, with West and North together, just as it does when circle casting. As you do so, say; "May the power of the elements of Water and Earth, the glory of the West and North, purify and protect this (name of tool)".

Your tool has now been purified through the connection with the four elements and it's time to dedicate it to its new purpose. It's now that you can use the meditations that you've been practicing for some time through this book. Draw up energy from the ground below you as you've been doing with the energising meditation. Feel the energy fill you completely and then push it into the tool that you hold in your hand. Wait till you feel it being full of white light, the purest of sacred energy. When you're ready, hold the tool up to the sky as though you are offering it to the Divine saying; "Lord and Lady. Here before you is the sacred (name of tool). Before you now I dedicate this (name of tool) to your honour, to be used to fulfil my intent as I work with the Divine love within and around me. In the name of the sacred ones, I consecrate this (name of tool). So mote it be."

If you're consecrating other tools at the same time, then you'd now do the next tool in the same way you just did the first one and so on.

Read
There's a myriad of ways to cleanse and consecrate tools depending on the tool itself, the tradition to which you aspire and your own preferences. Having read many Wiccan books, I still recommend Scott Cunningham's "Wicca: A Guide for the Solitary Practitioner". It is without doubt a wonderful book for the eclectic newcomer because it's so easy to read and full of common sense approaches.
If you can borrow this book from the library or better still, purchase one for yourself, so much the better. Please read his chapter on tools in Section I and also the ritual on consecrating tools in Section III.

Your Fifth Visualisation

This month we're going to begin connecting more deeply with the elements, the first one being Air from the East. For the next four months, you'll meditate on the elements, one each month as we work our way round the elements in a deosil fashion..

Remember to prepare as instructed in the first lesson and make sure that you're comfortable and won't be disturbed. As usual, read the energisation visualisation below first, and also remember to ground again afterwards.

Activity
Close your eyes, breathe deeply and slowly for a few seconds feeling the breath draw into your lungs and slowly back out again. Imagine a tap root growing from the base of your spine,your base chakra, downward toward the ground. It's a nice strong tap root and it slowly, gently but deliberately grows down through your

chair, through the floor covering, on through the floor structure and then down toward the ground below. See your tap root forcing its way into the earth below you and remaining strong and willing. Keep it growing, further and further. Push it further still, right down into the planet, right down into the dirt, the rocks and the substrata below your feet. Your tap root is strong and it's now anchoring you safely to the Earth. You're comfortable, you're connected to the planet and safe.

Now ask the glorious Goddess Gaia if she would allow you to draw into your tap root some of her pure, white, clean, fresh energy. She willingly gives you this energy. She always does because it's your pure white light too. See the pure white light, the cleansing, energising light being sucked up through your tap root and coming up closer and closer toward you. Draw it up toward you. Pull the energy up towards the base of your spine.

As it comes up through the tap root and enters your body, see it begin to tumble around at the base of your torso and then begin falling down your legs towards your feet. See the energy fill your toes up and any dark patches of negative energy are washed away as you breathe out. The energy just keeps streaming up through your tap root and flooding into your legs. Your lower legs, your thighs are now flooded with pure, white, clean, fresh light. Your legs feel cleansed and revitalised.

The energy keeps coming in and now it fills your lower torso, forcing away any dark and negative patches as you breathe out. Keep drawing up the energy, lots more yet, so much more yet. Your whole tummy area is now filled with white light and you feel comfortable, rested and calm. More white light, this time tumbling up into your chest and shoulders. The pure, white, cleansing light rolls down your arms and into your hands and fingers filling them with light. Yet more light, still coming into your body and now it fills your lower and upper arms and your shoulders feel relaxed and you feel safe and calm and peaceful. The white light then reaches up into your neck and as the light fills your body, it pushes any negative patches of old, faded, worn out, dirty energy away with each breath. Your head is filling with white light and so is your face and now, as you scan your body, you see all the parts of it are filled to the brim with wonderful, refreshing, rejuvenating, pure white energy. You feel alive, you feel calm, you feel peaceful and happy. Check your body for any last remaining patches of old, dark energy you don't need and breathe them away. Spend a few moments luxuriating in the bliss of being bathed in pure, clean energy from the Goddess.

Now draw up yet more pure, clean, white light and now see that extra energy flowing through from within your body, through the pores of your skin and gradually out into the air immediately around you. From head to toe, front and back the energy is wisping its way through your skin and into your aura. Let the wonderful clean and fresh, white light filter into it cleaning out any muddy, dirty patches of old, worn out energies. See the white light wisping through the pores of your skin and penetrating and washing clean your aura. Breathe away any dark patches of old negativity from your aura, make it clean and fresh and calm and peaceful.

As you sit basking in the purity of the purest of the universe's energy, imagine in front of you a door. This door will become the door you always come to when you go to other realms in meditation. It may be a heavy wooden door, perhaps it's a garden gate or a velvet curtain you draw back. Imagine your door and decide that it's your door and is the portal between the now and the other planes.

Slowly and gently, open your door and step through. You are now in the realm of the Air element and this is the home of sylphs, the winds and the breezes. Feel the wind on your face. Feel the caress of the breeze as it passes over your skin. Its gentle touch is comforting and warm as the element of Air shows you its wonder and gentle magic. The wind gets stronger now and begins pushing against you. Feel its strength, feel its power. It gets stronger again and now it buffets your body with surges of power and rage. You're safe and you cannot be harmed but you still feel the wind as it becomes a gale, howling around you in fearsome strength. Feel the torrent of air that rages all around you as you hold your body fast against its wrath. The Air is showing you its awesome strength and overwhelming power.

The gales subside and the gentle breeze returns. The air around you calms and becomes still. You notice in front of you a presence, you sense and feel someone with you. It's a sylph, one of the elementals of Air. See the sylph before you. What does it look like, or is it just a presence that you can't see and can only feel like the breeze on your skin?

Take a moment to ask the sylph a question. What do you need to know about the element and power of Air? What would you like to learn, to take away with you? Listen to the answers and feel your connection with this wonderful being grow and deepen.

The sylph lets you know that it has given you the knowledge and understanding that you seek and so you offer thanks and respect. Now turn back to your door and gently walk through and close it behind you. You are back where you were, in the now, in the here. Slowly bring your attention back to the room you're in and gradually open your eyes.

Ground yourself by bending or kneeling down on the ground, preferably outside on the grass or dirt, and place the palms of your hands flat on the ground. See the excess energy you drew up flowing smoothly back into the ground below you through your open palms.

Your Homework This Month

This month's lesson has been an important step forward in two ways. You're now acquainted with the tools of the Wiccan trade and you are ready to move into much more defined practice with those tools. You've also introduced yourself to Air and you should spend this month deepening that connection. For the next month ahead;

🦋 If you have any tools, consecrate them this month. It's highly likely that you do have tools and even if you don't, then you can cleanse and consecrate your Dream, Meditation and Nature Diary.

🦋 Keep practicing the energisation visualisation including the aura cleansing and in it, this month repeat the connection with the element of Air. Ask different questions of the element and generate a deeper relationship with this refreshing element of beginnings. Write the results in your Learning Journal.

🦋 Write regularly in your diary and include any significant dreams you had, any meditations that offered you insights and look at what's happening around you in nature and write that down too.

6

The Sixth Lesson
Exploring Magick

S we move deeper into your Wiccan training program, we also move deeper into how to 'do' Wicca and one of those doing things is how to create and conduct magick.

By the time you've finished this sixth lesson you should be able to;

- Explain what magick is,
- Explore the relationship between the Wiccan Rede, the Law of Return and your magickal practice,
- Describe the different types of magick,
- Create and conduct a magickal working.

What is Magick?

To begin our conversation about magick, I'm going to explain the 'k' at the end of what would normally be the spelling for this word. Most Wiccans, Witches and magicians tend to favour the term 'magick' rather than 'magic' because it differentiates spell craft from the entertainment that a performance magician might create for his audience. Magick is not for entertainment and is something much deeper and profound than the tricks and illusions presented by stage magicians. So whenever we talk about the spell craft that supports the religion of Wicca, we often use the term 'magick'.

Aleister Crowley 1943

So with the magic versus magick explanation set, I think it's absolutely crucial, before we get into types of magick and how to work it that we need to have a very clear, down to earth understanding about what magick actually is. Aleister Crowley, who was one of the biggest influences on Gerald Gardner as he created Wicca, described magick as "The science and art of causing change to occur in conformity with the will". Crowley was arguably one of the most prolific and certainly the most public occultists of the early 20th century so he had a huge influence over the way magick developed and the way Gerald Gardner would have viewed it. In a nutshell, he argued that magick was the manipulation of energies through the use of pre-defined determination that brought about a resultant change.

It's fair to say that we're not studying Aleister Crowley here but his influence contributes significant content to current Wiccan magickal practice, and in many instances ritual. In chapter 2 we talked through the history of contemporary Wicca and you should by now have a very clear understanding of where modern day Wicca inherits its contemporary practice from. Aleister Crowley is a huge part of that history even if only as its prime influencer.

Research
Just as an aside and as part of your overall training in the context of Wicca, please spend just a short time looking through some of the information available about Aleister Crowley. Some suggested places to look include;
http://www.controverscial.com/Aleister%20Crowley.htm
http://en.wikipedia.org/wiki/Aleister_Crowley
Booth, M. (2000). "A Magick Life: A Biography of Aleister Crowley). London: Hodder and Stoughton.

Predictably, as an eclectic Wiccan, Scott Cunningham by comparison saw magick as an act of religious practice and so he described it as "the projection of natural energies to produce needed effects". He proposed that there were three sources of this energy which included personal power, earth power and divine power. His input to the way contemporary and eclectic magick is conducted is one of the most significant contributions of any single person to date and is held worldwide as one of the most sensible and down to earth approaches of modern day Wicca.

Read
If I were to dictate a prescribed text for this Toward First Degree training program, apart from The Seeker's Guide to Learning Wicca, I would undoubtedly suggest "Wicca: A Guide for the Solitary Practitioner" by the now sadly deceased Scott Cunningham. His book is without doubt a foundational text for any new seeker to contemporary, eclectic Wicca.
Please take the time to get a copy of his book and in particular read chapter 3 – Magic.

So with a brief smattering of the Wiccan history of magick, what I would emphasise here is that magick is not some airy fairy, nonsensical wish list that we can romantically apply to our desires. It's is not a child's toy, it's not something to play with and use light heartedly. I can't stress this enough to you. It's a serious practice with serious outcomes and a means of working with the power and energy of the planet to bring about serious, tangible and often massive outcomes. There are a set of ethics around magick that we encountered in chapter 1 with the Wiccan Rede and the Law of Return that govern both how you should ethically conduct magick and what repercussions you should be prepared to take as a result. We'll look at these again shortly in relation to magickal workings. However, before doing so, it's foundational that you understand that magick is not a trivial pursuit that you can dabble in and use to create ridiculous outcomes like changing your hair colour and turning the ex into a toad.

So, if magick is not to be used for trivial matters, what is it actually then? If we think about what Aleister Crowley and Scott Cunningham suggested magick is, then we have a great discussion starting point. Magick is the action you apply to bring about a result you desire, having infused that action and desire with intent and will. So in other words, starting from the beginning, you have a serious desire to achieve something, to heal something, to bring about a particular result or whatever. With that desire, you embed your absolute will, your utter dedication and commitment to that outcome and this will is what helps fuel the magick. Then you take some magickal actions in a way that loads them with your commitment, with your committed desire and will and the coupling of this action with your will helps to shift the planet's natural energies toward bringing about your desired outcomes.

Note I said here 'shift the planet's natural energies'. I didn't say create energies or manipulate energies or worse still, work against natural energies. When you work magick properly, you're harnessing the naturally occurring energy and power that already exists all around us and shifting it to work in a more focused way toward bringing about the result you were after. A good analogy of this is to think about when you last brought a new car. Let's say it was a pale blue Ford. Before you brought that car, you never really took much of notice of Fords on the road, much less pale blue ones. Cars were cars and there were lots of them around, period. But now you have a pale blue Ford and all of a sudden, there seem to be a whole bunch of pale blue Fords on the road that were never there before. You notice them quite frequently. The truth is they were always there, you just never noticed them but now your thoughts are focused on pale blue Fords and now you see them more frequently.

Magick is similar. Its energy, the fuel of magick, is everywhere, all around us, within us but we don't always notice it. We notice the occasional serendipitous moment or coincidence but that's about it. So, like the pale blue Ford, energy is all around us all the time, we just don't notice it much. Let's take this one step further. When we use magick to harness energy, we focus our thoughts and we tune our personal energies with those naturally occurring energies around us and suddenly they all work together to bring about our end result. Magickal action shifts or brings in tune natural energies so they work together and so that we can see opportunities more clearly. More than that though; because magickal action tunes your energy with the naturally occurring energies, it strengthens it, focuses it and pushes it toward actually creating the opportunities that you can then grasp to bring about your results. This strengthened and tuned in energy actually creates and brings about your desired outcomes. You thus become the centre of energetic workings aimed at developing the outcome you wanted. *You* are the master, the architect, the designer of your outcomes and of your life. Powerful stuff eh? Do you begin to see why you shouldn't trivialise magick with silly spells to turn ex lovers into toads or whatever? Before long your garden would be overrun with ex toads that have mated, gone through a population explosion and turned your fish pond into toad central! As I said earlier, magick is serious stuff with serious outcomes.

With that thought, let's turn to the topic of white and black magick. As a fairly well known Wiccan and Witch around the world, I frequently get asked if I'm a 'White Witch' which I have to admit annoys the heck out of me. Let me say up front, right now that there is no such thing as white and black magick. Magick is in fact grey. What do I mean by that?

Magick, by its very nature, is the harnessing of natural energies to bring about a desired result. The natural energies around us are both gentle and powerful. When you practiced the last mediation in chapter 5, you were working closely with the Air element and the meditation showed you both the gentle, supportive and useful side of that element with its warm breeze and then you also saw the awe inspiring magnificence of its power when it raged into wild winds like those in tornados and hurricanes. Air, Fire, Water and Earth can be both gentle (white if you like) and destructively powerful (black) and for the planet to have balance we need both aspects to the elemental energy. Magick, which uses these energies as part of its fuel is both black and white because it uses all aspects of the elements. In addition, what is good magick for you may be not so good for someone else and when you conduct magick, you need to consider this ethical responsibility.

As a simple example, if you conduct magick to help you secure a job you really want, that's great, or white, magick for you and hopefully for your potential employer who will benefit from your skills, but it's a disappointment to the other applicants who missed out. From sitting in their shoes, it's not nice and probably a little more black than white. From your perspective though it's definitely white. So magick is a little like a coin with the heads or white on one side and the tails or black on the other. For a coin to be a true coin it has two sides just as magick is both good and bad, particularly depending upon what your relationship to it is.

This means that I, and many other magickal practitioners, prefer to see magick as grey rather than black or white. We're realistic enough to know that as much as we apply ethical responsibilities to our magickal practice, it's likely that someone or something, somewhere may be negatively affected. It's the degree of that effect we need to consider and this leads us nicely into a discussion about the ethics and repercussions of magick within the Wiccan religious framework.

Activity
In your Learning Journal, write down what you now understand to be the fundamental concept of Wiccan magick. Disregard other systems of magick at this point such as Thelemic or Hermetic and just concentrate on magick within the Wiccan context. What do you think magick actually is?

The Ethics of Magick

So with the basic makeup of magick understood, let's turn to the ethics and religiosity of magick. We've determined that magick is really an action that harnesses the power of the universe around us and focuses it to create a desired result. It's the way that a Wiccan manifests their life's desires and it's similar (but with notable differences) to the way a Christian might use prayer to ask for their life's desires. The major difference though between magick and prayer, quite apart from the fact that a Christian is communicating with a God that we know is not a Wiccan God, is that Christian prayer generally asks an external God to bring about their wish. It's a request of a God 'out there somewhere' to do something for them. In contrast, Wiccan magick determines that the practitioner is the architect of their own life because they hold the power and energy of the Gods within themselves. So magick doesn't ask the Gods and Goddesses to bring something about, it determines of itself that the result will be achieved anyway. Magick is thus not dependent on the benevolence of an external deity like Christian prayer is. It's a much more organic, internal and direct relationship with universal energies than prayer is.

But with this direct relationship with the organic energy of the universe comes responsibility. In asking an external, 'out there' God to bring about a result for me allows me the opportunity to say later that he didn't let it happen, if it didn't work. Alternatively, if the prayer is answered and the outcome is achieved, I can't take the credit for that because it happened as a result of 'my God' letting it happen. With Wiccan magick, you cannot give credit to the Gods for success or shove the responsibility on to them if it goes pear shaped. You created the magick, you were the owner of the energy that was raised and focused, *you* therefore own the outcome, be that good or bad. This is the underpinning reality of the Law of Return.

This Law argues that whatever happens in your life is usually the result of a string of thoughts, words, actions, behaviours that you alone orchestrated. Notwithstanding that serendipity does pop up sometimes and random things occur that you had no part in creating in this life, like child rape for instance, in virtually everything that happens to you, you were the major contributor to that outcome. In other words, your life is your responsibility and yours alone. You can't fob off the blame to the Gods and Goddesses when it goes sour because you were the one who created the result, not them. Damn difficult concept when things aren't working out too well to know that you alone are the reason why things aren't working out too well!

Let's think this through though. If you're the reason (and have the responsibility) for the state of your current life, then you're also the reason (and have the responsibility) for your future life as well. So the Law of Return reflects this concept by saying that if you want a great, productive, happy, peaceful life, then sow the seeds to live a great, productive, happy, peaceful life. What you sow is what you reap, what you put out is what you get back and you can't blame or credit anyone else with the result except yourself. The Law of Return places the responsibility for your life directly in your lap and directs you to make sure that you understand that when doing magickal work, when engaging with people, when doing anything at all in fact, you need to be aware that what you put out is what you'll get back. So in a nutshell, if you do really bad magick that harms others, then you're going to cop a whole barrowful of bad crap as a result.

The Law of Return is the descriptor of the broader ramifications of your magickal life then. It tells you that you have not only the responsibility for your outcomes but that you also have to live that responsibility and those outcomes. You can't just acknowledge the responsibility, you actually also have to live it. That's great if you only do productive magick, but pretty crap if you do crap magick!

The problem with this is that we've already decided that magick is not simply just good or bad, white or black but instead it's grey. So the responsibility and the outcomes you get will also be grey on many occasions.

To put some perspective on that though, the balance of outcome is determined by you. The degree or depth of the colour grey is up to you. You can, and indeed will, have a very muddy, dark grey life with hurt, anger, pain and frustration if that's the type of magick you conduct. Put bluntly, you create havoc then you'll get havoc. In contrast, you can have a very pale grey life, with the odd (and quite normal) frustration and upset but generally a life you love filled with happiness, laughter, peace and joy if that's the type of magick you conduct. I know which shade of grey I prefer.

Research

Like all the topics in this book, you don't get away with not doing your own work! Please now spend a considerable period of time reading through as many resources as you can about the Wiccan Law of Return as also known as The Threefold Law or the Rule of Three. I'd prefer you dismiss the quantification of three for the reasons discussed above and in earlier chapters but regardless of that, the principle remains the same. This is a very serious and important aspect of magickal work and deserves considerable research, thought and consideration. Some great resources I thoroughly recommend to get you started include;

http://en.wikipedia.org/wiki/Threefold_law
http://wicca.timerift.net/three.shtml
http://wicca.timerift.net/wicca101/ethics.shtml
http://www.cuew.org/thefivepoints.html
http://www.witchvox.com/va/dt_va.html?a=usfl&c=basics&id=2872

While the Law of Return is part of the 'justice system' that polices the outcomes to our magick, the Wiccan Rede is the front end of that same justice system which tells us what we should be doing in the first place. Where the Law of Return says "You deserve this!" the Wiccan Rede says "Make sure you don't deserve any nasty crap!" You might recall from the first chapter that the Rede says, "An it harm none, do what thou will" which in essence means don't do anything that's likely to harm anything or anyone including you. If you couple that with the Law of Return, it would mean that you'd only do magick that was positive and that as a result you'd only have positive outcomes and repercussions. This is the ideal but of course we've already seen that magick is grey and that no matter how hard you try, how well you plan and how much you consider, there's likely to be a negative outcome somewhere for someone at some point. So what do you do about that? The answer I think is about relativity and minimisation.

If we agree that all magick is grey and thus has a degree of both positive, good or white to it as well as negative, bad or black depending on what your relationship to the magick is, then your responsibility as the magickal creator is to minimise wherever possible any negative impact your magick might have, maximise the positive for everyone and everything that could possibly be affected and thus balance the relativities. Creating a magickal working to get yourself a dream job is all very well if that job is the right one for you. A great example of this principle is with magick around love. You must never do any magick that affects someone else's ability to use their free will so you would never do a magickal working to make a particular person love you. You're messing with, and violating, their right to their own freedom of will for your own desires and this is unethical and totally against the Rede. Instead, you might develop some magick to make yourself more lovable or to generally attract people to you but you would never direct this at one person. In terms of the dream job, you might create magick that takes you to the job which is right for you but you wouldn't create a spell working that demands a particular employer offers you the job. Like the specific love spells, this is removing someone else's right to their own free will and is thus harmful.

On a broader note around free will, many magickal practitioners believe that you must never do any magick on behalf of, or for, anyone else without their permission, even if it's a simple healing spell because you remove the recipient's right of free will. I'll give you an example of this to better explain what I mean here because this is an important point.

This example happened to a student of mine who's been practicing magick for several years and involved her doing some healing magick for her grandmother. Her grandmother was an elderly woman who was suffering dreadfully from illness and body degeneration as a result simply of old age. Her body was simply breaking down and she was hospitalised and expected to die in the not too distant future. Because my friend, her granddaughter, loved the elderly woman dearly and because she sympathised with her pain, she did some magickal workings to help her feel better and in fact to keep her alive thinking this is what she wanted. She didn't talk to her grandmother about it and just went ahead with the working.

On reflection later, the student admitted that her grandmother might actually be waiting to die so she could be with her husband who'd passed over several years before. It may also have been that my student's grandmother could have been suffering pain that she'd been hiding from the family to minimise worry and by keeping her alive with magick, my friend was denying her the desire and right to be with her beloved husband and to relieve herself of her possible never ending pain. While my student thought she might be helping, she later realised that she could in fact have been causing more long term harm than good.

I'm not suggesting that she engaged in unethical magick per se but rather that she may well have engaged in unethical magick, not deliberately, but because she didn't think through her reasons and the potential repercussions for herself and her grandmother. Working magick comes with serious responsibilities which must be considered from all angles before any spell work is crafted. If you conduct magick for someone else without asking their permission, you run the very real risk of creating effects that are unwanted or at least unconsidered and not prepared for. While you might have your heart in the right place and think you're doing the right thing, it may be that there are points you haven't considered in the current situation and that any magickal working you conduct may deliver uncalled for, unwanted and even damaging results.

The lesson here is to *think* before you act and to do so from as many points of view as you possibly can so that you're absolutely aware of all the ramifications on everyone of the spell work you're about to do. Never rush into magick, never craft a spell working that has implications for another particular person without asking their permission first and never, ever do spell work on someone else without telling them where it is only for your own gain. This is utterly unforgivable, immoral and unethical and I doubt that any Wiccan or Craft teacher would accept your argument that it was anything other than improper.

Research
This time your task is to research the Wiccan Rede from the viewpoint of using it as your ethical measuring tool for the practice of magick. There are an absolute myriad of resources available on the Rede but some of the best I've found include; http://www.religioustolerance.org/wicrede.htm
http://www.cuew.org/thefivepoints.html
http://realmagick.com/articles/12/12.html
http://www.witchvox.com/va/dt_va.html?a=usfl&c=basics&id=2876
http://www.realmagick.com/articles/66/1566.html

The Different Ways of Magick
There are of course a huge variety of types of magick and I'm not talking here about mechanically how you craft a spell but rather the

Exploring Magick

fundamental type of magick you're engaging with. There are three main areas of magick that I'd like you to consider, learn about and become familiar with so that you can develop a much keener sense of where the magick you finally craft sits. One area is an exploration into systems of magick, the second area is to discuss the styles of magick within the Wiccan magickal system and then finally we'll explore in more detail the actual mechanical forms that Wiccan magick can take.

Magickal Systems
Let's start at the broad end of the spectrum first and look at a few of the systems that heavily influenced Gardner as he developed Wicca. We'll look at ceremonial or high magick first and compare those magickal formats to the more 'hedge witch' forms that Wiccan magick tends to take.

Ceremonial or high magick sounds rather grandiose and perhaps something you should be aiming for in your Wicca practice. I tend to disagree with this aim largely because ceremonial magick is complex and is usually linked to highly ritualised styles of magick such as Thelemic and Hermetic. These styles of magick relate to, and are an intricate part of, a whole other esoteric set of orders such as Ordo Templi Orientus the Rosicrucians and Golden Dawn. As such, practicing ceremonial magick is in effect working magick within a different spiritual and practical framework than Wicca. It's termed ceremonial because it's exactly that, highly ceremonial. The magick is intricate, elaborate, very formal and extraordinarily complex.

Depending on your view point, ceremonial or high magick is also a branch of magick that's aimed much more at self improvement and enlightenment than ritual magick conducted during Wiccan based practice. Ceremonial magik's main aim is to bring the practitioner closer to their ideal, higher self whereas Wiccan ritual magick, while very often aimed at the same outcome, can also be used for more practical and day to day purposes such as healing, prosperity, safety, and personal well being and so on. Thus ceremonial magick is not really akin to Wiccan magick because of its relationship with other spiritual systems. However, it's true to say that Wiccan ritual magick is born from ceremonial magick because Gardner was heavily influenced by people like Aleister Crowley who was a ceremonial magician and adept at several systems of high magick. The scripts and content of Wiccan ritual and magick therefore come from the original texts as used by ceremonial magicians and so while we, as Wiccans, may not practice it in its original format, we must acknowledge the long and credible history from which our magick comes.

Read

Ceremonial and high magick are fascinating branches of the ritual magick we sometimes use within Wicca. I'm not too concerned that you should study them fully but they do make for excellent background reading. With that in mind, spend a few moments now exploring these excellent sites which discuss these magickal approaches.

http://www.ecauldron.net/cmagick00.php
http://www.rahoorkhuit.net/library/ceremonial/
http://magick-voodoo.suite101.com/article.cfm/ceremonial_magick

The history of the various esoteric and magickal orders and systems is amazingly complex and intriguing. Many of the orders originated more than a thousand years ago but have changed their name, been remodelled and adjusted as new teachers and philosophers adopted them. A study of the relationships between all these differing, yet extraordinarily related approaches would take a book on its own so for the purpose of introducing the magickal systems as a background to modern Wicca, I'm just going to provide a synopsis of the approaches that were most influential on Gardner and thus on the formulation of Wicca.

The first major influencer that's important is that of the Hermetic magickal system. The Hermetic Order of the Golden Dawn was first created in 1888 by Dr. William Robert Woodman, Dr. William Wynn Westcott and Samuel Liddel MacGregor Mathers in England. Whilst the name of the order was new, its content and philosophy was constructed from the works and texts of even earlier esoteric practices, some of which date back hundreds of years. The Golden Dawn is not a religious order per se, but it does include some religious symbology and concepts from those earlier writings. Golden Dawn magicians come from many different religions in fact and the concept of the Hermetic Golden Dawn approach is less about religion and much more about the ceremonial magick that it teaches which is designed to bring the practitioner closer to their true and higher self.

Golden Dawn encompasses quite a few different esoteric constructs including those from Egyptian origins, as well as Greek, Rosicrucian and Masonic amongst others. Hermes Trismegistus, after which the various Hermetic traditions are named including the Hermetic Order of the Golden Dawn, was supposedly an Egyptian philosopher and sage from around the 1st century BC but the historical data has been clouded by legend and conflicting writings. Golden Dawn students primarily learn how to work with the Qabalah or the Tree of Life and this forms a substantial framework to their learning journey. They also gain skills in divination, alchemy, Enochian magick and even astrology.

There are a series of grades within the order, similar to but more complex than the Inner and Outer Court system within Wicca, wherein the practitioner comes gradually closer to an ever deeper set of teachings and insights. Aleister Crowley joined the Order in 1898 and worked his way through the grades fairly quickly but broke away after some damaging internal politics within the Golden Dawn leadership and of course to pursue his own practices. He later wrote rituals which were often based on the Golden Dawn rituals he learnt and of course Gardner was heavily influenced by these texts.

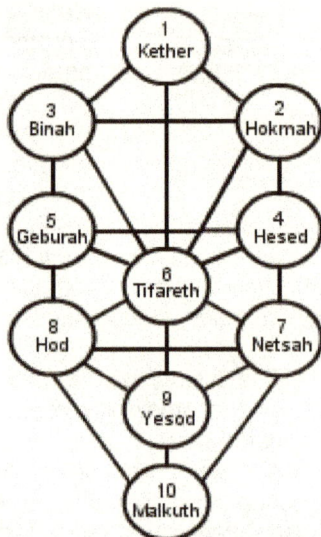

The Ordo Templi Orientus (OTO) was formed in 1895 by Karl Kellner and its practitioners use largely Masonic based rituals and also tantric based sex magic. By 1922, Aleister Crowley had gained sufficient expertise and skills to take the role of Outer Head of the Order. It was at this point that he rewrote a considerable proportion of the OTO rituals and essentially remodelled it to his more Thelemic practices which were based in part on Rosicrucian principles.

The Law of Thelema is "Do what thou wilt" and this comes from "The Book of Law" that he wrote in 1904. It was on this text that OTO was reformulated and remodelled into a religion and graded fraternity, much like those of Golden Dawn and Freemasonry. However, because of the inter politics of the esoteric community, the Golden Dawn practitioners and the Thelemic practitioners became two distinct and often opposed groups and so the magickal landscape moved yet another step forward.

OTO has three grades called the Hermit, the Lover and the Man of Earth and within those there are 25 different levels through which the practitioner passes. This is similar to the Freemasonry grading system in fact so again we can see the relationships and similarities between different groups. However, one of the main things that stands out about OTO is that it has a fully hierarchical church structure complete with different levels of clergy right up to Bishops in Amity and the Grand Lodges are presided over by the international headquarters.

We'll turn now to Enochian magick which is a fairly old magickal system, created by Dr John Dee who was a magician and an advisor to Queen Elizabeth I. We met John Dee in chapter 3 when we were learning about the history of circles. Under Dee's direction and supervision, Edward Kelly received messages supposedly from the angels which describe a magickal system that enabled the practitioner to become closer to their higher and true self. Remember that in these times, England was a Christian regulated state and both John Dee and Edward Kelly, while practicing magicians, were also heavily influenced by the dogma of the Christian faith. Thus they saw their system as being related to the angels, and to a sincerely Christian form of closeness with the mystery of their God.

Centuries later, various Golden Dawn practitioners developed Dee and Kelly's work even further and integrated it into their own Order. Thus we can see that Wiccan circles and ritual practice, while the invention of Gardner in the 1940s, was a remodelling of work much earlier than his own. Enochian principles were carried over into the original Wiccan circle but because they were also adopted and modelled by the Golden Dawn practitioners which were subsequently remodelled by OTO, Gardner was working with some seriously old, albeit fragmented material.

While all that was going on in Europe, over in New York, the Theosophical Society was founded in 1875 by Helen Blavatsky, Henry Steel Olcott and William Quan Judge. While much less focused on religion and far more on esoteric practice, this group had what would be considered now some radical viewpoints on the origin of humans. They believed that current mankind came from a series of 'root races', one of which was the Ayran race supposedly from Atlantis. The group argued and fought for equality of all humankind regardless of race, colour or creed suggesting that we're all descended from this series of root races and thus equal. Indeed, this philosophy is one of the foundational principles upon which the movement is built and thus brotherhood of all mankind is of extreme importance in following the group's credo.

However, history shows us how some others later grabbed this concept some sixty years later and turned it into the holocaust. It's that series of tragic events that changed the meaning of the swastika which still forms part of the emblem of the Theosophical Society from its previous spiritual meaning into something more sinister and unforgiving.

Theosophical Society practitioners learn about a number of esoteric skills, most notably those techniques around mediumship and events not explained within science. It's these concepts that Gardner drew upon when he formulated Wicca and so the work of Blavatsky in particular was a heavy influence on Gardner's creation of the esoteric arts within Wicca.

Let's turn now and take a quick tour of the very old and respected Rosicrucian approach. Legend has it that the Rosicrucian Order originated in 46CE when Ormus, who was an Alexandrian Gnostic sage, met and was converted to Christianity by Mark, one of Jesus' disciples. Given that Alexandria was an Egyptian territory, he merged Christianity with his Egyptian mysteries and formed the Rosicrucian Order.

This is, of course, legend rather than verifiable fact and the modern day Rosicrucian Order, like many others underwent centuries of change and rejuvenation before it reached its current state. Much of that change was based on national politics, the religious landscape at the time and of course esoteric advancement and the blending of different practices.

Like virtually any other esoteric group, there are a number of different traditions within the Rosicrucian Order but most suggest that their verifiable origin dates from around the 15th century when Christian Rosenkreuz opened his first House of the Holy Spirit. Rosenkeuz had travelled to the East and learnt the mysteries of esoteric practice there. He brought this knowledge back with him and initially went to Spain and then later to Germany. Realising that what he had learnt and wanted to teach went against the political formulations of the church at that time, he chose to teach in secret, thus creating another secret society similar to the Knights Templar. After his death, he was buried in a secret tomb as was the custom of his faith and was buried with his manuscripts. These were supposedly later unearthed when the secret tomb was relocated centuries later.

There's considerable evidence to suggest that the rites and structure of the Rosicrucian Order were the primary influences for the Freemasons and that they built their fraternity on Rosicrucian principles. The United Grand Lodge of England of Freemasonry was formed in 1717 and of course branched out across the world thereafter. Its rituals and structure remained secret for centuries but we know from text comparisons that Gardner used many of the Freemasonry ingredients in his formulation of Wicca. Given that it's highly likely that Freemasonry borrowed some of the Rosicrucian practices, we can see again how Wicca has become the modern day reincarnation of many very old ritual practices.

Let me point out at this stage, as I have at various points of this book, that whilst I might promote that Wicca is a modern day religion and not a rebirth of an ancient religion, there's considerable evidence to suggest that some of its content comes from the fragmented work of centuries old philosophies and wisdom. That's not to say we can jump to the conclusion that we're regenerating old works because we clearly are not. We may be using tiny fragments and sections of old works of course and we can be proud of that, but we must always remember the truth; which is that Wicca is a modern day religion and magickal practice with some influences and possible inclusions from ancient practices and philosophies.

Activity
Like the ceremonial and high magick background work, learning the history and influence of other magickal systems is not vital to Wiccan practice but it is helpful. Take some time to look through some of these locations to learn a little more about the various approaches described here. In your Learning Journal, write a few sentences describing what you think the relationship between Wicca and the ancient magickal systems actually is. Some sites of interest to inform those sentences are given for you here.

http://en.wikipedia.org/wiki/Theosophical_Society
http://www.austheos.org.au/
http://oto-usa.org/faq.html
http://altreligion.about.com/od/ritualmagick/MagickOccult.htm
http://en.wikipedia.org/wiki/Spell_(paranormal)
http://www.hermetics.org/home.html
http://www.hermeticfellowship.org/
http://www.http://www.hermeticgoldendawn.org/index.shtml
http://www.golden-dawn.org/
http://en.wikipedia.org/wiki/Hermetic_Order_of_the_Golden_Dawn
http://www.golden-dawn.com/eu/index.aspx
http://www.mysteriousbritain.co.uk/occult/the-golden-dawn.html
http://www.osogd.org/
http://www.themystica.com/mystica/articles/h/hermetic_order_of_the
_golden_dawn.html

Wiccan Magickal Styles

Wiccan magick uses some old rules that, not surprisingly, are consistent with many other magickal systems around the world. Essentially Wiccan magick adopts five styles.

- Sympathetic magick
- Contagious magick
- Attraction magick
- Binding magick
- Banishing and protection magick

Starting from the top and working our way down, sympathetic magick is probably one of the most prevalent styles of magick and essentially draws direct comparisons between the spell that's crafted and the desired end result. Like affects like in other words. In this style of magick, often termed 'imitative magick' the practitioner creates a relationship between a spell ingredient and the object of the magick. As an example, a poppet doll that's been created to resemble a particular person might be filled with certain herbs to help heal them (with their permission of course!). Any spell work done to the poppet, the energy for which resides in the magickal plane, results in healing for the actual person who resides in the material plane. A direct relationship is created between the spell ingredient, a poppet, and the person, or end result in the 'real' world.

Another example might be where you wanted to attract more money so you might dress a green candle with Cinnamon oil and burn it. That oil is known for attracting money and green is the money and abundance colour. The action of dressing and lighting the candle draws a distinct and deliberate link and relationship between the candle and the need to attract money. The real world is sympathising with the magickal world and so creates the outcome in the material world that was started in the magickal world.

Research

Spend some time looking on the web and through books to learn more about sympathetic magick. What do other authors say about this style of magick? What other systems of magick incorporate sympathetic magick?

Contagious magic is similar to sympathetic magick in that there's a relationship between a spell ingredient and the end result but the difference here is that the magickal ingredient becomes the catalyst for the transference of its major strength into the end result. Talismans and amulets are good examples of contagious magic.

Different crystals have different properties and the clear quartz crystal for example is known as a powerful healing stone. By carrying a quartz crystal with you to help you heal an illness, a wound or even a psychological scar, you're engaging in contagious magick. You're asking the magickal object you're using to duplicate and transfer some its strengths and powers to you. It becomes a contagious object that 'infects' you with its strength.

Attraction magick is a combination of both sympathetic and contagious magick and essentially is created to bring something to you. This is often the style of magic used in commercial, and often dangerous, spells available on the internet and in books to attract a lover to you. But attraction magick can be used for all manner of ethical and wonderful outcomes. You can attract love to you generally without the need to draw a particular person to you. Similarly you can attract abundance, happiness and health when you create well crafted magickal workings that respect the natural energies around us. The dangers with attraction magick is that it can be seen as the fast and easy option to resolve problems when in fact attracting what you think you need is only a bandaid over the real problem underneath. Let me explain.

If you desperately need more money in your life and you did magick to bring that about, what would it result in? More money of course but the underlying reason why you needed more money in the first place still exists. It may be that you don't actually need more money but instead need to learn how to budget better, or to rid yourself of your partner who takes you for granted and spends all your money or perhaps to learn to live a more frugal and sensible life. Research shows that even the great lotto winners more often than not are flat broke again within two years of winning squillions because they didn't learn how to control their new found money.

Similarly, while you may think it will solve all your problems to attract more love in your life, it may in fact be that you need to gain much more self confidence and love for yourself rather than trying to gain that confidence from the love of someone else.

Research
Have a look on the internet for sites that offer spells. Look in particular for spells which you'd classify as attraction spells. What sort of things are they normally trying to attract and do you consider the things they're attracting as appropriate?

Binding magick is a piece of spell craft where you deliberately stop someone from hurting themselves or someone else or even something else. Now there needs to be a few words of caution here with regard to ethics yet again. Yes I know I keep harping on about ethics but appropriate, effective practice has to be tempered against what's morally just. Far too many injustices, wars and depravities have occurred in the name of religion over the last few thousand years and it would be wonderful to think that in our own small way we can help to swing that tide of selfish, irresponsible history.

The Wiccan Rede you already know prohibits you from doing any magick which may result in harm to someone else and you must always consider that in doing binding magick. You may in fact be restricting someone's will and this goes against the Rede. Having said that, binding magick is a good way to restrict someone who may be about to harm you. My personal preference in this situation is banishing or protective magick but I can very much understand the need for something a little stronger like binding magick in certain circumstances.

Whereas a binding spell directly restricts the actions of someone, a protection spell does not stop them from acting but it does protect you, and anyone else, from the repercussions of that action. In other words you haven't harmed anyone else by restricting their will but you have stopped any of their actions having an effect on you. This is a much more ethical approach to this kind of a problem and one that gives you more freedom to act magickally without breaking the Rede.

Banishing magick is in effect the opposite of attraction magick and instead of drawing something toward you, it pushes away from you any negativity, any internal, psychological or emotional attributes you no longer want. It may also push away from you other more material situations you don't want or need. Some really simple examples of banishing magick are gargoyles on the rooves of houses which were originally put there to ward off evil spirits. Even the jack-o-lanterns with their odd carved faces were originally created to drive away any nasty spirits that might be hanging around at that time of year. The old superstition of throwing salt over your shoulder is in fact banishing magick so you can see that this kind of 'get the heck away from me' magick is quite old and you've probably been doing it without realising it for years!

Wiccan Magickal Forms
Within those five styles of magick, there are so many different forms of it throughout the Wiccan tradition that there's bound to be a spell working or two that suits your needs. I generally find that practitioners use a variety of different magickal forms but they often have a favourite form they use repeatedly albeit with variations to meet the needs of a particular spell. Some of the more common forms of magick within Wicca include;

- Meditative or doorway magick
- Cord or knot magick
- Candle magic
- Sex magick
- Poppet magick
- Talisman or amulet magick

Now before we go into what each of these magick forms are and how they're worked, it's worth noting that you can do magick within the circle and without it. Personally I prefer to cast a circle first so that I'm working within the sacred space of the Divine because for me this makes my magick stronger and more robust. However, magick can be created at any time and at any place really. The choice, location and timing are yours to decide.

I'm suggesting you use the circle as a venue for magick for a number of reasons however, not least of which is the greater degree of control you have over when you release the power. When you create your circle space, you're also creating a sphere in which magickal energy is captured and retained until you're ready to let it go. This magickal containment shell is an inherent part of the circle erection process and is deliberately done so to capture any magickal energy you create.

When you create magickal energy within the circle either through the forms indicated here or perhaps through the more traditional dancing and chanting, you build up a 'cloud' of energy, a sort of charge like static electricity that builds and surges. You aim is to grow that cloud of energy around you till it reaches its peak and then right at that moment, you focus and point it at its destination and release it through the circle shell. Creating this magickal energy inside the circle is a much safer space to do it in and because the circle area is holding your magickal cloud inside itself for you, you've got time to focus it and point it to its destination before you let it go. If you were working outside a sacred space, the cloud of energy you create might leak off in all sorts of directions before you were ready to point it to its destination and release it.

One last note before we look at each of these magickal forms. I've not included specific spells here for several reasons. The first is because to include spells here would change this book from a training program into a magickal grimoire and that's not what the aim of this material is. There are many good magickal books out there already that serve that purpose. The second is that this chapter is primarily to teach you *about* magick and not to teach you *specific* magic. Everyone has a form of magick they prefer and you won't know what form of magick suits you till you've tried them all. Furthermore, any spell I might publish here suits me and my circumstances and may not suit you and your needs specifically.

Lastly I've not included spells here because as part of your training, I want to teach you how to craft your own spells. To be a well trained, effective Wiccan, you need to learn how to create magick that suits your needs rather than just copy someone else's spell. So with those provisos set, let's move into the explanations for the most popular forms of Wiccan magick.

Meditative or doorway magic is a very gentle magick form that can be conducted anywhere without the need for any tools so it's especially good when you're at work or somewhere where you can't create a sacred circle. Essentially you follow the visualisation process you've already become accustomed to and 'see' what you desire after going through your energisation visualisation door. This door should have become your personal doorway to other planes by now and you can use it as a passageway to many different realms. With doorway magick, you meditate and visualise your door, walk through it and see the end result you're trying to create. So for example, if you wanted to heal some emotional pain, you'd walk through your doorway and see yourself in a beautiful, calm and happy place as a healthy, fully functional person.

With any form of magick it's important that you always focus on the desired end result and not actually on what you want changed. If instead with this example you focused and saw your pain, you'd just be creating magickal energy to reinforce and grow that pain. So instead you focus on the desired result which is a happy, healthy, emotionally free you.

This form of magick actually underpins all other magick simply because it's deliberately making you focus on your end result without the tools and ingredients and correspondences. It's defined, it's direct and very strong when you practice it repeatedly. This form of magick should always be one of your major strengths, not just as a magickal practitioner but also as a Wiccan or Witch.

Cord or knot magick are really one form of magick but you can use your cords because they store magickal energy or you can use string, wool or ribbon. Many Wiccans and Witches have a set of cords and indeed, cords are a vital part of the initiation process so they have magickal properties and it's for this reason that knot magick is often called cord magick.

The aim of cord or knot magick is to generate energy and to tie it up inside the knots of the cord (or string, ribbon, rope, wool etc). The magic is then stored inside the knots for when you need it. Depending on whether you're creating a banishing spell or an attraction spell, you might either bury or burn the cord straight after the magic or for an attraction spell, you'd keep the cord with you and untie the knots in the opposite order they were created in once you had received the end result. Alternatively, you can keep the cord with you and untie a knot each time you need a piece of the magick you created and stored within it. The cord becomes your pantry of magick in effect and holds your stock of magick until you need it.

When crafting this type of magick, you sit with your cord in your hands and visualise your desire, stroking the cord within your grasp and seeing your desire infusing itself into the cord. You'll keep pushing your desire and will into the cord as you tie nine knots and with each knot you'll say a single sentence.

For the first knot, tied in the position illustrated below, you say; "By knot of one, the spell's begun".

For the second knot, tied in the position illustrated below, you say; "By knot of two, it cometh true".

For the third knot, tied in the position illustrated below, you say; "By knot of three, so mote it be".

For the fourth knot, tied in the position illustrated below, you say; "By knot of four, this power I store".

For the fifth knot, tied in the position illustrated below, you say; "By knot of five, the spell's alive".

For the sixth knot, tied in the position illustrated below, you say; "By knot of six, this spell I fix".

For the seventh knot, tied in the position illustrated below, you say; "By knot of seven, events I'll leaven".

For the eighth knot, tied in the position illustrated below, you say; "By knot of eight, it will be fate".

For the ninth and final knot, tied in the position illustrated below, you say; "By knot of none, what's done is mine".

Another of my favourite forms of magick is candle magick, because it's so versatile, so quick and so easy to prepare and do.

It's a misunderstood art however because you don't just buy a candle, light it and expect to achieve the end result. There is a little more to it than that!

Candle magick has been conducted for centuries, possibly because the flame from a candle is so enchanting and mesmerising. The aim is to infuse your will into the candle and the act of burning it releases the magickal intent to the planet through the flame and smoke. The two important factors are to choose the correct candle colour and to dress it first. Let's talk through colours first.

We've discussed correspondences before and now we're going to extend that conversation just a little further. We'll talk through the practicalities of correspondences even further later in this chapter.

Each magickal ingredient, in this case a candle, has a correspondence with a number of other factors which will strengthen it to a particular outcome. So for example, the colour green corresponds to finances and so if you wanted to attract more money toward you, you'd burn a green candle. To take that even further, Friday is associated with green so you'd burn a green candle on Friday. As an attraction spell, you're trying to increase your wealth so you'd also do it on a waxing moon, probably just after the new moon as she's slowly growing bigger toward the full moon. This is so that as the moon grows bigger, the global energy increases and so your magickal intent within the spell grows bigger and stronger. If instead you were trying to do some banishing magick, perhaps to rid yourself of sadness, you'd do this just after a full moon as she's getting smaller so that as she diminishes, so too does your sadness.

So with any magickal ingredient, you attach to it relevant correspondences like herbs, colours, days of the week, cycles of the moon, essential oils, times of the day or night or whatever correspondences feel right and appear to work well with what you want to achieve. The tables in the next section of this chapter gives you an introductory matching of correspondences so you'll be much better placed to draw different factors together to strengthen your outcomes.

Once you've decided the colour of your candle, the next thing is to dress it using a suitably corresponding essential oil. Take your candle and oil, place a little oil on your fingertips and starting in the middle of the candle, roll your fingers laced with oil up along the sides of the candle toward the tip. Make sure you try and cover all the candle sides. Then put just a little more oil on your fingertips and again starting from the middle, coat the candle from the middle down to the base with oil trying to make

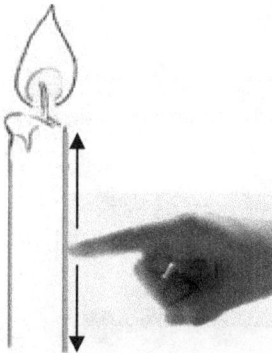

sure you have coated all the sides. As you do this, think about the outcome you want your magick to achieve, focus on the desired end result and infuse the candle with that outcome through the oil. What you're doing is pushing your will into that oil which is then coating the candle.

Some candle spells require you to burn the candle completely down in one sitting and if so you need to place the candle somewhere safe where it can't set light to anything else like curtains and where it can't be knocked over by your curious pets or blown out by a breeze. Other spells expect you to relight the same candle every day for a few days, often a week or more and gradually burn the candle down each day. This approach sets the magick, then adds to it each day to bring it greater strength and longevity.

While candle magick is quite common, one of the most misunderstood, and occasionally misused, forms of magick is that of sex magick. In any form of magick, the working consists of generating energy or power and then when that energy is at its peak, 'pointing' it at the desired outcome and releasing it. The compassion and passion of lovemaking between two consenting adults is similar in that the couple generate considerable energy and power together and when that energy peaks, they orgasm and the power is released. The concept of sex magick is therefore to raise power through lovemaking and when both people are almost at orgasm (nice if this happens at the same time!) they turn their attention to the object or desired result of their magick, allow the orgasm to flood over them and in so doing release the power and energy to that outcome.

Now, there's obviously a few provisos with this form of magick that you could argue go without saying because their obvious but I'm going to say them anyway. Sex magick, because of the potential repercussions and social expectations, should never be conducted forcibly on someone. That is not sex magick; it's rape, pure and simple. Never, ever consent to conducting sex magick with someone if it's under duress, if you feel uncomfortable or if you have any concerns of any description.

Moreover, I'd suggest you never conduct sex magick with anyone you don't know. Having sex with a stranger is fraught with danger anyway and is just plain silly. Always use a condom when conducting sex magick with someone who's not your partner for the very obvious reasons of minimising transmittable diseases and preventing unwanted pregnancies.

I absolutely recommend that sex magick only be done between couples who are already enjoying a stable, peaceful relationship together. Sex magick can sometimes throw up some unwanted and unexpected emotional side effects and you can minimise these substantially by conducting the magick only with a trusted life partner.

As a further suggestion, I'd recommend that you don't conduct sex magick when you're stressed, miserable or sad. Quite apart from the difficulty of actually having meaningful lovemaking when you're miserable, as I mentioned before, sex magick can generate some surprising emotional side effects and if you conduct sex magick when you're in a negative state, you're likely to fuel that negativity further.

I'd also suggest that you talk through your magickal intent prior to beginning lovemaking. It may be that you are both magickal practitioners and if so the magickal intent should be agreed and shared. If only one of you is a practitioner, then ethically you really should discuss the purpose of your proposed magick with your non practicing partner. It may be that they would not agree with what you're doing and this has ramifications for your adherence to the Wiccan Rede.

Lastly, sex magick can be done either alone for an individual or in fact with a group of people if you're comfortable with that. Where a group performs sex magick together, it must be clearly discussed and agreed to first and everyone should be made aware that if they feel uncomfortable at any time, they're free to remove themselves from the activity without question or without the need to explain or justify their withdrawal. If you're single, you can easily conduct sex magick with masturbation and this can often be an extremely rewarding experience.

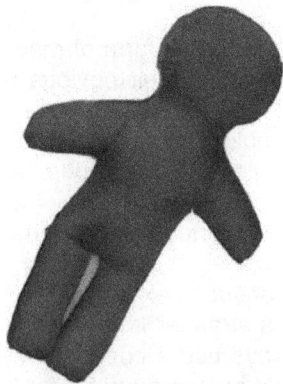

From sex magick, we move into poppet magick which is a great example of the sympathetic style of magic. What you generate with the poppet in the magickal world is what occurs for the person represented by the poppet in the physical world. What is a poppet though I hear you ask? A poppet is simply a doll that represents someone. It could be made from felt, corn, wax or any material that can be fashioned into the likeness of someone. It might even be a doll that represents your pet dog or your friend's budgie.

Now, let's get something straight here. Please don't conjure up images of Voodoo dolls with pins poking out of them. Poppet magick is not Vodun (the correct and original name for the anglicised term Voodoo) which is the legitimate magickal system of the ancient Yoruba people of West Africa.

Poppet dolls are indeed dolls crafted deliberately to form the likeness of someone and to strengthen the connection to the person represented, they'll often hold a lock of that person's hair or perhaps nail clippings. But because we work within the Wiccan Rede, we never use poppets to create negative magick so you won't find any little dolls with pins sticking out of them within Wiccan magick! Even in the Vodun system, the dolls they use are not always used for negative purposes and this classic representation of Voodoo dolls as items used to hurt and kill people has just been totally taken out of proportion and sensationalised in order to sell newspapers and movies.

In terms of actually making your poppet, there are several ways but one I've found useful is to cut out two person, or appropriate animal type shapes if you're doing this for a pet, from felt and then sew them together. Leave one part open because you can put inside herbs, crystals or even something from the person or animal and then sew up the last part. Use felt in a colour that corresponds with what you want to achieve for that person (green for more money, purple for wisdom etc) and if you're using herbs or crystals, check the correspondences so that you're using appropriate ones that strengthen what you want the magick to result in.

You can now draw on the poppet any particular markings or a face so that you can begin to really see who the poppet is supposed to represent. If it's for your dog or a cat or similar animal, draw onto it some of the markings or colours of the pet. Your aim here is to personify the poppet so that it really becomes a likeness.

Your next step is to use the poppet as the major tool in your spell work in whatever way the spell demands. It may be that you move the poppet toward a money talisman in order to create greater prosperity. Perhaps you tie the poppet with appropriately coloured string or wool to bind the person's actions having made sure you're not falling foul of the Rede. Perhaps you use the poppet as a representation of yourself and you create a shield around it to protect you from the actions of others. This might mean putting it inside a glass or an enclosed box for safety. You may have to bury the poppet once the magick has worked and this is quite common for this type of spell work.

Poppets can be made using other materials as well quite adequately. You can use ears of corn, a large wax candle carved into the shape you want, pastry, modelling clay, cloth or plasticine. The material you make it from is not as important as the intent you infuse it with and the only suggestion I would make about the actual material is that you try and use natural rather than manmade materials like plastic or nylon. Natural products and materials tend to hold and transfer naturally occurring energies and powers much more than sterile, factory developed and chemically derived products like vinyl, plastics and imitation products.

A last note on poppet magick before we move on and that again is around ethics. If you're doing any poppet spell work for, or about, someone else, please make sure you've sought permission where possible first. Remember the Rede and the Law of Return and make sure your magickal actions are positive and that you won't be contributing to harm in any way. It's really easy with poppet magick to fall into the trap of over stepping the ethical mark. Poppets are an easy tool to use in representing yourself or someone else and so it's very easy to trip up morally with this magickal form.

Finally we look at talismans and amulets as tools in spell craft. These two things are actually one and the same thing and they're quite simply an item that's charged with a certain attribute, usually good luck but often health or healing, and it's then used to keep bringing about that same outcome. The more you use a talisman or amulet, sometimes called a charm, the more powerful it becomes. It's as though you charge it up with power to begin with and the more practice it gets at bringing about its designated task, the better it gets at bringing the result home.

Do you remember the lucky rabbit's foot or the four leafed clover? The poor rabbit probably wasn't too keen on the outcome but you can see from these types of items that they've been around for centuries. A thousand years ago, unscrupulous tradespeople would roam the European countryside selling fragments of bone reputed to be those of Jesus and also tiny sections of old cloth supposedly being from his clothing or whatever. Of course this was all absolute rubbish but these items were treasured none the less as Christian talismans of good luck and prosperity.

You can make your own talisman for a particular purpose using a number of different methods. For example, I have a tiny scrap of green cotton cloth, rolled up and tied fast with corresponding green cotton which I keep in my purse. Several years ago, when I was a bit down on my financial luck, I got the material and tied it, infused it with the power to keep my spending in check and then put it in my purse. It's been there now for several years and rather than being free with my money as I used to be, I'm now much more careful. I see that simple little talisman almost every day as I use my purse and it constantly reminds me to remain sensible with spending.

Your talisman can be anything from a shell for emotional strength, to a crystal to help with communication. Perhaps your talisman is a tiny drawstring bag that holds a couple or crystals, perhaps a scroll of paper with a message on it, perhaps a rune or piece of stone. Your talisman in effect can be any small item that's meaningful to you and which you charge with a certain strength or power. You then keep this talisman with you as your personal charm and in so doing you strengthen it even further. You can have several talismans; each one charged with a different purpose, that you keep with you always.

Research
Take some time now to go and do a fair bit of research on the different forms of Wiccan magick. Do searches on the internet for knot magick, poppets and amulets. Read as many books as you can that describe the different ways you can craft magick. Work out what forms of magick appeal to you and study those in more depth. The longer you spend on this task, the more helpful it will become.

How to Craft a Magickal Spell

So after all that, you should now be in a much better place to understand what magick is, how the different styles and forms of it are generated and what the ethical implications are for magick making. The next step is to actually give it a go yourself.

There are numerous resources like grimoires, spell books, supposed Books of Shadows and even web sites to buy readymade spells or kits for magickal workings out there. Needless to say some of these are suspect at best, downright dangerous at worst. One of their strengths though is to give you a boundless supply of ideas to work from and this is the purpose that I'd rather you see them as. Personally I have a massive library of Wiccan, Craft and Pagan related materials with many of them being magickal texts and rather than use them verbatim, I prefer to use them as a resource to give me ideas and to provide input to any spell work I feel the need to do. As such these books and texts make a valuable contribution to my workings but I don't follow them without question, nor without modification to suit my needs.

Spells and magickal workings will work best when the ingredients and process are designed with your needs and purpose in mind. In other words, a personalised spell will have much more charge than an 'off the shelf' version that someone else created. That's not to say that all published spells are useless. That's not the case at all but rather they're the skeleton ready for you to add your own requirements to. Many of these published spells contain residual power because they've been created and crafted thousands of times and there's a certain amount of benefit in using those spells but by adding your own touches to them, you make them work even better toward your own needs.

So, what are the steps we need to follow when crafting a spell? While the actual steps might be modified as required, essentially the process is as follows;

- Determine that a magickal working actually has to be designed and crafted,
- Explore the ethical considerations of any magickal working for the purpose required,
- Consider the style of magick best suited to the task,
- Think about, then meditate on the form of magick that's most appropriate,
- Draft out your spell,
- Develop a list of the correspondences that fit with the spell working,
- Finalise your spell ingredients, correspondences and process,
- Cast a circle with all the magickal requirements at the ready,
- Do an energisation visualisation to prepare yourself and to see the end result,
- Raise the power,
- Focus and point the magickal power,
- Release the magickal power,
- Write the spell working in your Book of Shadows,
- Remain silent about the magickal working conducted.

Let's take a look at each of these steps in more detail. The first step, that of determining if a spell is actually required, is vitally important. This may sound silly but just because there's a problem or an issue to resolve, doesn't mean that magick is the best or only way to approach the situation. It may well help but there may also be other, more mundane things that can be done as well or instead. As an example, if you're feeling particularly unwell, while magick might benefit you and indeed go a considerable way to healing you, so might a visit to your doctor or health care professional. Similarly if you want to do some spell work to stop your otherwise wonderful pet dog from digging up your precious vegetable patch, a chicken wire fence round the garden might actually do a better job than crafting an elaborate or time consuming spell.

Look, I'm not trying to stop anyone from doing magick per se but what I am suggesting is rather controversial. Just because you have magickal opportunities at your disposal, please don't discount other, probably more boring but equally as effective solutions. Magick should never be an escape route where the mundane might work. It's unethical in my opinion to use magick for unnecessary purposes or simply because you can. During a discussion on magick with a sceptic, they asked me to magickally move a pencil from one side of the desk that was in front of us to the other. My initial response was "why"? What on earth was the reason or purpose for such a ridiculous request? It was simply to see if it could be done and so was of no purpose whatsoever. I picked the pencil up with my mundane fingers at the end of my mundane arm and gently moved it from one side of the desk to the other. So just because you can do magick, doesn't mean you always have to.

Having decided however that magick will help, your next step is to thoroughly examine all the ethical considerations and determine if you can do the magick with minimal harm. Magick should generally be done to create a better world to live in for everyone, not to make it worse.

With all that preliminary work completed, you can now start the crafting process. This is when you work out what style and form of magick will suit your purpose. Do you need sympathetic magick or protection magick? Would candle magick work best as the form, poppet magick maybe, perhaps a talisman? I've found at this point that meditating on the magick form to take often helps me clear my head of cognitive interference and 'feel' what would work best for this spell rather than 'think' what would work best. Magick is best done when it comes from the soul and the essence of who you are, not when it comes from your brain that's rational and sensible but not always intuitive and instinctive.

With the rough draft ready, write down what you want to do just in dot point form at this stage. You're still crafting the spell and it will probably change a little yet. With the basic spell written down, think through and research what correspondences apply. What colours work well with what you want to do? What day of the week is best? Are you doing a minimising spell or an attraction spell so should it be on a waning moon or a waxing one? What herbs and oils might help that are relevant? The correspondences really add power and concentrate the spell into a much more intensive and effective outcome. In the next section you'll find some tables to help you bring together different ingredients that gel together and correspond well with one another.

With all that, you should now have a complete spell ready to work. Gather what you need together, check it all fits well together and then when you're ready cast your circle. I've mentioned before that this step isn't always necessary and indeed in many quick fix spells, a circle casting simply isn't necessary. If you were at work for instance or somewhere that it might be difficult to do a spell casting, then you'll have to do it without the circle around you. Where you're doing the magick with a group of people, it's always wise to do the working after a circle casting however. This is because when lots of people raise magickal power together, they tend to raise a considerable amount and you need to capture that so you can focus it and release it all at once rather than letting it wander off into the environment around you before you're ready.

Just before you raise the power, I suggest you do the energisation visualisation you've already become used to here. There's a number of reasons for this, not least of which is that it enables you to clear yourself of any negative and muddy energy that's stuck to you and so helps you channel that energy much more efficiently. In addition, you can also use the visualisation to actually do the next step as well and raise the energy, particularly if you're doing this working somewhere where it might be embarrassing or difficult to go dancing and chanting to raise the power.

As a last point on visualising, it also gives you the opportunity, just before raising the power, to 'see' the end result again of your magick. It helps you focus one more time on your objective and this will strengthen that magickal intent and outcome even further.

Now you can raise the magickal power and this might be just an extension of the visualisation so that you see the energy streaming from the palms of your hands into a ball in front of you which grows and grows. Alternatively, this is where you do the dancing, the chanting, the singing, the drum beating or any other physical activity. It might also be that you dress the candle at this time and charge the candle with the power you channel through from the planet. You'll already have designed this section of the spell work earlier so you'll know what to do here.

When your gut instinct tells you that you can't raise anymore power and that it's at its peak, you quickly refocus again on the intended outcome. Remember here to see the desired outcome, not the problem. Focusing on the problem, be that ill health, a rowdy neighbour, an empty wallet, means that all you're doing is sending energy to the problem which will magnify it. Instead focus on the desired outcome which might be a healthy body, a calm and peaceful neighbour or a wallet and bank account with an abundance of money in it. You want to magnify the desired outcome, not the problem you're trying to resolve.

With the outcome firmly embedded in your will, release the power. See the power you raised stream off into the atmosphere towards its target. If you're the target, see that built up energy race toward you and into you. At this point, you're directing that energy like a magick bullet to its intended recipient so it can bring about the result you loaded it with.

Now you can write the spell working in your Book of Shadows so that you can use the spell again if needed and also so you can track the success of the outcome over time. With the spell recorded, your last task is to remain silent about the magick and let it do its job. It's said that the more you discuss the magick, the more it loses its power and amongst magickal practitioners therefore not talking about any workings is an important feature of practice.

All this might seem to be a rather laborious script of tasks that would take days, if not weeks. In some cases, yes it might take weeks. It may be that the best time to cast the spell is during a waxing moon but that might be two weeks away, so be it. If the magick's worth doing, it's worth doing well.

Not all magick is so intense, directed and prepared though. It may be that you need to do a spell quickly and without much preparation. It could be that you need to do it now. Again, so be it. Magick should be a tool that suits your needs and not one that sticks to a timetable just because the book, or indeed I, said so. If you've got everything prepared and one of the correspondences is a waxing moon but it needs to be done now during a waning moon, then do it now. Just substitute more correspondences in to counteract what is lacking from the moon's power.

What I'm saying here is that magick should come from the soul, not from the head so if there's a need to do the magick at a time not usually recommended or if you can't get a green candle even though the book says so, then modify things to suit. This is *your* magick. Make sure your intent is strong, make sure you've focused well and give it a go. The more you practice, the more your gut instinct will help and tell you what will work best.

Activity
Think about something you'd like to create a magickal working for. Keep it simple at this early stage. Make sure it can be done without causing harm and consider any repercussions.

Think about how you could best create that spell and what style it fits into. Is it sympathetic magick or some other style? What form should it take? Will it be poppet magick or a simple candle spell? Write you spell out in your Learning Journal and then conduct it. Record how you think the spell worked for you and what you'd do differently if you repeated it.

Correspondences

By now, you should be well prepared to experiment and try new ways of casting magick that suits your needs. Now you just need to gather more information about the various correspondences that will enhance your magickal workings so you can test out ways to strengthen your outcomes.

Correspondences as briefly mentioned earlier are all the add-ons that will intensify a spell. They're the colours, oils, herbs, timeframes, days of the week, star signs, moon phases, elements, crystals and any other factor that can add value to your spell. You don't need to use them all but the more you choose to weld and weave into your work that fit with what you want to do, the better.

Their purpose really is to intensify your work and to bring together a range of subtle and complimentary powers that enhance and exaggerate the outcome. Because these correspondences come from a variety of sources, they each bring a different set of magickal vibrations that when brought together create a richer sense of energy. To make the example easier to understand, imagine a string quartet. The musicians are playing beautiful music and it's serene and gentle. Now add a percussion section to the musical group as well and see how the music becomes richer, stronger, broader. Just to boost it a little further, now add a brass section and then finally a woodwind section. You now have a whole orchestra and the music will sound very different than it did from just the original string quartet. The music is now louder, stronger, richer and captures your heart with greater clarity and depth.

Magick done with a broad range of correspondences is similar. The more correspondences you add, just like the more instruments, the stronger, richer and more robust becomes the magick, just like the music. However, you need to keep the correspondences on target. So for instance, if you were playing baroque music, you wouldn't use an electric guitar or if you were playing folk music, you wouldn't use a trombone would you? Designing magick follows much the same principles so that you use the best correspondences together and avoid using ones that clash or minimise the strength of other correspondences.

All this may sound rather complicated but the more you experiment with magick, the easier it becomes. I'll suggest to you though that the best way to learn about correspondences is to read lots and then use your heart and instinct through meditation to give you answers about what correspondences are best. I mentioned it earlier but it's worth repeating. Magick is certainly a skill that requires cognitive input but ultimately it's an art that requires your heart and soul as the major contributor. *Feel* your magick, don't always *think* it. The more you practice, the more it will become a natural part of who you are.

The introductory tables below provide some simple ideas to get you started with different correspondences and how you can match up different ingredients into a complementary whole. Use them as simple stepping stones to designing your own lists of correspondences that work well for you. Remember that you don't have to use everything all at once but the more you can draw together in harmony, the better the magickal outcome.

Colour	Meaning	Day
Yellow/Gold	Beginnings, confidence, communication	Sunday
White	Purity, truth	Monday
Red	Strength, sex, action, power	Tuesday
Purple	Wisdom, psychic ability,	Wednesday
Blue	Business, travel, justice	Thursday
Green	Finances, peace, fertility	Friday
Black	Regeneration, banishing, forgiveness	Saturday
Brown	Finding lost things, security	Saturday
Pink	Friendship, Healing emotional hurts	Friday

Colour	Element	Quarter	Sun Sign
Yellow	Air	East	Virgo/Sagittarius
White			Pisces/Aries
Red	Fire	South	Taurus/Gemini/Leo/Capricorn
Purple			
Blue	Water	West	Aquarius
Green	Earth	North	Cancer
Black			Libra
Brown	Earth	North	Scorpio

Research
There are literally thousands of different correspondences across the range of ingredients, times, elements and so on. Take some time over the next couple of weeks to search the internet and various books for lists of correspondences. When you find any, copy them out into your Learning Journal so you'll always have them handy.
Some sources for you include;
http://herbalmusings.com/herb-magic.htm
http://www.controverscial.com/Colour%20Correspondence%20Table.htm
http://www.sticksstonesnbeyond.com/wittancrystal.htm
http://www.wejees.net/crystals.html
http://www.asiya.org/bos/corroils.html

Your Sixth Visualisation

Having started with the element of Air last month which corresponds to East and beginnings, we're now going to move deosil (clockwise) to the South quarter where the element of Fire resides. This month you'll be working with and getting to know this element which is quite masculine and synonymous with passion and action.

Remember to prepare as instructed in the first lesson and make sure that you're comfortable and won't be disturbed. As usual, read the energisation visualisation below first, and also remember to ground again afterwards.

Activity
Close your eyes, breathe deeply and slowly for a few seconds feeling the breath draw into your lungs and slowly back out again. Imagine a tap root growing from the base of your spine,your base chakra, downward toward the ground. It's a nice strong tap root and it slowly, gently but deliberately grows down through your chair, through the floor covering, on through the floor structure and then down toward the ground below.

See your tap root forcing its way into the earth below you and remaining strong and willing. Keep it growing, further and further. Push it further still, right down into the planet, right down into the dirt, the rocks and the substrata below your feet. Your tap root is strong and it's now anchoring you safely to the Earth. You're comfortable, you're connected to the planet and you're safe.

Now ask the glorious Goddess Gaia if she would allow you to draw into your tap root some of her pure, white, clean, fresh energy. She willingly gives you this energy. She always does because it's your pure white light too. See the pure white light, the cleansing, energising light being sucked up through your tap root and coming up closer and closer toward you. Draw it up toward you. Pull the energy up towards the base of your spine.

As it comes up through the tap root and enters your body, see it begin to tumble around at the base of your torso and then begin falling down your legs towards your feet. See the energy fill your toes up and any dark patches of negative energy are washed away as you breathe out. The energy just keeps streaming up through your tap root and flooding into your legs. Your lower legs, your thighs are now flooded with pure, white, clean, fresh light. Your legs feel cleansed and revitalised.

The energy keeps coming in and now it fills your lower torso, forcing away any dark and negative patches as you breathe out. Keep drawing up the energy, lots more yet, so much more yet. Your whole tummy area is now filled with white light and you feel comfortable, rested and calm. More white light, this time tumbling up into your chest and shoulders. The pure, white, cleansing light rolls down your arms and into your hands and fingers filling them with light. Yet more light, still coming into your body and now it fills your lower and upper arms and your shoulders feel relaxed and you feel safe and calm and peaceful. The white light then reaches up into your neck and as the light fills your body, it pushes any negative patches of old, faded, worn out, dirty energy away with each breath. Your head is filling with white light and so is your face and now, as you scan your body, you see all the parts of it are filled to the brim with wonderful, refreshing, rejuvenating, pure white energy. You feel alive, you feel calm, you feel peaceful and happy.

Check your body for any last remaining patches of old, dark energy you don't need and breathe them away. Spend a few moments luxuriating in the bliss of being bathed in pure, clean energy from the Goddess.

Now draw up yet more pure, clean, white light and now see that extra energy flowing through from within your body, through the pores of your skin and gradually out into the air immediately around you. From head to toe, front and back the energy is wisping its way through your skin and into your aura. Let the wonderful clean and fresh, white light filter into it cleaning out any muddy, dirty patches of old, worn out energies. See the white light wisping through the pores of your skin and penetrating and washing clean your aura. Breathe away any dark patches of negativity from your aura, make it clean and fresh and bright and calm and peaceful.

As you sit basking in the purity of the cleanest universal energy, imagine in front of you the same door you created and became familiar with last month.

Slowly and gently, open your door and step through. You are now in the realm of the Fire element and this is the home of flame, heat, the destructive power of raging fire and necessary gentle warmth to sustain life. Feel the gentle and soothing caress of warmth around you and see before you the flicker of a single candle flame. The flame casts a soft glow across the room and provides a comforting sense of safety and direction.

Before you several more candles appear, some large, some tall, some small, some round, some coloured, some white. They're all alight and now a sea of flame is raised. The light in the room brightens dramatically. Move your hand over the candles quickly and feel the strength of the heat rising from their individual flames. The wax from several candles drips to the floor and catches fire. The flames rise up through the mass of candles and within a few seconds, the flames engulf the inflammable wax and a full on fire develops in front of you. The heat becomes intense and threatening. You're safe and cannot be harmed but feel the strength and power of the raging inferno. Feel the light and heat singe the air around you and note the difference between the gentle and supporting caress of a single flame and the awesome power and rage of the mighty fire.

The flames die back till all that remains is a single candle flame again. Once more, you're cocooned within the gentle light of the soft candle flame. You notice in front of you a presence; you sense and feel someone with you. It's the element of Fire, the spirit of the flame. What does it look like or is it just a presence that you cannot see and can only feel like the flicker of light from the flame? Take a moment to ask the Fire element a question. What do you need to know about the element and power of Fire? What would you like to learn to take away with you? Listen to the answers and feel your connection with this wonderful being grow and deepen.

The Fire element lets you know that it has given you the knowledge and understanding that you seek and so you offer your thanks and respect. Now turn back to your door and gently walk through and close it behind you.

You're back where you were, in the now, in the here. Slowly bring your attention back to the room you're in and gradually open your eyes.

Ground yourself by bending or kneeling down on the ground, preferably outside on the grass or dirt, and place the palms of your hands flat on the ground. See the excess energy you drew up flowing smoothly back into the ground below you through your open palms.

Your Homework This Month

The art of magick, like with ritual design, is probably one of the most complex areas of Witchcraft and one that can take years to master and be comfortable with. This month's homework is all about focusing on developing the underpinning skills to help you get to grips with magick as a part of your religious Wiccan practice.

For the next month ahead;

- Make a list in your Learning Journal of the things you would like to change, heal or create for yourself. Then craft at least four spells to bring the things on that list to fruition. Try to do different kinds of magick using different forms. Record the results in your Learning Journal.
- Keep practicing the energisation visualisation including the aura cleansing and the connection with the Fire element this month. Finish off by grounding and write the results in your Learning Journal.
- Write regularly in your diary and include any significant dreams you had, any meditations that offered you insights and look at what's happening around you in nature and write that down too.

7

The Seventh Lesson

Exploring Divination

ere we are heading toward the final stages of learning about the practicalities of Wicca and Witchcraft. With magick under our belt, it's now time to look at divination and to explore the forms of that skill.

By the time you've finished this seventh lesson you should be able to;

* Explain what divination is,
* Describe the differences between magick and divination,
* Discuss the different types of divination,
* Begin to explore your own preferred skills in divination or build upon those skills you already have.

What is a Divination?

One of the most publicised, yet misconstrued parts of Wicca and Witchcraft is that of divination. Many members of mainstream society and indeed some Witches as well, consider divination to be one of the central arts of Witchcraft when in fact it's merely one of the many talents that Wiccans and Witches may possess. Please note I said 'may' and not 'do'. Like magick, divination is a practice of the Craft which some people may skill themselves in or not. It's *not* a required art of Wicca or Witchcraft, merely an added skill that many people choose to use.

Divination essentially is the ability to use a tool, usually in conjunction with an inherent gift, to see factors and events about people or situations that may not be immediately and obviously apparent otherwise. This doesn't always mean that practitioners can see into the future and may instead mean they're able to see elements of an individual that might be hidden, parts of their personality not normally on show, sections of their history not usually known or feel the energy of people long since departed but who continue to have a connection with a current place, a person or an event. Divination is thus the ability to sense in some way energy, spirit or the matter on other planes, using tools that act as doorways. These tools can include things like tarot cards, runes, scrying mirrors or even simply just actions that prepare the third eye for more insightful access.

Let's make sure we have a clear understanding of the difference between divination and magick before we go any further. Magick you've already learnt is the art of bringing about change by using the natural energies of the universe in a prepared and intended manner. Divination of itself doesn't bring about any change whatsoever and instead is just the ability to see hidden things or sense otherwise hidden energies. That's not to say that as a result of seeing something through divination that you don't then do something to bring about a change or to heed the warning of an event that divination might provide, but the divination itself was not the agent that brought about that change.

Divination Revealed

So what sorts of divination are there? The answer to that incorporates a huge list of tools and abilities, some unique to the practitioner, some more generic in nature. The list includes things as common and as well known as astrology and as vague and obscure as padomancy. Given this is an Outer Court training program, we'll just focus on the primary forms of divination here so you can then explore further and begin to find your own divination synergies. Later on in the second degree within Inner Court, training in divination and magick is reinforced and extended should you wish to go that far.

Tarot

The origins of tarot, like many of the esoteric arts has long since been lost but there is evidence of some Jewish based cards being used for fortune telling in the Western world as far back as 1392. Modern tarot decks however often are derivatives of the Ryder Waite deck which was designed by Arthur Edward Waite with the artwork done by Pamela Colman Smith and it was published by

Ryder. This deck, like most other modern decks has 78 cards that form the major and minor arcarna. Each card has a specific meaning and when the deck is laid out in a specific spread, the relationship between the meanings of each

card becomes even more significant. For example if one card refers to an imminent change, the card next to it might indicate what sort of change is in the wind and the location of the change card within the spread might indicate the expected timeframe.

While the Ryder Waite deck still probably remains the beginners' deck of choice, it's important to remember that the name of the card in the major arcana is not necessarily a reflection of the expected outcome. For example the death card certainly does not mean death and the Hermit card doesn't mean you're going to be a lonely old person living in a cave up in the Tibetan mountains! The names of the cards refer to a symbolic language and to the archetypes of meanings significant with the card itself and the placement within the spread. Many practitioners also use the inherent card meanings along with their own internal talents and blend the two together to get an even deeper reading result.

There are now a vast array of tarot decks available to suit the creative bent and needs of almost every practitioner. My favourite is the Witches Tarot which substitutes the names of some of the original cards for Wiccan names and therefore is more suitable for readings in a Witchcraft context.

However, there are tonnes of choices. When choosing a deck, always try and sense the cards as well as look at their aesthetic qualities. A tarot deck should speak to you and while learning its secrets takes time, if it's right for you, you should know it immediately.

Research

Tarot is one the most well known forms of divination and certainly one you should be at least familiar with if you eventually want to take your Craft studies further. Take some time now to research the different tarot decks available, not necessarily to decide which deck to buy, but more as a means of deciding what style of deck suits your personal needs. Some sites to try are;

http://www.aeclectic.net/tarot/cards/reviews.shtml
http://www.tarotpassages.com/deckrev.html
http://www.angelfire.com/la2/tarotdeevah/tarot/tarot.html

Runes

Yet another very popular form of divination for Wiccans and Witches alike are the runes. While there are different forms of runes, born from slightly different runic alphabets such as the Germanic, Anglo-Saxon and Norse, essentially they're blocks of wood, crystal or stone, each marked with a particular letter of the runic alphabet that are drawn from a bag to develop a reading of clarification. Unlike tarot which can be used to predict the future, runes are cast more to clarify a current situation so that the reader can then work on ways to improve or change it for the better.

The origins of the runes, like that of tarot are somewhat vague but there are considerable blocks of evidence across Europe that indicate the use of a mystery alphabet, often associated with different tree species, that was used as both a means of general communication between tribes but also as a method of divination. Many sites of spiritual connection are dotted with carved stones showing runic symbols and antiquities have been located with runes engraved on them.

There are usually 24 runes in each set (although this can differ slightly with different alphabets) and they're kept within a pouch. The reader decides on a particular question they need answering or focuses on a situation at hand. Then one by one they draw a rune from the pouch and they lay it out in a specific pattern. Each rune is used as an oracle to bring clarification and insight to the situation being examined and the position of each rune can alter its meaning so that each reading will be different depending on the runes drawn out and the layout used.

Like tarot, learning to use runes is a lengthy affair and one that requires dedication and commitment. It's not something you can pick up within a few days and in fact is akin to learning a whole new alphabet and related correspondences. Once learnt though, the runic symbols can be applied to your tools, you can recreate your name in runes and you can even write rituals in runes.

Read
The runes are a fascinating topic worthy of further study especially if you want to take your Wiccan study further in the future. As a precursor I'd suggest you spend some time reading through the information on these sites; http://www.sunnyway.com/runes/
http://www.uponreflection.co.uk/runes/index.htm
http://www.rune-scripts.arollo.com/

Astrology

This form of divination, like the others, has been around for thousands of years and its practitioners can provide evidence of its use in various texts, grimoires and materials across several different continents. It's certainly one of the popular forms of commercially available and acceptable divination in the Western world and many people will check out their stars in the local newspaper daily, even if they don't actually believe what the astrologer says!

Astrology is the process of defining a person's personality attributes, strengths and weaknesses by the correlation of the sun, moon and planets at the time and place of their birth. With a birth or natal chart in place, the expert astrologer can then predict planetary trends applicable to everyone but these can be aligned to the personal attributes of the individual so that a better prediction of their responses to those trends might be ascertained.

In other words, each planet has a particular set of correspondences that when lined up with Earth can influence meta energies to bring about general outcomes for everyone. But because most people were born at a different time and place, their personality, as it corresponds with their birth chart, will help define how they cope with those meta trends. So while Mars in a certain aspect might influence a considerable increase in action and activity across the planet Earth, one person whose star sign indicates they're a positive person with a clear intent to better themselves might use that Mars energy to increase their wealth, while another whose star sign shows them to be less decisive might completely miss the opportunities Mars was presenting them with. The underpinning Mars energy was the same for everyone but the birth chart of the individual defined how they coped and responded to that meta energy.

Like tarot and the runes, becoming an expert astrologer can take years and the study to do so is intense and complex. Having a birth or natal chart completed for yourself is one way to get a clearer understanding of who you are so that you're better prepared to deal with emerging situations. You can get a basic natal chart online and while this is fun, it's very basic.

Activity

Having your birth chart done can be expensive but a synoptic version can be done free and quickly online. Take a few moments now to go to the site indicated below and input your own personal data to get your free birth chart. This URL provided is probably the best available online because it comes minus the advertising and it's quick, simple and comprehensive.
http://www.alabe.com/freechart/

Numerology

This quite popular form of divination was once regarded as an essential component of scientific mathematics several hundred years ago. It ascribes certain characteristics to numbers and correlates them with physical objects, environmental factors, personality traits and resultant actions.

This skill is not quite as difficult to learn as tarot, runes and astrology and is often a quick way to come up with clarification about a particular topic when time is limited and you don't have skills in more complex divination methodologies.

Like astrology, you can describe your personality trends but this time you do it through the addition of numerical digits assigned to the letters of the alphabet that correspond with your name or even your date of birth. Using your birth name as an example, you assign numbers to your name (usually your full name), add them up and calculate your final birth number and then read what that says about your personality type. There are at least two different ways to add up the alphabetically defined numbers of your name but one of the most prolific is that indicated below.

A-I	J-R	S-Z
A=1	J=10 (1)	S=19(10)(1)
B=2	K=11(2)	T=20(2)
C=3	L=12(3)	U=21(3)
D=4	M=13(4)	V=22(4)
E=5	N=14(5)	W=23(5)
F=6	O=15(6)	X=24(6)
G=7	P=16(7)	Y=25(7)
H=8	Q=17(8)	Z=26(8)
I=9	R=18(9)	

Using the table above, we can now define the numeric value of a given name. Rather than use the full name as you'd usually do, for simplicity's sake, let's just use a first name and we'll take 'Julie' as our example ;

J=10, U=21, L=12, I=9, E=5.
Now add the numbers all together like this;
1+0+2+1+1+2+9+5=21

Now add 21 together like this;
2+1=3

What you've done is to convert the letters of the alphabet to numbers then added them all up and re-added them till they eventually become a single digit. That single digit (of which there are only be nine of course) will then describe your personality strengths and weaknesses. In certain systems, you can also use the numbers 11, 22, 33 and so on. Knowing these attributes will then help you better understand who you are and help you make more appropriate decisions about events in the future.

Activity
It's your turn again now. Take your full birth name including any middle and family names and convert and reduce it to a single number. Write this number in your Learning Journal and then go to the sites indicated below to get an idea of how your birth number defines your personality;
http://www.numberquest.com/knowledge_number_meaning.php
http://www.whats-your-sign.com/spiritual-meaning-of-numbers.html

There are of course a myriad of ways to use numerology and to combine that with astrology or indeed any other form of self divination. Your lifepath number for instance is the number derived from your full birth date and indicates other factors specific to you. When coupled with your destiny number (the number derived from your name) and applied to complimentary divination methods, you can get a much more holistic appreciation of who you are and how you're likely to approach certain issues. The Chinese also have a very well regarded version of numerology which they use extensively in conjunction with the Chinese calendar of animal and elemental years.

Scrying
This very simple form of divination is one synonymous with Witches the world over. Gazing into crystal balls, black mirrors, pools of water and crystals has been a popular method for defining future events for hundreds of years, not just in Europe but in Eastern countries as well.

While many people think that the tool used holds the visions of the future, the fact is that the practitioner actually holds the visions or messages and the tool just turns them into a more tangible and observable action. In other words, the practitioner already possesses the visions she may see in the crystal ball but the ball enables her to focus and zero in on that vision to make it clearer and more accessible.

Scrying can be used in a number of different ways using a plethora of techniques. It can be used to clarify an issue, to solve a problem, to predict a future event, to make meaning out of a past event, to explain a dream or even to describe the strengths and

weaknesses of a particular person. Different mediums can bring up different answers or at least focus on different aspects of the same answer. A tea leaf reading for instance might bring up a more concrete answer than perhaps a crystal reading. Different mediums are often used to approach a similar issue because each medium holds a different correspondence with the natural environment and thus transmits slightly different energy. A crystal ball for instance feels quite different to a dowsing rod. So when used together, these different mediums can generate a much broader, more useful picture so that a clearer final answer can be ascertained. Some of the mediums include those already mentioned such as crystal balls, crystal chunks, black mirrors, still water and tea leaves. But there's a long list of other mediums such as the pendulum, clouds, shells, smoke signals, candle flames, oil, auras, wind and so on. The list is virtually endless, especially when you consider that the individual practitioner may develop a specific talent for reading the meaning in a tool that's notable just for him or her.

How Do I Explore Divination?

Let's get something straight here before we take this chapter further. As mentioned earlier and in the same vein as magick, divination does not identify you as a Wiccan or Witch. You don't have to do divination in order to be a Wiccan or Witch. It's not a pre-requisite to the Craft. It does help round out your esoteric skills and that's helpful so you're generally encouraged to find a form of divination that serves you best but it's not a defining attribute of a Wiccan or Witch.

With that said, anyone intending to take their study further once they become a member of an Inner Court, will be encouraged to pursue a divination form, along with magick and any other speciality that the particular coven holds as being their strength. Divination is most definitely a wonderful aid to the Craft practitioner for a number of reasons.

Being skilled in at least one area of divination helps you to better understand your own attributes, your strengths and weaknesses and therefore enables you to understand why you might respond to situations in certain ways. Armed with this knowledge you're in a much better position to be able to modify your behaviours for the better when you can clearly identify what those behaviours actually are.

If you provide a service for others in any area such as naturopathy, reiki or spiritual counselling, being a skilled practitioner in a couple of fields of divination can aid you by helping you focus and 'feel' what service speciality is best for your client or friend or family member. For example, if you're using reiki to help heal a close friend, by also being able to use tarot to focus in on any underlying issues, you might be better positioned to use your reiki sills to zero in on the right part of the body that requires targeted healing.

Having divination skills can also help you design and conduct more effective magick as well. By using divination as a clarifying oracle, you're much better placed to work out exactly what magick might be needed to resolve an issue. It becomes your preparatory method in effect

It's important to note however that not everyone can use all forms of divination. Each person will be suited to a particular form of divination. It's a bit like our individual tastes for food. One person might love broccoli and ham sandwiches while their sister or best friend can't stand either. I'm a chocoholic while I have work colleagues who can take or leave the stuff. Divination formats are the same. What works for one person may not work for another. I can read tarot almost intuitively but I can't make head nor tail of runes. Numerology makes no sense for me personally but I really love astrology and crystal work.

What's important for you is to determine the right form of scrying for you and not lose confidence if the first method doesn't work. Many years ago, my partner brought me an absolutely beautiful set of handcrafted amethyst runes thinking that I'd be able to work with them because of my Craft name and my affinity with crystals. It was one of the first divination tools I tried and I was devastated when I just couldn't connect with them. I really doubted my abilities at that point. However, I later picked up a tarot deck and within days was able to accurately connect and use them to define people, events and predict future actions.

This same disappointment might happen to you but please understand that if this does happen, it's just a message to say that your real divination methodology is just round the corner. Keep trying with different methods till you find the ones that work for you and use the learnings you got from the previous methodology to build on your skills for the next.

You may also find that even within the same divination method, certain tools work better than others. One tarot deck may have more affinity with you than another while one crystal type may resonate much more effectively with you than another.

Activity
The list of divination methods given above includes the more popular ones but there are a myriad of others including I Ching and dream interpretation to name just two. You may already be adept at one form or another, maybe without even realising it.

Take some time now to consider the different divination forms and write down in your Learning Journal the order in which you'll explore and practice with each one. Then spend the next few months playing with them in turn till you find one that works for you. Record your outcomes in your Learning Journal.

Your Seventh Visualisation

This month we keep moving deosil and go from the Fire element in the South to Water in the West. This element corresponds to emotions and is quite feminine. It's a cleansing, purifying element and one that works with the emotional relationship between action and humanity.

Remember as always to prepare as instructed in the first lesson and make sure that you're comfortable and won't be disturbed. As usual, read the energisation visualisation below first, and also remember to ground again afterwards.

Activity
Close your eyes, breathe deeply and slowly for a few seconds feeling the breath draw into your lungs and slowly back out again. Imagine a tap root growing from the base of your spine,your base chakra, downward toward the ground. It's a nice strong tap root and it slowly, gently but deliberately grows down through your chair, through the floor covering, on through the floor structure and then down toward the ground below. See your tap root forcing its way into the earth below you and remaining strong and willing. Keep it growing, further and further. Push it further still, right down into the planet, right down into the dirt, the rocks and the substrata below your feet. Your tap root is strong and it's now anchoring you safely to the Earth. You're comfortable, you're connected to the planet and you're safe.

Now ask the glorious Goddess Gaia if she would allow you to draw into your tap root some of her pure, white, clean, fresh energy. She willingly gives you this energy. She always does because it's your pure white light too. See the pure white light, the cleansing, energising light being sucked up through your tap root and coming up closer and closer toward you. Draw it up toward you. Pull the energy up towards the base of your spine.

As it comes up through the tap root and enters your body, see it begin to tumble around at the base of your torso and then begin falling down your legs towards your feet. See the energy fill your toes up and any dark patches of negative energy are washed away as you breathe out. The energy just keeps streaming up through your tap root and flooding into your legs. Your lower legs, your thighs are now flooded with pure, white, clean, fresh light. Your legs feel cleansed and revitalised.

The energy keeps coming in and now it fills your lower torso, forcing away any dark and negative patches as you breathe out. Keep drawing up the energy, lots more yet, so much more yet. Your whole tummy area is now filled with white light and you feel comfortable, rested and calm. More white light, this time tumbling up into your chest and shoulders. The pure, white, cleansing light rolls down your arms and into your hands and fingers filling them with light. Yet more light, still coming into your body and now it fills your lower and upper arms and your shoulders feel relaxed and you feel safe and calm and peaceful. The white light then reaches up into your neck and as the light fills your body, it pushes any negative patches of old, faded, worn out, dirty energy away with each breath. Your head is filling with white light and so is your face and now, as you scan your body, you see all the parts of it are filled to the brim with wonderful, refreshing, rejuvenating, pure white energy. You feel alive, you feel calm, you feel peaceful and happy. Check your body for any last remaining patches of old, dark energy you don't need and breathe them away.

Spend a few moments luxuriating in the bliss of being bathed in pure, clean energy from the Goddess. Now draw up yet more pure, clean, white light and now see that extra energy flowing through from within your body, through the pores of your skin and gradually out into the air immediately around you. From head to toe, front and back the energy is wisping its way through your skin and into your aura. Let the wonderful clean and fresh, white light filter into it cleaning out any muddy, dirty patches of old, worn out energies. See the white light wisping through the pores of your skin and penetrating and washing clean your aura. Breathe away any dark patches of negativity from your aura, make it clean and fresh and bright and calm and peaceful.

As you sit basking in the purity of the purest of the universe's energy, imagine in front of you the door you created and should now be familiar with. Slowly and gently, open your door and step through. You are now in the presence of the Water element, Salamanders and water spirits and nymphs. Just before you is a quiet, peaceful lake and its tiny waves lap gently onto the ground in front of your feet. Take your shoes off and step lightly into the caressing waves of warm water. Feel the water envelop your feet and ripple over your skin. How does the water feel as it gently touches your feet?

Step further into the water until you're in the lake up to your waist. You're safe and the water is calm and relaxing. Lay back and let the water take your weight. You float effortlessly within the supporting liquid and it holds you safe and warm. Feel how the water touches your body all over, soothing it, holding it up, refreshing it.

Stand back up again in the lake so that the water reaches your waist. The waves begin to get a little taller and instead of lapping gently against you, they begin to buffet and pull at your clothes. You feel the strength of the current rip at your legs and tear at your skin. You remain safe always but as the waves begin to push up against your chest and the water level rises and falls dramatically with the waves, you can sense and feel the awesome power and strength of the torrential waters around you. Feel the rain as it begins to pound on your skin, cast down upon you like spears of water, feel the power of the current around your body. How does the water feel now? Can you feel its anger and overpowering will? Can you feel the rain stinging your face and beating against your body?

The rain slows, the waves begin to recede and gradually the torrential currents and rips die back. The lake begins to soothe itself and calms and once again you feel the gentle rhythm of the tiny laps of water as they caress your body. You notice in front of you a presence; you sense and feel someone with you. It's the element of Water and is perhaps a salamander or the water nymph. What does it look like or is it just a presence that you cannot see and can only feel like the gentle lapping of the waves?

Take a moment to ask the Water element a question. What do you need to know about this element and power of Water? What would you like to learn to take away with you? Listen to the answers and feel your connection with this wonderful being grow and deepen.

The Water spirit lets you know that it has given you the knowledge and understanding that you seek and so you offer your thanks and respect. Now turn back to your door and gently walk through and close it behind you. You are back where you were, in the now, in the here. Slowly bring your attention back to the room you're in and gradually open your eyes.

Ground yourself by bending or kneeling down on the ground, preferably outside on the grass or dirt, and place the palms of your hands flat on the ground. See the excess energy you drew up flowing smoothly back into the ground below you through your open palms.

Your Homework This Month

As you head towards the end of your Outer Court learning journey, your task is to continue to consolidate your theory with practical exercises and 'doing' Wicca. For the next month ahead;

- Spend this month practicing the first form of divination you prioritised in your Learning Journal. Explore how your chosen method works and get to know it well.
- Keep practicing the energisation visualisation including the aura cleansing and the Water Elemental, finishing off by grounding. Write the results in your Learning Journal.
- Write regularly in your diary and include any significant dreams you had, any meditations that offered you insights and look at what's happening around you in nature and write that down too.

The Eighth Lesson
Living as a Wiccan

*W*ell, it's been an interesting journey this last seven months hasn't it? With all you know now, and with all the activities and practice you've put in, you should now be that much closer to being a Wiccan, a Witch and/or a Pagan as opposed to simply knowing about Wicca, Witchcraft and Paganism. Your journey hereafter includes making choices about whether this is a philosophy, religion and life practice that you want to commit to. To help you do that, by the end of this last lesson you should be able to;

- More clearly explain what a commitment to Wicca and Witchcraft means,
- Create and conduct your own self dedication ritual,
- Discuss the fundamentals of initiation and be better placed to decide if that's something you want to commit to,
- Have a program of further reading,
- Explore the option of visits to other covens for festivals if you feel the need,
- Consider additional study where you feel this is a path you'd like to follow.

What does living as a Wiccan Mean?

This is a good question for you to seriously contemplate at this point because while it may seem simple, it's actually not. A decision to commit to a life of spiritual and religious consideration is one that takes some deep thought, lots of meditation and a whole pile of dedication. In other words, like marriage where you commit yourself to another person, this is not a decision to take lightly or without due thought.

I say this because far too many people jump blindly into dedication or initiation simply because it's fashionable, or because their best friend did it or worse still because it will upset Mum and Dad or the neighbours or whatever. This is a serious decision requiring serious contemplation. You wouldn't marry someone just because it was fun (or you shouldn't anyway) and neither should you dedicate yourself to the Craft because it sounds fun. Let's think through then why you would want to dedicate yourself to a spiritual life of Wicca and a practical life of Witchcraft.

Being Wiccan, being a Witch is far more of a life choice than simply knowing about it and dabbling at the edges. As a dedicated practitioner, you join a global community that identifies itself with certain life philosophies and approaches largely focusing on respect and love for deity, for each other and for our planet. You have a set of ethical principles to live your life by that can help you identify what behaviours, language and thoughts are helpful to you, and the world around you and what the repercussions are when you either follow or deny those principles. You have the opportunity to be the master and architect of your own life and to design both who you are and what you do. Your magickal skills open the door to a world that you don't just contribute to, but that you're actively involved in the outcome of.

What it doesn't mean necessarily is that you should run around in black gothic clothing, pretending to shock people with your 'secret' powers and abilities. It doesn't mean you can turn the ex into a frog and it doesn't mean you eat babies and sacrifice goats under a full moon while dancing naked in the forest. (That would be funny if it wasn't still a popular misconception!) Wicca and Witchcraft are not secret cults or secret societies that you can use as a badge of honour or a title you can use when it suits you. Serious practitioners get a little peeved when newcomers suddenly become 'media Witches' and espouse to the world that now they're initiated, they know the secrets of the esoteric world and can show everyone else how clever they are. Similarly, they get just as annoyed when newcomers profess to have all the knowledge and therefore start teaching before they've even cut their teeth on a few years of good practice.

At this stage, you've learnt about Wicca and Witchcraft and you've begun your practice as a Wiccan or Witch but becoming a well grounded, skilled practitioner takes years of dedication and commitment. And that's what this question is really asking. How much dedication and commitment are you willing to give this new life? If it's just for show or just for shock or just for mild curiosity, admit that right now you shouldn't dedicate. If instead you're prepared to spend years practicing, years trying and years learning, then by all means dedicate yourself.

Self Dedication

Ok, now that I've got back down from the soapbox about taking the decision to dedicate yourself seriously, let's assume at this point that it's something you want to do and talk through how you can do that. The first thing to talk through and revisit is this continuing debate within the Wiccan community about initiation versus dedication and what you can and can't do yourself. I'm going to spend some time talking through initiation in the next section so for now, let's focus on dedication.

A Wiccan dedication is, by its very nature, an event and resultant lifelong process that clearly speaks to the Divine, to the world around you and to your own being that says you're prepared to, and committed to, dedicate your life and its purpose to honouring the Lord and Lady, yourself, others and the world around you. It's your public (public before the Divine even if done alone) declaration that you are making a choice to live your life in respect and according to the principles and framework that are Wiccan by nature and practice. You're openly declaring and promising that you are now a Wiccan and a Witch. So why do some traditions say you can't self dedicate?

Well the issue is around training and the validity of dedication if you've not been trained appropriately. To be fair, there's a degree of common sense to the argument that says if you've not been trained properly then you can't legitimately self dedicate because you may have no idea, or the wrong idea, and so you don't really know what you're dedicating yourself to. This is really important and valid, especially when you think through exactly what you are dedicating yourself to.

If for example I were advocating that you dedicate yourself as a Gardnerian or Alexandrian having read this book, the suggestion would in fact be invalid. This is not a Gardnerian or Alexandrian training program and that's been stated clearly and repeatedly throughout this work. So, when you dedicate yourself, based on this material, you dedicate yourself to the Inclusive tradition, and more precisely to your own tradition, not to the more strict oath bound traditions. You can't call yourself an Alexandrian after dedicating yourself to the principles in this program and this tradition but you can still call yourself a Wiccan and a Witch and of course an Inclusive Wiccan and Witch because the Inclusive tradition is absolutely Wiccan, it's just not an oath bound one.

So the argument from the fundamentalists that says you can never self dedicate is indeed true of people who want to self dedicate to traditions without undertaking the required coven based training within an oath bound tradition. However, for traditions like Inclusive, also like Universal Eclectic Wicca and other more progressive and flexible traditions, you can self dedicate and indeed will be encouraged to do so where that fits with your life choices. From our perspective, we argue that you have every right to dedicate yourself to your tradition where you've received appropriate, effective and ethical training (as this program is recognised as) and where you are ready for the responsibility and commitment that dedication entails. So with that said, I'd encourage you to self dedicate after considerable thought and contemplation on the brevity and importance of your life choice.

Research

Before you move forward to read the self dedication ritual offered below, spend some time looking through the internet and various books at the self dedication rituals available. As you read them, think about what the common themes are and what seems familiar across the different dedication rituals.

As a preliminary opening to this self dedication rite, I want to raise two points. The first is that a dedication ritual can be conducted within a coven setting or for a single person working alone. Where it's conducted within a coven, usually everyone is involved in the ritual as a sort of welcoming committee, very much like the Christian christening of a baby as it's welcomed into its Christian family. The role of the dedication in that sense is to welcome the newcomer into the family of that coven as well as allowing the seeker to publically declare their commitment to the Wiccan path before the Divine and before their Wiccan family. The coven is very much a spiritual family whose task is to nurture each other and to create an environment of mutual support and shared respect and honour of the Divine. However, the dedication rite I've suggested below is more apt for a solitary practitioner largely because an existing coven will probably already have a dedication ritual recorded within its coven Book of Shadows. That dedication rite, often a precursor to initiation, can be modified to meet your personal requirements but within the coven setting, will often include elements specific to that group.

The second point is that a self dedication should really be designed by the dedicant themselves. It's a personal, often very private affair and when done in this manner, is intimate and extremely moving. Because it's so personal, many practitioners want to design their own rite and this could be as simple as sitting before a rising sun, contemplating the birth of your new life. Maybe it's meditating at the full moon on the meaning of your dedication. Alternatively, you might want something more elaborate or more ceremonial to show the depth of your commitment and that's Ok too. This is your self dedication and it has to meet your needs.

What I'm saying here is that the rite offered below is by no means the prescribed self dedication rite for the Inclusive tradition. It's a guide only and you can modify it to suit your needs or throw it out all together and design something that means something more relevant and personal to you.

Self Dedication Ritual
Required
The normal circle casting equipment.

Prior to the Ritual
Have all the usual materials for a normal circle ready and prepare the circle area according the normal practices.

Cleanse yourself in a stream or the sea by silently basking in the glory that is a natural water source. If this isn't possible (and for many people it won't be) bathe yourself instead in a salted bath. As a last resort shower yourself. As you feel the water lapping over your body and caressing your skin, rid your mind of mundane tasks and worries. See any negativity wash away with the waves or down the drain. Soothe your racing brain by doing the energisation visualisation just to the point of cleansing your aura. Feel your mind open to other consciousness planes. *Feel* the experience of the cleansing bath, don't think it.

When you've done that, it's very helpful to spend some time outside in the open connecting with nature and feeling yourself meld into the environment around you. Try and choose a quiet place amongst trees, or perhaps the beach or somewhere that feels right for you and where you won't be disturbed. Spend some time meditating on your decision. Then when you're ready cast your circle as normal.

Ritual Opening
With your circle cast, you're ready to declare your intention. Your first task is to introduce yourself to the Lord and Lady so you can use your chosen Craft name or your birth name here. Sitting in the centre of the circle facing East you open by saying; "Blessed Lady, mother of Earth, Blessed Lord, Father of the Heavens, I ask that you honour me this day/night with your presence. Here before you I offer myself, (say your Craft or birth name here) in love, in respect and with humility."

Stand and walk toward the East quarter. Raise your arms out wide and introduce yourself to the elementals of the East quarter saying; "To the sacred element of Air, that presides over and governs the East, I offer myself, (say your Craft or birth name here) in love, in respect and with humility."

Bow to the East elementals then walk to the South quarter. Raise your arms out wide and introduce yourself to the elementals of the South quarter saying; "To the sacred element of Fire, that presides over and governs the South, I offer myself, (say your Craft or birth name here) in love, in respect and with humility."

Bow to the South elementals then walk to the West quarter. Raise your arms out wide and introduce yourself to the elementals of the West quarter saying; "To the sacred element of Water, that presides over and governs the West, I offer myself, (say your Craft or birth name here) in love, in respect and with humility."

Bow to the West elementals then walk to the North quarter. Raise your arms out wide and introduce yourself to the elementals of the North quarter saying; "To the sacred element of Earth, that presides over and governs the North, I offer myself, (say your Craft or birth name here) in love, in respect and with humility."

Bow to the North elementals then return to sitting in the centre of the circle. Spend some time in meditation considering your commitment and what your promise means.

When you're ready, it's time to make your promise before the Lord and Lady. This is the essence or crux of your self dedication and it should be heartfelt and said in earnest.

"Blessed Lord and Lady, Mother and Father, my sacred God and Goddess, before you now I pledge my dedication and devotion. I promise to walk the Wiccan path from this day forward, to honour you in all I say and do and to grow stronger in my love and respect for you and the world that lives around me. To you I dedicate myself this day/night. May I always walk your path. So mote it be."

Have the cakes and ale at this time and as you do so, make a toast to the Lord and Lady and thank them for attending and hearing your dedication to them. Make sure you leave an offering of both some cake and some ale and then close the circle again.

Activity
Scott Cunningham has a wonderful self dedication rite in his book "Wicca: A Guide for the Solitary Practitioner". Please read this ritual and compare it to some of the other suggested self dedication rites in other books and on the internet.

With all this information to hand, design your own self dedication ritual and write it in your Learning Journal.

The Purpose and Role of Initiation

Dedication as we've determined is your public declaration of commitment to the principles and practices of Wicca and it's something that the Inclusive tradition encourages and supports where the student is ready and committed. So what's the difference between that and initiation?

There are some fundamental differences between these two rituals and ones that whether we like it or not have ramifications for whether they can or can't be conducted by a solitary practitioner. Let's get the technical aspects out of the way first given that we did discuss these briefly earlier on in this program. Initiation is what's called a mystery rite by the anthropologists which means that it contains an element of mystery or a degree of the unknown for the person undertaking the ritual. While virtually anyone going through an initiation will have a basic idea of what they're about to do, for it to be absolutely successful, there will be large portions of it that they won't know about and won't have had explained to them. This is because for a mystery rite to have the effect that it can have, including the personal gnosis that comes with initiation, there has to be an element of surprise and of course mystery.

As a mystery rite, the initiation has three phases, each of which can be different lengths depending on the tradition and indeed the coven within that tradition. The first stage is the preparation stage where the student undertakes a regime of gearing up toward the actual event and in a process of stripping away the layers that make up who they are. This isn't as scary as it sounds but in order for the Divine to make a direct connection with the initiate, the layers that cover up that person need to be stripped away as much as possible. These layers are the social persona we adopt when we interact with the world around us. So in this process, which often takes up to a week prior to the event, the initiate might be required to eat certain foods on certain days, to contemplate what their life has meant to date, to consider what they think their life should actually mean and to strip away any hierarchical identifiers that label them as parent, manager, university educated, wealthy or indeed any other layer that's a social label and not in fact who they actually are.

One of the last parts of this stage is to have their clothing removed (where the coven does this ritual skyclad) because clothing is one of those social labels that can give you a 'station' in life. Someone well dressed might be seen as being more educated, wealthier or even better than someone wearing ill fitting or dirty clothing. Someone wearing a particular style of clothing might be looked down on by someone else wearing some other type of clothing. We all do it. We all judge people by the way they look, by the clothes they wear, by the quality and amount of jewellery or accessories they have, by the car they drive, by where they live, by the education level they have. These are all labels that raise us up or drop us down in the hierarchy of social importance. Before you go into a mystery rite and connect with the Gods and Goddesses, these labels have to be stripped away.

Just before moving into the second stage of the ritual, the initiate is subjected to a challenge which might be a simple or even difficult activity depending on the coven, the tradition and the degree level to which they are being initiated. This challenge serves to strip away the very last of the layers and prepares the person's sense of nervousness and anticipation for the rite ahead. This is the stage where any explanation they were given of the ritual stops. From here on in, they know nothing so this is truly the point at which the trepidation and nervousness starts. Most people are a little nervous where they're expected to do something they know nothing about. Becoming a parent for the first time fills people with both joy but also trepidation sometimes. Speaking before an audience if you've never done it before can invoke fear. The mystery rite invokes that same level of fear partly because the initiate is entering the unknown from this point forward, as indeed they should for it to have the effect it was designed to.

The next stage happens within the rite itself and traditionally across most societies and religions, this part of the rite is where the initiate is introduced to deity. As part of this introduction, the initiate is often given the opportunity to learn something from deity that will be a fundamental piece of information or philosophy that will give them purpose in their life going forward. So it's a significant piece of information or insight they didn't have before. It might be, given the tradition, their new Craft name or a secret name known only to the initiate and the Gods. It might be a personal insight or the answer to a long held question or it may be simply a sense of knowing that their initiation is perfect for them at this time of their life.

The important factor here is that deity would not be able to give this information or insight unless the public and social layers of that person had been stripped away first. So the information is direct, straight to the heart and soul, and profound. During meditation, people will often receive information and messages from other planes and from the Lord and Lady and this is valid and important. However, because the initiate is stripped of any social labelling, they're in fact absolutely bare before the Divine so the Lord and Lady can speak straight to the initiate and not have the message clouded by cognition and rationality and common sense. This information and insight then is heartfelt, not head felt.

The third and final stage of the mystery rite is the return to the physical, social, hierarchical built world as a new person, with a new set of social labels and with new insight and strength. The anthropologists determine this stage as the emergence of a new person, with a new station in life and with a new set of principles and ideals that identify them to the world in a new way. What this means for the Wiccan initiation is that the person undertaking the rite entered the process as a parent, manager, dog owner, fireman, Volvo driver or whatever and came out the other side as a Wiccan. This is their new life label in effect and helps them identify with the

Wiccan community and with the expectations and behaviour set that is Wicca.

These three stages are the classic anthropological description of initiation rites worldwide, regardless of the society or belief framework in which it takes place. One of the most important factors in that is the secrecy that surrounds the stages, and in particular stage two. It's the stripping away of the labels that have identified who the person is and the fear and anticipation, coupled with, and as a result of, not knowing what's about to happen that raises the initiate's sense of connection with deity and so enables them to better receive the insights that come during stage two. So if the person knows everything that's about to happen to them and has the script of the ritual process, then they have less fear and this reduces their ability to connect with deity. Their initiation rite is less powerful, less moving and has less impact. The mystery is therefore a deliberate measure to give them a much greater ritual effect and provide them with a much more powerful sense of occasion.

It's for that reason that you won't find an initiation ritual inside this program. This tradition believes that for initiation to work the way it was intended, the initiate should enter into it without knowing what's about to happen. Having said that, just a few minutes research on the internet and in many books will give you a quite detailed description of an initiation, in many cases even an oath bound initiation sadly.

But all isn't lost. You can be initiated into this tradition in two ways if this is something you absolutely want to do. The first is that you can ask someone already in the tradition to initiate you. This might be your tutor or a local Inclusive coven where that's geographically available for you. The person you ask, if not your tutor, will quite rightly want to ask you a number of questions including how you trained and who your tutor was. They will probably want to talk with your tutor to get evidence that you did in fact go through the training program and got some effective learning from it. They'll ask these questions because there's generally a belief amongst Wiccans that the person who initiates another is forever karmically linked with that initiate. So the actions of that initiate later on will reflect on, and have repercussions for, the person who initiated them. This means your initiator will probably want to make sure they're doing the right thing for both you and themselves.

The second option is to ask a friend or trusted person to initiate you using a process that's Inclusive friendly but that meets your needs. They way this can happen is that you ask that person to be your initiator, you refer them to us and after ascertaining that they are suitable to initiate you, we can work with them to provide a ritual that meets the requirements of the Inclusive tradition, meets your needs but does so without you knowing the full details. This is sometimes a complex process but in order for it to be meaningful and not reduced to simply a tick and flick exercise with no validity, the more the parties work together to get the best result, the better the outcome for you.

Research
Now that you understand the purpose of initiation, please take a good measure of time researching how other traditions do their initiations. What traditions do oath bound initiations? Which ones don't? Identify the main stages and components of initiation rituals published on the internet and in books. Write what you find in your Learning Journal.

Expanding Your Reading

After all these months, my hope is that you would already have supplemented this book with additional reading from a variety of sources. Making a commitment to a Wiccan and Craft life should be taken only after you've consulted a number of different texts and thus a number of different opinions.

Regardless of your achieved reading so far, I'd very much recommend you read the books in the List of References at the back of this book. The more you read, the more you'll be able to make decisions about what works for you and what doesn't work. The books on that list are the most valuable I've found to date in terms of ethical, unbiased information aimed at providing the student with basic facts and ideas to develop their own practice.

You'll probably notice that the list doesn't contain some of the popular books available and there's a very good reason for that. While I'd encourage you to read everything you can, you also need to do so using your common sense. There are a number of commercially available books that are extremely popular, a portion of those are rather commercial in approach and less concerned with accuracy and ethical, appropriate information provision than they are about making money for the publishing company and the author. I don't have any problem with an author and publishing house being paid for their efforts and talents but I do draw the line at works that are blatantly aimed at a market that's not really able to discern between quality and commerciality yet. So if I've not included a book on this list that you think should be there, I encourage you to read it anyway but balance it against materials that are probably a little more respected by the very community that you're aiming to be part of.

Working With Covens

Many Wiccans and Witches choose to work alone either before or after initiation for a huge variety of reasons and that's quite legitimate. But, what if you work alone at home yet now and again want to attend the Sabbat of a local coven? Can you do that and if so how?

Just like a party, a wedding or any other celebration of people you don't know, it would be pretty bad form if you gate crashed, even if you really loved weddings or birthday parties, or even if you did actually know someone there. The same is true of the Sabbats held by covens. Many covens hold what's called 'open' festivals or Sabbats where local Pagan friendly people are welcome to attend either through invitation or because they know someone in the coven already.

If you want to strike up a relationship with a coven that holds open festivals but not actually become a member of the group, then you need to do your homework and be up front with the coven leadership about your aims. Some covens simply won't allow this unless you're committed to their tradition or their way of doing things. Other covens will welcome you with open arms but will want to know a little about you first, maybe meet you before a festival to make sure you fit with them and they with you. The final decision on attendance at a festival by an outsider belongs to the coven leadership so you need to be on your best behaviour and make a good impression or they'll never invite you. Just like that wedding or party invite, you don't get one unless the wedding or party organiser thinks you'll fit in and should be there.

So how do you find a coven that might let you attend their festivals? This is where your homework comes in again. Check out local web sites, Pagan supply shops and the local Pagan related organisations to see what covens are in your area. Witchvox is a really good start at www.witchvox.com. They're a great resource for locating covens and groups in your area no matter where you are in the world.

Activity
Go to www.witchvox.com and see if you can locate any covens close by to where you live. You may not want to do the occasional work with a coven yet but it's handy to know if there are any around ready for if you change your mind. Write any potential contacts down in your Learning Journal.
Look around your local metaphysical shops and see if there are any contacts you can find there too.

When you do approach a coven to ask if you could occasionally participate in festivals with them, make sure you know what style or tradition of Wicca you're akin to. Assuming you want to dedicate or even initiate within the Inclusive tradition, then you'll have a tradition name to offer and from this program, you'll have a description of the eclectic approach that fits you.

As an Inclusive Wiccan, there's no point approaching a fundamental Gardnerian coven because their style of Wicca doesn't equate to the Inclusive style and they simply won't appreciate your attendance. If you want to venture into other styles, please do so but make sure you're always able to articulate what you're doing so that your hosts can make an informed decision about your fit with them. For example, if your preference is for an eclectic Egyptian sympathetic style, then don't approach a Dianic group. Similarly, if the group you approach is Asatru and you love the Wittan tradition, then again you're just not going to fit. Make sure you can explain what you want, what you feel is important and what style of Wicca appeals to you so that when asked (and you will be!) you can be clear, articulate and up front.

Your next step is to simply to ask. Email, or telephone the coven contact if a number is provided, and politely ask if you would be able to attend any open festivals the coven might hold in the future. Explain that you prefer solitary work and why and talk through how you'd like some community feel to your practice on occasions. The coven leadership will probably ask to meet you first, probably over a cuppa in a public place somewhere before they offer you an invite. If you can offer a reference from a past Wiccan teacher, including your Inclusive tutor, or a local practicing Wiccan the coven leadership might know of, they may be a little more accommodating to your request especially if that reference is someone they respect. Be prepared for questions and to be 'on probation' for a few months. Wiccans are notorious for being a little hesitant to allow outsiders into the fold, particularly from a tradition they're not familiar with and that's not necessarily because they think you're a nasty kind of person but because they've heard it all before from people who declare they want to be a part of something and who then never turn up!

Finally, when you do get an invitation, do two things. Accept or respectfully decline giving a reason why you can't attend and secondly, be polite when you get there. A coven leader takes a risk inviting a new person to a festival because they never really know how things will pan out so please respect their trust. If you can't attend, let them know in good time and explain why. Ask if you could attend the next festival instead.

Before you do attend, make sure you've asked beforehand if you need to bring anything with you. Most festival attendees will bring a plate of food to share and they might also be required to bring items for the ritual as well. If you're requested to contribute with something like this, please do. Coven leaders usually don't charge to teach and they often cover most of the ritual and coven costs themselves out of pure dedication so blatant freeloaders won't be appreciated for too long. Check also if robes are required or if the ritual will be done in street clothing.

Finally, when you get there, it's a case of 'When in Rome...' Show respect for the ritual, for those present and follow instructions. Unless the ritual involves something that makes you feel particularly uncomfortable or is simply immoral or illegal, it's good manners to 'follow the leader' and do what everyone else does. If all that goes according to plan, then hopefully they'll invite you back again and you'll have started a warm and friendly relationship of Wiccan community support.

There's one other option open to you and that's to start your own coven or study group. The Inclusive tradition encourages people to grow their own covens when they've received enough training and if they feel ready and able. To be honest, it's a huge undertaking and takes a considerable amount of time and effort but the rewards are often worth it. I'd suggest waiting to do this till you've got at least a second degree under your belt at which point the Inclusive tradition offers a range of support options for new coven leaders.

Where To From Here – Second Degree

Well, you've just about finished your first degree journey and after this month's homework, you can pretty much title yourself a first degree Inclusive Wiccan and Witch. Congratulations! You have even more choices now around the options for further study or whether to just enjoy what you've learnt for a while.

If you decide to self dedicate or choose to undertake initiation through the methods described earlier, then you're able to become an Inner Court member of the coven you've trained with and been initiated into, which of course will need to be an Inclusive associated coven, or indeed through Oak and Mistletoe if you went through the Toward First Degree program that this book is the text for.

If you choose to move into the next stage, that of Toward Second Degree either now or sometime in the future, then you'll need to consider that you'll be studying again for at least a year and your studies will be in greater depth. It's a very rewarding program and one that can direct you into teaching others where you choose to do that and it also serves to provide you with greater opportunities to work even more closely with the Inclusive tradition and with the people who've dedicated themselves to a Wiccan and Craft life.

I would very much encourage you now to make or buy your Book of Shadows. After this quite intense first degree program, you're more than ready to begin your own journey, supported by Oak and Mistletoe of course but your journey none the less. The best way to record that journey is within the pages of your very own Book of Shadows that will serve as your record and your own sacred text.

The last message I would leave you with is this. Welcome to the wonderful, but often controversial, world of Wicca and Witchcraft. Know always that your contribution to that world is as valid, as important, as crucial and as precious as anybody else's. Know as well that as a Wiccan and a Witch, you are the master of your own life and future and that this comes with responsibilities as well as challenges, joys and wisdom. I am honoured that you chose Oak and Mistletoe as the venue for your learning and I hope that this book will serve as the platform from which you'll enjoy a life filled with laughter, happiness, peace and love.

Your Eighth Visualisation

This is the last month of the Outer Court training program and as we move further deosil from West and Water, we finish now with Earth in the North. This element is the ultimate feminine correspondence and one associated with home, with fertility and with the absolute purity of Gaia.

Remember to prepare as instructed in the first lesson and make sure that you're comfortable and won't be disturbed. As usual, first read the energisation visualisation and also remember to ground again afterwards.

Activity
Close your eyes, breathe deeply and slowly for a few seconds feeling the breath draw into your lungs and slowly back out again. Imagine a tap root growing from the base of your spine,your base chakra, downward toward the ground. It's a nice strong tap root and it slowly, gently but deliberately grows down through your chair, through the floor covering, on through the floor structure and then down toward the ground below. See your tap root forcing its way into the earth below you and remaining strong and willing. Keep it growing, further and further. Push it further still, right down into the planet, right down into the dirt, the rocks and the substrata below your feet. Your tap root is strong and it's now anchoring you safely

to the Earth. You're comfortable, you're connected to the planet and you're safe.

Now ask the glorious Goddess Gaia if she would allow you to draw into your tap root some of her pure, white, clean, fresh energy. She willingly gives you this energy. She always does because it's your pure white light too. See the pure white light, the cleansing, energising light being sucked up through your tap root and coming up closer and closer toward you. Draw it up toward you. Pull the energy up towards the base of your spine.

As it comes up through the tap root and enters your body, see it begin to tumble around at the base of your torso and then begin falling down your legs towards your feet. See the energy fill your toes up and any dark patches of negative energy are washed away as you breathe out. The energy just keeps streaming up through your tap root and flooding into your legs. Your lower legs, your thighs are now flooded with pure, white, clean, fresh light. Your legs feel cleansed and revitalised.

The energy keeps coming in and now it fills your lower torso, forcing away any dark and negative patches as you breathe out. Keep drawing up the energy, lots more yet, so much more yet. Your whole tummy area is now filled with white light and you feel comfortable, rested and calm. More white light, this time tumbling up into your chest and shoulders. The pure, white, cleansing light rolls down your arms and into your hands and fingers filling them with light. Yet more light, still coming into your body and now it fills your lower and upper arms and your shoulders feel relaxed and you feel safe and calm and peaceful. The white light then reaches up into your neck and as the light fills your body, it pushes any negative patches of old, faded, worn out, dirty energy away with each breath. Your head is filling with white light and so is your face and now, as you scan your body, you see all the parts of it are filled to the brim with wonderful, refreshing, rejuvenating, pure white energy. You feel alive, you feel calm, you feel peaceful and happy. Check your body for any last remaining patches of old, dark energy you don't need and breathe them away.

Spend a few moments luxuriating in the bliss of being bathed in pure, clean energy from the Goddess.

Now draw up yet more pure, clean, white light and now see that extra energy flowing through from within your body, through the pores of your skin and gradually out into your aura. Let the wonderful clean and fresh, white light filter into it cleaning out any muddy, dirty patches of old, worn out energies. See the white light wisping through the pores of your skin and penetrating and washing clean your aura. Breathe away any dark patches of negativity from your aura; make it clean and fresh and bright and calm and peaceful.

As you sit basking in the purity of the purest of the universe's energy, imagine in front of you your door. Slowly and gently, open it and step through. You are now in the presence of the Earth element and the home of the Earth gnomes and spirits. Before you is a cave with a curious and inviting entrance that beckons you to enter. As you walk inside the cave, you notice it's round and the walls are a wonderful colour of ancient rustic rock. The floor is smooth and the air is warm and still. The cave has a sense of comfort, like the womb of a great mother as she grows the foetus of new life within her. You hear the rhythm of a deep and tremendous heartbeat somewhere in the distance and it brings you great comfort and a sense of security. You feel safe and nurtured here. As you sit on the ground, against the wall of the cave you can feel the ancient wisdom of the planet within the rock all around you. The rock floor and walls feel smooth and worn from a long and fruitful life. Listen to her heartbeat, feel her wisdom, feel her nurturing your growth and wellbeing.

You hear a gentle rumble in the distance, coming closer, getting louder. It's a deep, growling noise and as it gets nearer, it begins to roar like a thousand trains coming your way. You feel the rock below you tremble and the walls around you shudder. You remain safe and cannot be harmed but you can feel the growing power of an earthquake deep within the planet. You hear the deafening roar of the rock as it tears against itself, ripping the womb of the great mother in two in awesome power and global rage. The cave walls sway and shudder; they slide apart, screaming at you and close back together again. The floor before you splits apart and reveals the horror of the chasm that leads to the planet's fiery core. You grip at the smooth rock to keep yourself stable as the walls and floor shake violently all around you. As you glimpse the red hot power of Gaia's heart, the split on the rock floor comes together again before you and closes off to form a scar in her surface. Rocks fall from the cave roof and walls all around you and the scream of the earthquake hurts your ears as it feels as though it comes from the very earth below you.

Just as your fear begins to engulf you, the noise begins to abate, the shaking, shuddering cave walls being to calm and the cave settles into peace once more. Listen; you can hear the rhythmic heartbeat of Mother Earth once more and the rock walls feel smooth and gentle and caressing again. You begin to feel nurtured and loved and at peace once more, safe in the womb of the great mother. You notice in front of you a presence; you sense and feel someone with you. It's the element of Earth and is perhaps a spirit or gnome of the planet. What does it look like or is it just a presence that you cannot see and can only feel like the comforting rhythm of the Earth's heartbeat?

Take a moment to ask the Earth element a question. What do you need to know about this element and power of Earth? What would you like to learn to take away with you? Listen to the answers and feel your connection with this wonderful being grow and deepen.

The Earth gnome lets you know that it has given you the knowledge and understanding that you seek and so you offer your thanks and respect. Now turn back to your door and gently walk through and close it behind you. You are back where you were, in the now, in the here. Slowly bring your attention back to the room you're in and gradually open your eyes.

Ground yourself by bending or kneeling down on the ground, preferably outside on the grass or dirt, and place the palms of your hands flat on the ground. See the excess energy you drew up flowing smoothly back into the ground below you through your open palms.

Your Homework This Month

For your final month in this program;

- Now's the time to go and locate your Book of Shadows, work out how you're going to use it and begin writing within it recording your Wiccan life's journey ahead.
- Keep practicing the energisation visualisation including the aura cleansing and the Earth elemental connection, finishing off by grounding. Write the results in your Learning Journal.
- Take up the second choice of divination you prioritised last month and practice that as well. Explore how your chosen method works and get to know it well.
- Consider if you want to move into the next stage of training which is the Toward Second Degree program offered by Oak and Mistletoe or simply enjoy your new found learning for a while.
- Continue to write regularly in your diary and include any significant dreams you had, any meditations that offered you insights and look at what's happening around you in nature and write that down too.

Glossary

Alexandrian – This is one of the original traditions (or forms) of Wicca named after its founder Alex Sanders.

Amulets – Small items that symbolically hold magickal intent. These allow the owner to remain connected with the magick conducted that the item represents and helps to reinforce the power of the spell.

Athame – A small, black handled, double edged dagger used as a tool to cast a sacred circle and in other various Wiccan rituals.

Beltaine/Beltane – One of the four major festivals celebrated by Wiccans.

Besom – A broom which is used to symbolically sweep the sacred space clear of negative energy before a circle is cast.

Book of Shadows – A sacred book in which rituals, practice, dreams, meditations and magick are written.

Chalice – A ritual cup that holds wine and/or water and which is used during Wiccan rituals.

Circle – A sacred space in which rituals take place.

Correspondences – Ingredients in magickal workings that match similar items related to the four elements of Earth, Air, Fire and Water.

Coven – A group of people who share similar philosophies and rules of practice and who work together in Wiccan rituals.

Craft – An shortened version of the word 'Witchcraft'.

Dedicant – Someone who is learning about Wicca and who has not yet been initiated.

Deosil – The direction (clockwise) in which many rituals take place within the Circle. This follows the direction across the sky that the sun takes in the northern hemisphere.

Elements – Earth, Air, Fire and Water which are the four substances that together make up the physical and spiritual planes of the planet.

Esbat – A routine ritual often held on or near the night of each Full Moon.

Gardnerian – This is the original tradition (or form) of Wicca named after its founder and the father of modern Wicca, Gerald Gardener.

Hex – A magickal spell specifically designed to result in negative outcomes for someone or something.

High Priest – The title given to a man who has reached the level of 3rd degree initiate. The High Priest usually hives off to lead his own coven.

High Priestess – The title given to a woman who has reached the level of 3rd degree initiate. The High Priestess usually hives off to lead her own coven.

Imbolg – One of the four major festivals celebrated by Wiccans.

Inner Court – The members of a coven who have undergone the groups' initiation process.

Lughnasadh – One of the four major festivals celebrated by Wiccans.

Magick – The practise of deliberately creating outcomes with intent using spells. Wiccans often add the "k" at the end of the word to separate their practice from that of stage magic.

Neophyte – Someone who is learning about Wicca and who has not yet been initiated.

Outer Court – A teaching program provided by a working coven to a group of seekers who want to learn about Wicca.

Pagan – A self defined title for anyone who sympathises with nature based religions such as Wicca or Druidism.

Pentacle – A ritual tool, usually a plate or tile, marked with a pentagram, on which salt or other magickal ingredients are laid for ritual use.

Pentagram – The symbolic five pointed star, often enclosed with a circle, which represents Wicca much as the cross represents Christianity.

Sabbat – The major festivals of Wicca made up of four Greater and four lesser Sabbats.

Samhain – One of the four major festivals celebrated by Wiccans.

Seeker – Someone who is learning about Wicca and who has not yet been initiated.

Spell – A magickal ritual written to deliberately bring about a particular outcome.

Skyclad – Participating in a ritual naked.

Solitary – A Wiccan or Witch who does not belong to a coven and works alone.

Tradition– A form of Wicca, similar to a denomination within the broader Christian faith.

Wheel of the Year – The cyclic list of festivals that mark the spiritual year for Wiccans, Witches and many Pagans.

Wicca – A religion, originally developed by Gerald Gardner in the late 1940s, that focuses on a polytheistic connection with deity and nature.

Wiccan – A person who self titles and adopts the philosophy and practices of Wicca.

Widdershins – The direction (anti-clockwise) in which many rituals take place within the Circle.

Witch – A person who self titles and adopts the practices of magick, often inclusively of the philosophy of Wicca.

List of Resources

Bibliography

Adler, M. (2006). *Drawing Down the Moon: Witches, Druids, Goddess-Worshippers and Other Pagans in America.* New York: Penguin Group.

Amber K. (1998). *Covencraft: Witchcraft for Three or More.* Saint Paul, Minnesota: Llewellyn Publications.

Bodsworth, R. (1999). *Sunwyse: Celebrating the Sacred Wheel of the Year in Australia.* Victoria: Hihorse.

Buckland, R. (1986), *Buckland's Complete Book of Witchcraft* (2nd ed.). St Paul, Minnesota: Llewellyn Publications.

Cotterell, A. (1996). *The Encyclopaedia of Mythology.* London: Anness Publishing Ltd.

Crowley, V. (2001). *Way of Wicca.* London: Thorsons.

Cunningham, S. (2004). *Wicca: A Guide for the Solitary Practitioner* (1st ed. revised). St Paul, Minnesota: Llewellyn Publications.

Eason, C. (2001). *A Practical Guide Witchcraft and Magick Spells.* Berkshire: Quantum.

Ezzy, D. (2003). What is a Witch? In Ezzy, D (Ed.) *Practising the Witch's Craft: Real magic under a southern sky* (pp. 1-22) St Leonards, NSW: Allen & Unwin.

Farrar, J., Farrar, S. (1981). *A Witches' Bible: The Complete Witches' Handbook.* Washington: Phoenix Publishing.

Gardner, G. (2004). *Witchcraft Today.* (50th anniversary ed.).New York: Citadel Press.

Hume, L. (1997). *Witchcraft and Paganism in Australia.* Carlton South, Victoria: Melbourne University Press.

Hutton, R. (1999). *The Triumph of the Moon: A History of Modern Pagan Witchcraft.* Oxford: Oxford University Press.

Kelly, A. (2007). *Inventing Witchcraft: A Case Study in the Creation of a New Religion.* London: Thoth Publications.

MacMorgan-Douglas, K. (2007). *All One Wicca: A Study in the Universal Eclectic Wiccan Tradition.* New York: Covenstead Press.

Sabin, T. (2006). *Wicca for Beginners: Fundamentals of Philosophy and Practice.* St Paul, Minnesota: Llewellyn Publications.

Smith, Z. (2009). *How and What Witches Learn: Modern Witchcraft in Suburban Australia.* Adelaide, Australia: Oak and Mistletoe.

Web Pages

http://www.oakandmistletoe.com.au

http://www.cciwi.org

http://www.religioustolerance.org/witchcra.htm

http://en.wikipedia.org/wiki/Wicca

http://wicca.timerift.net/wicca101/index.shtml

http://gamma.faithweb.com

http://www.geraldgardner.com/

Index

www.ingramcontent.com/pod-product-compliance
Lightning Source LLC
Chambersburg PA
CBHW031253090426
42742CB00007B/437